The Impossible Friendship

The Impossible Friendship

BOSWELL AND
MRS. THRALE

MARY HYDE

HARVARD UNIVERSITY PRESS
CAMBRIDGE, MASSACHUSETTS
1972

TO L. F. POWELL

Johnsonianissimus

CONTENTS

ILLUSTRATIONS

INTRODUCTION

One often hears of Johnson's Mrs. Thrale, his protective hostess, recorder of his anecdotes, and editor of his letters; and far more often one hears of Johnson's Boswell, the faithful friend and dedicated biographer. The closeness of both to the great man is vividly and minutely shown in the books they wrote — and in books which many others have written — but one has never heard the full story of Boswell and Mrs. Thrale themselves, such opposite personalities. How friendly were they in the early days, and how did they come to be enemies? Their interesting and complex relationship is the subject of this book. It is based upon fresh manuscript material, in particular, the correspondence between Boswell and both Mr. and Mrs. Thrale.

Letters and actual encounters are the sources of information for the period of 1769–1781, from the time of their meeting until the death of Thrale. During these years, the acquaintance seemed entirely agreeable; the wealthy brewer and his wife entertained Boswell with unfailing kindness at their home near the brewery, at delightful Streatham Park in the country, and at other places as well — wherever they happened to be when he came down from Scotland. On almost every occasion Dr. Johnson was present, the magnet that brought them together and held them fast; he was devoted to all three. Thrale, blunt and generous, expected nothing from Johnson except his steady friendship; but the deep admiration and affection in which Boswell and Mrs. Thrale held Johnson also contained a dash of self-interest, for each had early been given his blessing to write a biography, and both were collecting material at the same time they were enjoying his company.

In this pursuit Mrs. Thrale had the advantage of being able to observe Johnson closely, as he was a virtual member of their household for most of the Thrales' married life. Boswell, though he had professional literary experience which Mrs. Thrale lacked, was at a disadvantage in being separated from Johnson much of the time. Boswell was well aware of this unfortunate situation, and even in his first letter playfully called Mrs. Thrale "a generous rival," for he had wished to hold Johnson in London, when she wished to take him to the country — and of course, she had won — a spirited beginning for their acquaintance. Indeed, it was this particular letter which first set me to work. The letter was in the Four Oaks Farm library, with two other letters from Boswell to Mrs. Thrale, and one from him to Henry Thrale. All four had formerly belonged to R. B. Adam, the distinguished Buffalo Johnsonian whose library some years before had become the nucleus of our book and manuscript collection of Johnson, Boswell, Mrs. Thrale, and other eighteenth century authors. How many more letters, I wondered, did Boswell write to the Thrales? Where were their answers? And how long did the correspondence continue?

In a short while our friend, Colonel Ralph Isham, owner of the vast collection of Boswell Papers from Malahide Castle (now at Yale University), was able to answer my questions in part, and with great generosity, for he allowed me to acquire his four letters from Mrs. Thrale to Boswell, and also five retained Boswell letters to her (three drafts and two copies; one draft and one copy were of letters already at Four Oaks). Soon, in various institutions, I was able to locate seven more letters: three from Boswell, two from Mrs. Thrale, and one from Henry Thrale, all written in the 1770's; also an enigmatic letter from Boswell in 1781, written a few days after Henry Thrale's death. Photocopies of these letters were kindly sent to me by the libraries, and study of the material began. During the course of this, I was able to acquire two additional holograph notes: Mrs. Thrale's first communication to Boswell (1769), and a note in 1781 from Thrale to Boswell, written by Johnson.

By this time, counting originals and photocopies, there were texts for twenty letters, summaries of six from Boswell's Letter Register, and also mentions of two, one in a Boswell letter and one in his Journal. (See the "Chronological List of the Correspondence between Boswell and the Thrales," p. 175.) In addition, there were two of Boswell's letter drafts and five copies of his letters, two in his hand and three in the hand of his clerk, John Lawrie. I found no drafts of letters from

Mrs. Thrale; the one transcription of a letter of hers, her first note, Boswell had incorporated into the manuscript of the *Life of Johnson*, introducing it with a gracious compliment; he later deleted both compliment and note.

The Boswell-Thrale correspondence gave an unusual view of Johnson, and an extremely revealing picture of Boswell and the Thrales, disclosing the personalities of all three and their methods of approaching each other; Thrale liberal, open, hearty; Boswell polite, guarded, asking a favor; Mrs. Thrale self-conscious, evasive, her letters curiously brief and restrained. Between Boswell and Henry Thrale communication was clear and easy; between Boswell and Mrs. Thrale it was obscure and tense.

In the beginning, I planned simply to present this important unpublished correspondence chronologically, filling in the periods of silence with pertinent comment, and giving an account of each actual encounter. I prepared tables of these encounters, year by year. Throughout the story, the emphasis would be on Boswell and Mrs. Thrale. They would be in the foreground; other characters — including Johnson — would remain in the background.

But a problem immediately presented itself: by the end of 1782, the year after Thrale's death, the correspondence between Boswell and Mrs. Thrale ceased. They did not see each other in this year, and in 1783, after meeting on March 21st, they never saw each other again.

Boswell's disapproval of Mrs. Thrale's marriage to the Italian music master, Gabriel Piozzi, and her desertion of Johnson precluded the possibility of any further meeting or exchange of letters. This was not, however, the end of their story; their social connection was over, but years of public confrontation, with even closer linking of their names, not in the "Johnsonian School" as heretofore, but in the Johnson market place, were about to begin. It was no longer polite rivalry, illustrated by letters and encounters, but bitter enmity and public warfare, carried on through successive publications: Boswell's *Journal of a Tour to the Hebrides* (1785); Mrs. Piozzi's *Anecdotes* (1786); her edition of *Johnson's Letters* (1788); and Boswell's *Life of Johnson* (1791). It was essential to cover this second phase, I soon realized, in order to give the full picture of their relationship.

For both parts of the story, certain published reference works have been my constant companions. The badly worn covers of the three most used sources are testimony of what these books have meant to me:

James L. Clifford's *Hester Lynch Piozzi (Mrs. Thrale)*; the eighteen
volumes of the *Private Papers of James Boswell from Malahide Castle,
in the Collection of Ralph Heyward Isham*; and the Hill-Powell
edition of Boswell's *Life of Johnson* (volume VI, the index, is in itself
a survey of Johnson's world, and has served at every turn).

Also of great assistance have been Katharine C. Balderston's *Thraliana, the Diary of Mrs. Hester Lynch Thrale (later Mrs. Piozzi)
1776–1809*; R. W. Chapman's edition of the *Letters of Samuel Johnson*; the published volumes of Boswell's *Journals (1769–1778)* in the
Yale edition; the biography by Frederick A. Pottle of *James Boswell,
the Earlier Years (1740–1769)*; and *The Correspondence and Other
Papers of James Boswell Relating to the Making of the Life of Johnson*, edited by Marshall Waingrow. The Limited Editions Club *Life
of Johnson* has also been helpful, with its marginal comments made by
Mrs. Piozzi in a fifth edition and an eighth edition of the *Life*.

Manuscript research began at home. The Boswell-Thrale letters
which are here were of course vital, but beyond these there was other
important manuscript material: Mrs. Thrale-Piozzi's correspondence
with Samuel Lysons, a young literary adviser for her Johnson publications, her manuscript journals, her *Commonplace Book*, some of her
verses, and a few of the Thrale family papers.

A number of letters from Boswell to Malone have contributed information, as have Boswell's *Book of Company* and various manuscript
memoranda. His corrections on first proof sheets and second proof
sheets of the *Life of Johnson* have also been valuable.

Of the Johnson letters at Four Oaks Farm, more than two hundred
are to the Thrales, and a study of these (including a close examination
of Johnson's handwriting) has been rewarding.

Manuscripts and letters concerned with other characters in the story
have also served a purpose. One small collection to be noted is a series
of complimentary letters and verses addressed to Elizabeth Montagu,
together with a few manuscript pages of her *Essay on the Writings and
Genius of Shakespeare*, the controversial work which precipitated the
public quarrel between Boswell and Mrs. Thrale. Portraits, drawings,
and other iconographic material at Four Oaks have been used as illustrations.

The first draft of *The Impossible Friendship* was written several
years ago and at that time the typescript was very kindly read by L. F.
Powell of Oxford and by Frederick A. Pottle and Marion S. Pottle of

Yale. Extensive notes from Dr. Powell and detailed corrections and suggestions from the Pottles, including valuable comments on my treatment of Boswell, prompted further research and revision. My visits to the Beinecke Library in New Haven have been filled with the warmth associated with Streatham itself. I am deeply indebted to Herman W. Liebert, Dr. James M. Osborn, Professor and Mrs. Pottle, and Miss Marjorie Wynne. The resources of the Boswell Papers have been made fully available: I am grateful for the opportunity to check references to the Thrales in the manuscript of the *Life of Johnson*, and to study the important section, certainly one of the most difficult for Boswell to handle in the entire biography, his treatment of Mrs. Thrale's marriage to Gabriel Piozzi and his "animadvisions" upon the accuracy of her Johnsonian anecdotes.

Also of interest to me in the Boswell Papers were numerous letters: the Boswell-Courtenay correspondence and even more important the Boswell-Malone correspondence, which Dr. Osborn will soon present in a definitive edition. Material collected by Boswell from Johnson's friends provided further points; this material has been well edited by Marshall Waingrow in his *Correspondence and Other Papers of James Boswell Relating to the Making of the Life of Johnson*, but in many instances passages on Mrs. Thrale-Piozzi were not chosen for publication, and these of course were vital to my purpose. To avoid misunderstanding, I have sometimes noted, "Not in Waingrow" for these quotations. Other letters which I found in the Boswell Papers had special bearing upon Mrs. Thrale-Piozzi; and helpful as well was Boswell's collection of newspaper clippings (with his own compositions starred). Boswell's *jeux d'esprit*, written about his rival, first as Mrs. Thrale, later as Signora Piozzi, added much to my story, and they are treated at some length in the pages which follow.

Permission to quote material in the Boswell Papers has been granted by Yale University and by the McGraw-Hill Book Company. In the Boswell-Thrale correspondence, seven letters which are not at Four Oaks Farm are quoted with the permission of Harvard University, the National Library of Scotland, the Rylands Library (two letters), and Yale University and the McGraw-Hill Book Company (three letters). Permission to give short quotations has been granted by Arthur A. Houghton, Jr., and the Pierpont Morgan Library. Permission to examine and to quote from Samuel Lysons' collection of newspaper cuttings was granted by the Columbia University Libraries. For assistance in securing permissions and for illumination on special points, I wish to thank William Beattie, William H. Bond, Kenneth Lohf, L. F. Powell, E. F. D. Roberts, Charles Ryskamp, Frank Taylor, and Marshall Waingrow.

Permission to reproduce illustrations has been given by the Beaverbrook Art Gallery, the Fitzwilliam Museum, Wilmarth S. Lewis, the National Portrait Gallery, the Rylands Library, the Scottish National Portrait Gallery, and Yale University; I wish also to give personal thanks, not only to Mr. Lewis, but also to Geoffrey Agnew, Leslie Cook, John Kerslake, Ian Lumsden, Frank Taylor, Clovis Whitfield, and Hugh Whitwell.

In the early phase of my work I was given sound direction and many suggestions by Donald Hyde. He read the original typescript, as did my friends Gabriel Austin, Jackson Bate, and Robert Metzdorf. The last has continued his help through every stage, including the reading of proof.

I owe a great debt to my understanding *Harvard Library Bulletin* editors, Rene Bryant and Edwin Williams, who saw to the serialization of "The Impossible Friendship" in the *Bulletin*, volume XX (1972). For help with the hardcover book, I am grateful to the editors of the Harvard University Press; Katherine Bruner has been responsible for the index. Finally, I shall always be grateful to Rose McTernan, who typed and retyped what seemed to be endless drafts of manuscript.

The composition of this small book over a number of years has tried and strengthened many friendships.

Mary Hyde

Four Oaks Farm
9 August 1972

The Impossible Friendship

CHAPTER I

RIVALRY

1763 through 1775

> "I told you, Madam, that you and I
> were rivals for that great man."
> — James Boswell's first letter to
> Mrs. Thrale, 5 September 1769

YOUNG BOSWELL had for several years read Samuel Johnson's writings with delight, his essays in the *Rambler* and the *Idler*, and the short novel, *Rasselas*. He admired the monumental *Dictionary of the English Language* as well, and had a consuming desire to meet the Great Cham of Literature. On two earlier visits from Scotland he had tried to secure an introduction to Johnson, but both times his friends had failed him.[1] Now, in May 1763, Boswell was in London again, still trying through important connections to obtain a commission in the Foot Guards, preferably one which would mean residence in London. His father, Lord Auchinleck, a respected Scottish judge, was set against this plan and refused to buy him a commission; he wished his son to follow the law, lead a settled and useful existence. If London were to be a residence, it should be in later life, when perhaps he might be a Member of Parliament.

On 16 May 1763, while still unsettled about his future plans, Boswell went to his friend Tom Davies' bookshop at tea time, and there one of the celebrated scenes in English literary history took place. Unexpectedly, the famous Dr. Johnson walked into the room. He was, Boswell recorded in his Journal, "of a most dreadful appearance . . . a very big man . . . troubled with sore eyes, the palsy, and the king's evil [scrofula] . . . slovenly in his dress . . . with a most

---

[1] The author, Samuel Derrick, promised to introduce him in 1760; Thomas Sheridan, the actor (father of Richard Brinsley), and Tom Davies, the bookseller, in 1761. None had been able to arrange a meeting.

uncouth voice." [2] Boswell was unprepared and flustered. He made an unfortunate attempt to hide the fact that he came from Scotland. Johnson parried this roughly. Boswell erred again and Johnson put him down dogmatically. It was a rude reception, not conducive to friendship, but Boswell accepted his reprimand with a cheerfulness that was one of his most endearing traits. Johnson still seemed heroic to him in knowledge and character, despite the hard blows he had delivered. And Davies consoled him by saying, "Don't be uneasy. I can see he likes you very well." [3]

Boswell persevered. He called upon Johnson on the 24th of May in his chambers in the Inner Temple, "where he [lived] in literary state, very solemn and very slovenly." [4] There was company with him and Boswell was afraid he was intruding. Johnson replied that "he was obliged to any man who visited him."

On the 13th of June Boswell waited upon Johnson again, and found him even more cordial. He shook his hand at parting and asked why he did not come oftener. [5] On the 25th of June Boswell dined in the same room at Clifton's and later the two went on to the Mitre Tavern in Fleet Street. There, as Boswell talked freely about himself, Johnson cried, "Give me your hand. I have taken a liking to you." They sat until almost two o'clock in the morning "and finished a couple of bottles of port," [6] Boswell in "high exultation," and Johnson exhilarated as well. Such an evening made Johnson forget the wretchedness of his existence. Since his wife's [7] death over ten years before he had

---

[2] *Boswell's London Journal, 1762–1763*. (New York: McGraw-Hill, 1950), p. 260. Hereafter referred to as *London Journal*.

[3] Boswell's *Life of Johnson*, Edited by George Birkbeck Hill, Revised by L. F. Powell, 6 v. (Oxford: Clarendon Press, 1934–1950), I, 395. Hereafter referred to as *Life*.

[4] *London Journal*, p. 267.

[5] *Ibid.*, p. 279.

[6] *Ibid.*, pp. 283, 285.

[7] Elizabeth (Tetty) Porter Johnson (1689–1752). In 1733, after Johnson had been forced to leave Oxford, and after his employment at Market Bosworth had ceased, he went to Birmingham. There he met Harry Porter, a woolen draper, and his wife. The Porters were a solid family with three children: Lucy, seventeen, and two sons, Henry Jervis, fifteen, and Joseph, eight. Harry Porter enjoyed company and Tetty had considerable charm and wit, an interest in literature, and a respect for the abilities of Johnson, an ungainly young man of twenty-three. Johnson enjoyed the hospitality of their house.

When Harry Porter died suddenly and insolvent, Johnson courted the widow, though he himself was without means of support, and was twenty years her junior.

moved to three different lodgings,[8] continuing to work in depression, disorder, and discomfort. His appraisal of a tavern as the height of human felicity shows the extent of his loneliness. Friends were his only solace and their company gave a brief respite of pleasure in a melancholy vacuum of wretchedness.

Johnson cultivated friendship and took its responsibilities seriously. He felt great kindness for men and women of widely divergent qualities, circumstances, and ages. The difference in Johnson's age, fifty-three, and Boswell's, twenty-two, was no barrier; in fact Johnson had a partiality for young people — they invigorated him: ". . . in the first place, I don't like to think myself turning old. In the next place, young acquaintances must last longest, if they do last; and in the next place, young men have more virtue than old men . . . I love the young dogs of this age . . ."[9]

Throughout the next month the two met frequently, for breakfast, dinner, tea; in Johnson's chambers, Boswell's lodging, at friends' houses, at the Mitre, the Turk's Head, and on the Strand. Their talk "ran over the grand scale of human knowledge":[10] issues of the day, personalities, rank, philosophy, preaching, poetry. Discussion was sometimes deeply personal. Boswell told his full story, his attraction to a religious life, then to the Guards; he told of his sexual dissipations, his love of literature, his compulsion to write. He gave a history of his family and described Auchinleck, the romantic seat of his ancestors. Johnson's response to this was enthusiastic, "I must be there, Sir, (said he) and we will live in the old castle; and if there is not a room in it remaining, we will build one."[11] Boswell explained his filial struggles and his recent capitulation on receiving Lord Auchinleck's firm letter of May 30th. He had agreed, he told Johnson, to follow his father's

They were married in 1736 against general opposition. With the few hundred pounds which Tetty had, Johnson set up a school at Edial. The two sons never saw their mother again, but Lucy came to live with them at Edial. The school was a failure and the following year Johnson came to London where he did hack work for *The Gentleman's Magazine*. It was a hard life for the Johnsons in London and little recognition came to him during Tetty's lifetime: the publication of his poem *London* in 1738, *The Vanity of Human Wishes* in 1749, and the conclusion of *The Rambler* in 1752, shortly before Tetty died. Her death left Johnson desolate, and the future seemed void.

[8] Staple Inn, Gray's Inn, Inner Temple-lane, No. 1. *Life*, III, 405, n. 4.
[9] *London Journal*, p. 319.
[10] *Life*, I, 461.
[11] *Ibid.*, 462.

plan and go to Holland for a winter's study of civil law at Utrecht on the condition that he later be allowed to visit Paris and some of the German courts. What did Johnson advise? He "begged for counsel." [12] Johnson took pleasure in discussing the problems and plans. He even suggested that "in the course of the following summer [he might] come over to Holland, and accompany [him] in a tour through the Netherlands." [13]

Johnson made the uncomfortable two days' journey from London to Harwich to see young Boswell off; and when on August 6th he boarded the boat for Holland, his "revered friend walked down with [him] to the beach, where [they] embraced and parted with tenderness." [14]

At the time Boswell departed for Utrecht, plans were going forward in London for the marriage of Henry Thrale and Hester Lynch Salusbury. Thrale was a businessman in his mid-thirties. He had inherited his father's fortune some years before and was now head of the brewery which had created this wealth. Henry had received every advantage: he had been educated at Oxford and had later made a grand tour of the Continent; he had generally enjoyed the life of a young man of position. He was a sensible person, handsome and amiable — something of a rake in the past, but now eager to settle down and raise a family. He was searching for a wife, someone of pleasing appearance and good family (but someone not too proud to live adjacent to the brewery in Southwark for part of the year). He was satisfied that he had found the right young lady in Hester Lynch Salusbury. She came from a distinguished Welsh family, both sides of which traced descent from Henry Tudor.

Hester was twenty-two, a slip of a thing, four feet eleven; not a beauty, but vivacious and attractive. She was an only child, adored and spoiled by her parents and relations. She had been precocious, an infant Blue Stocking: at seven reading books in French, and at ten reading Livy and Plutarch in the original. She was early led to believe that she had remarkable gifts as a writer; she was always ready to show her verses, and accustomed to hearing them praised.

[12] *James Boswell, The Earlier Years (1740–1769)*, by Frederick A. Pottle (New York: McGraw-Hill, 1966), p. 117. Hereafter referred to as *Boswell Earlier Years, Pottle*.

[13] *Life*, I, 470.

[14] *Ibid.*, 472.

During the courting by Henry Thrale, Hester was somewhat dazzled by the rich suitor but not much involved; her mother talked to him, and Hester continued her studies with Dr. Collier, her tutor, a sentimental bachelor of fifty-one, for whom she felt an innocent but tender regard.[15] Hester's father disliked Thrale, but his opinion was not overriding in the household. John Salusbury was a lovable but unsuccessful man; he had twice journeyed to Nova Scotia to improve the family fortunes, had failed, and now, back in London, faced financial ruin. As Thrale continued his advances, John Salusbury became violent in his opposition — Thrale was not worthy of his daughter. Mrs. Salusbury (who knew the hazards of following one's own heart) abetted the match. She saw in Thrale the solution of the family's financial plight, and also she genuinely liked him.

The conflict was settled when Hester's father died suddenly in December 1762. From then on Thrale received active encouragement, and on the 28th of June 1763 he sent a letter to both mother and daughter, ardently desiring an appointment to discuss the "very interesting subject" on his mind. The meeting took place, and after it, Mrs. Salusbury was able to mold her daughter's vague dreams of romance into a cast of prudence and practicality.

On the 11th of October 1763 (while Boswell was applying himself to the study of the law in Utrecht) the Salusbury-Thrale marriage took place at St. Anne's in Soho, near Mrs. Salusbury's small house. After the ceremony the wedding party proceeded to Mr. Thrale's country place a few miles away. This was the first time that Hester had seen Streatham Park, the fine house where she was to spend so much of her life.

Time passed slowly for the bride. There was not much for her to do. Thrale managed the kitchen, the household, and all matters concerning the estate of a hundred acres. Mrs. Salusbury provided some distraction for her daughter when the Thrales were at Streatham, for she resided with them when they were there, returning to her own house in London when they were in Southwark. The new Mrs. Thrale saw this brewery residence also for the first time after her marriage.

Both Thrale and Mrs. Salusbury were opposed to Hester entering London society and Thrale forbade her favorite exercise of riding as

[15] *Hester Lynch Piozzi (Mrs. Thrale)*, by James L. Clifford (Oxford: Clarendon Press, 1941), p. 25. Hereafter referred to as *Clifford*.

being too masculine (perhaps because a former mistress had been an expert horsewoman). Hester solaced herself with quieter interests such as extensive reading, which made her more familiar with Johnson's works. She also did some writing herself, notably poems of sentiment to Thrale, who did not show the appreciation for her verse [16] to which she was accustomed. But, though the bridegroom was not effusive, he was well satisfied. All was going well, and in time he was pleased to know that an heir was expected.

Thrale's numerous bachelor friends were a trial to his wife, as bachelor friends are to all brides, but there was one she liked very much, the playwright, Arthur Murphy.[17] Mrs. Thrale, knowing him to be a good friend of Dr. Johnson, begged for an introduction to the great man of letters; Thrale was eager for the meeting as well. The three made a plan: they would send an invitation for dinner to James Woodhouse — "the poetical shoemaker" [18] whose verses were the literary talk of the moment. His presence would be a temptation to draw Johnson, whom Murphy agreed to ask, but he warned them "not to be surprised at his figure, dress, or behaviour." [19]

Unlike Boswell's first meeting, the Thrales' was carefully planned and went off well,[20] though not without its share of irony. Johnson felt contempt for the public's critical notice of Woodhouse.[21] Still, he did not treat him too roughly upon this occasion, for what Mrs. Thrale remembered particularly was his telling Woodhouse to "Give

[16] Like many other authors, both Boswell and Mrs. Thrale began with verse.

[17] Arthur Murphy (1727–1805), actor, writer, and member of the bar. Murphy was much respected and a favorite in society. "Tall and well made . . . very gentlemanlike appearance . . . easy and polite" — Mme. D'Arblay's (Fanny Burney) *Diary*, quoted in *Life*, I, 357.

[18] James Woodhouse (1735–1820). Forced to leave school at the age of eight, Woodhouse became a shoemaker; marrying early, he added to his means by elementary teaching. In 1759 Woodhouse had addressed an elegy to William Shenstone, and this established poet had taken a sympathetic interest in him. Shortly before the dinner at the Thrales', Woodhouse's *Poems on Sundry Occasions* had been published.

[19] *Anecdotes of the Late Samuel Johnson, LL.D.*, by Hester Lynch Piozzi. (London: T. Cadell, 1786), p. 125. Hereafter referred to as *Anecdotes*.

[20] On January 9th, according to Johnson's Diary, the meeting took place. Boswell was in Turin that day, calling upon Mme. de St. Gilles, in whose company he was "tired to death." *Boswell on the Grand Tour, Italy, Corsica, and France (1765–1766)*, Edited by Frank Brady and Frederick A. Pottle. (Yale [Trade] Edition of the Boswell Papers, McGraw-Hill, 1955), p. 26.

[21] "He may make an excellent shoemaker, but can never make a good poet. A school-boy's exercise may be a pretty thing for a school-boy; but it is no treat for a man." *Life*, II, 127.

nights and days, Sir . . . to the study of Addison, if [he meant] either to be a good writer, or what is more worth, an honest man." [22] As for the Thrales, it was instant attraction. "We liked each other so well," Mrs. Thrale recorded in her Diary, "that the next Thursday was appointed for the same Company to meet — exclusive of the Shoemaker." [23] Regular meetings followed every Thursday during the winter. The Thrales were not put off by Johnson's grossness and eccentricity. They appreciated the force of his character and mind and greatly enjoyed his company. Johnson, in turn, enjoyed theirs. He appreciated Thrale's geniality and generosity, also his fondness for providing wars of words,[24] a sedentary sport in which Johnson revelled. Mrs. Thrale was an enchanting hostess, bright as a bird, and ready to talk on any subject without fear. It was not long before she showed Johnson some of her verses; he praised them warmly and said she should help him with his translation of Boethius. He set her the task of translating an "Ode" for him to correct each Thursday. This collaboration proceeded well for some weeks, but in the end was abandoned because Johnson discovered that an impoverished author was engaged in the same work and he did not want to jeopardize any profit the man might realize. Johnson continued, however, to beg verses from Mrs. Thrale and the next year asked for her tale of "The Three Warnings" to fill out the *Miscellanies*, a volume of poems by his blind friend, Anna Williams,[25] which he was seeing through the press.

Not only did Johnson appreciate the comforts and pleasures of the Thrale household, but he also took an affectionate interest in the family,

[22] *Anecdotes*, p. 125.

[23] *Thraliana, the Diary of Mrs. Hester Lynch Thrale (Later Mrs. Piozzi)*, 2 v., Edited by Katharine C. Balderston (Oxford: Clarendon Press, 1942), I, 159. Hereafter referred to as *Thraliana*.

[24] *Clifford*, p. 57.

[25] Anna Williams (1706–1783) was the daughter of Zachariah Williams, a Welsh physician. She was well educated, spoke French and Italian, knew a good deal about literature and had a talent for writing verse. About 1727 she had come to London with her father, and for a while she enjoyed the life of the city. She worked at translations and excelled in "the exercise of her needle"; but in the 1740's she was beset by failing eyesight and financial distress. She had become an intimate friend of Johnson's wife, and in 1752, the year of Tetty's death, Johnson had arranged for an operation upon Miss Williams' eyes. This was performed in the Johnsons' house in Gough Square, where it was thought that she would be more comfortable than in her own lodgings. The result was total blindness. From this time on, Johnson cared for Anna Williams. Whenever he had a house, there was a room in it reserved for her.

particularly the infant, who had been born on the 17th of September 1764 (the day before his own birthday) — not an heir, as Thrale had doubtless hoped at the time, but a baby girl, whom they had named Hester Maria, after Mrs. Salusbury. Johnson called her Queeney (Queen Hester) and this nickname remained with her always. He delighted in playing with Queeney, and soon he was endeavoring to make her an even greater prodigy than her mother had been.

In August the Thrales asked Johnson to join them in Brighton. Final work on his edition of Shakespeare prevented him from leaving London, but he wrote, "the week after the next . . . where should pleasure be sought but under Mrs. Thrale's influence?" [26]

When Johnson went to Brighton, as he had promised to do, but without communicating further with the Thrales, he was enraged to find that they had returned to London. He wrote an angry letter, and Murphy had to be called to straighten out matters. He explained that they had come back to London sooner than expected because Thrale had decided to run for Parliament upon the sudden death of one of the Members for the Borough of Southwark; and Mrs. Thrale had come to see her doctors. Her second child, Frances, was born on September 23rd and lived only four days — a dismal pattern which would be repeated frequently over the years to come. Johnson, upon hearing these reasons, was completely mollified and hastened to give sympathy to Mrs. Thrale, and to lend his literary talents to Thrale's election campaign. Their warm relationship was never again impaired so long as Thrale lived.

1766

Johnson had not been good about writing to Boswell during his year in Holland, nor during the next two when his young friend travelled through Germany, Switzerland, Italy, Corsica, and France — there was only one letter, in December 1763.[27] Now, as Boswell approached,

[26] Johnson to Mrs. Thrale, 13 August 1765. MS. Letter: Hyde. Letter #172 in *The Letters of Samuel Johnson*, Collected and edited by R. W. Chapman, 3 v. (Oxford: Clarendon Press, 1952), I, 174. Hereafter referred to as *Letters*. This is Johnson's first letter to Mrs. Thrale.

[27] Johnson to Boswell in Utrecht, 8 December 1763. Letter #163. *Letters*, I, 164–166. The present location of only a handful of Johnson's letters to Boswell is known. The source of the texts (with omissions indicated by Boswell) is in the *Life of Johnson*. I am citing the Chapman edition of Johnson's Letters, however, as a more convenient reference.

JAMES BOSWELL

BY GEORGE WILLISON, 1765

Reproduced by permission of the
Scottish National Portrait Gallery

Drawn by the late J. Smith.   Engraved by E. Finden.

Johnson's House
Johnson's Court, Fleet Street.

**JOHNSON'S HOUSE, JOHNSON'S COURT,
FLEET STREET**

Johnson wrote to him in Paris, apologizing, and assuring him that "nothing has lessened either the esteem or love with which I dismissed you at Harwich . . . when you return, you will return to an unaltered, and, I hope, unalterable friend." [28]

Boswell arrived in London on February 12th, full of his travels and adventures, particularly his recent visit to Corsica.[29] He had "wished for something more than just the common course of what is called the tour of Europe" and his new friend and mentor, the Swiss philosopher, Jean-Jacques Rousseau, had supplied the inspiration. He told him he must see Corsica,[30] a country in revolution, a country which would one day astonish Europe. Rousseau furnished an introduction to the brave Corsican general, Pasquale Paoli, and Boswell set off. Memorable days.

Now he was again to see his Swiss mentor, for Rousseau had been forced to leave the Continent and in January 1766 had taken up residence in Chiswick. Boswell had just performed the kindness of escorting the philosopher's mistress, Thérèse Le Vasseur, to London — not an entirely altruistic act, for during the journey Thérèse had become his mistress as well. On February 13th, the day after their arrival, Boswell accompanied Thérèse to Rousseau's house, promising not to tell of their affair. To Boswell's disappointment the meeting had little of the exhilaration of those abroad. He confessed in his Journal that he had lost his old enthusiasm for the ailing philosopher and concluded by saying: "[That over, went] back to London, [and hastened] immed[iately] to Johnson." [31] The Doctor was now living in Johnson's Court. Miss Williams, sixty, the blind poetess whom his wife had befriended during her lifetime, and whom Johnson now cared for, had an apartment on the ground floor, and Dr. Levett, sixty-one, a physician of doubtful reputation but an honest friend, occupied the garret. Francis Barber,[32] the Jamaican boy who had come to John-

---

[28] Johnson to Boswell in Paris, 14 January 1766. Letter #181. *Letters*, I, 183.

[29] See *Boswell Earlier Years*, Pottle, pp. 244–250.

[30] Matteo Buttafoco, a Corsican in the service of the French, had written Rousseau in the autumn of 1764, urging him to draw up a constitution for Corsica. *Ibid.*, p. 249.

[31] *Private Papers of James Boswell*, Edited by Geoffrey Scott and Frederick A. Pottle, 18 v. (Privately printed for Lt. Col. Ralph H. Isham by William Edwin Rudge, 1928–1934), VII, 68 (13 February 1766). Hereafter referred to as *Boswell Papers*.

[32] Francis Barber (1745?–1801) had been brought to England in 1750 by Colonel Bathurst, a West Indian planter, the father of Johnson's intimate friend, Dr. Bathurst. Except for brief employment elsewhere, a stint at sea, and a try at school, Francis

son in 1752 (when he was about seven) was the only young person in the household.

Miss Williams was in the room when Boswell arrived and she seemed glad at his return; when she left the room Johnson hugged Boswell "like a sack, and grumbl'd, 'I hope we shall pass many years of regard [together].' [Boswell] for some minutes saw him not so immense as before, but it came back." [33] And after a dinner at the Mitre, with discussion of religion, science, and the law, of friends, Corsica, and self, he found his early mentor "as great as ever." [34]

Boswell knew he must leave for Edinburgh shortly. His mother had died during his long absence; his father was ill and urged his speedy return. During Boswell's brief stay in London Johnson made no effort to introduce him to the Thrales, and there is no evidence that Boswell knew how important this family had become to Johnson. Had he stayed in London longer he could not have helped being aware of the fact.

The Thrale relationship, indeed, became even closer during this year, for sometime then, according to Mrs. Thrale,[35] Johnson suffered a severe breakdown and became so morbidly depressed that he would not stir out of his room for weeks together. When the Thrales visited him at Johnson's Court, they were so shocked by his condition, physical and mental, that they brought him back to Streatham, where they could watch over him. With loving care they restored his health and sanity, and from this time on a room was set aside for him in their house at Southwark, as well as a room at Streatham Park.

Johnson did not give up his own house in Johnson's Court. There he continued to support his curious household, and his door was open to other unfortunates as well. He stayed certain days in this cheerless

stayed with Johnson until the Doctor's death in 1784; and only death separated the other members of the household.

[33] *Boswell Papers*, VII, 68 (13 February 1766).

[34] *Ibid.*, 70 (13 February 1766). Again at the Mitre on the 15th of February, Johnson upbraided Boswell for keeping bad company abroad — both Rousseau and John Wilkes, the political firebrand, had been expelled from their countries. *Life*, II, 11.

[35] *Anecdotes*, pp. 126–128. Also see Appendix F in *Life*, I, 520–522; and Dr. William Adams' report to Boswell on Johnson's melancholia in *The Correspondence and Other Papers of James Boswell Relating to the Making of the Life of Johnson*, Edited by Marshall Waingrow (Yale Research Edition; McGraw-Hill: New York, 1969), p. 24. Hereafter referred to as *Waingrow*.

dwelling, but it is easy to see why he came to spend more and more time with the Thrales, for he delighted in their lively and affectionate company and the conventional comforts they provided. For the first time ever, he was able to enjoy a regular and agreeable family life. He settled in with pleasure, calling both Southwark and Streatham "home"; Thrale, "Master," and Mrs. Thrale, "Mistress"; her mother, "honoured Madam"; and Queeney, "little Miss." From 1766 on, Johnson became a virtual member of the Thrale family.

Boswell was not aware of this domestication for two years. The few letters he received from Johnson did not mention the Thrales, and Boswell was fully occupied with his legal practice in Edinburgh; beyond this, he was busy writing *The Douglas Cause, Dorando*, and *An Account of Corsica*. He also had personal problems concerning a Mrs. Dodds, and her child, Sally, whom he had fathered.

1768

It was 1768 before Boswell became conscious of Johnson's new life. Boswell arrived in London on the 22nd of March; his volume on Corsica [36] had been published in February and he was delighted by its reception; he was now something of a literary figure himself. He called at Johnson's Court, eager to have the great critic's approval of his success. [37] To his disappointment he was told that Johnson was in Oxford, visiting Robert Chambers, the Vinerian Professor of Law. Even Francis, the black servant, was not there; Johnson had sent him to school at Bishop's Stortford to learn Latin and Greek (Francis was not to return until 1772). [38]

Boswell consoled himself by enjoying his fame for a few days; he also indulged his "roaring" spirits, with unhappy results. A cure was in order but he postponed this for a few days, going on the 26th of March to see Johnson and Chambers in Oxford. Boswell wrote full accounts of the great man's wide-ranging conversation, and among the many subjects discussed was the idea of their tour to Scotland and

[36] *An Account of Corsica, the Journal of a Tour to that Island; and Memoirs of Pascal Paoli.* By James Boswell, Esq. Glasgow:by Robert and Andrew Foulis for Edward and Charles Dilly, London. 1768.

[37] "I wish you would empty your head of Corsica, which I think has filled it rather too long." Johnson to Boswell, 23 March 1768; but this letter was sent to Scotland and had not yet been received.

[38] *Life*, II, 62, n. 1.

the Hebrides. Undoubtedly, during these days Boswell heard mention of the Thrales; and surely he heard much more about them when he returned on the 29th to his London lodgings in Half-Moon Street. There he secluded himself for the cure, which took several weeks. Many callers came to see him, congratulating him upon his book and entertaining him with news and gossip. His curiosity about the Thrales was roused.

And one day, when Boswell was in circulation again, he did an impulsive thing — he jumped into Mrs. Thrale's coach at Johnson's Court as she came to fetch the great man to Streatham. He wrote to her later that the impulsive leap had been prompted by "that agreeable kind of attraction which makes one forget ceremony." [39] Presumably Johnson was in the coach when Boswell leaped into it, for he wrote in notes for the *Life* that Johnson had introduced him to Mrs. Thrale.[40] Boswell talked to her with assurance, showing that he "was as Johnsonian as herself." [41] He was far more at ease than he had been in his first encounter with Johnson.

The exact date of the incident in the coach is not known but it must have been in early June, before Boswell returned to Scotland.[42]

1769

From the time that Boswell left London in June 1768 until he came back in the autumn of 1769, his thoughts did not often turn to Johnson. He was deeply involved with personal matters; his long search for a wife had finally ended — and with surprising good fortune; he was engaged to Margaret Montgomerie,[43] his understanding and devoted cousin. He could not have made a better choice.

[39] Boswell to Mrs. Thrale, 9 July 1782. (Lawrie MS. Copy: Hyde — MS. Letter was W. K. Bixby; present location not known.)

[40] "He had introduced me to Mrs. Thrale in 1768. But I returned to Scotland so soon after I was not at their house." Material for the *Life*, Yale: (M153, p. 3).

[41] MS. of the *Life of Johnson* at Yale (Papers Apart 349). Under 30 September 1769: "I had last year had the pleasure of seeing Mʳˢ Thrale at Dʳ Johnson's for a short while in a morning, and had conversation enough with her to admire her talents and to shew her that I was as Johnsonian as herself." (Also *Life*, II, 77).

The greatest part of the manuscript of the *Life* is at Yale. The manuscript is hereafter referred to as MS. *Life*.

[42] *Life*, II, 66.

[43] Margaret Montgomerie of Lainshaw (1738–1789) was Boswell's first cousin; her mother, Lord Auchinleck's only sister. Her parents were dead and she was thirty-one — two years older than Boswell. Some might have questioned Boswell's

Drawn and Engraved by William Ellis.

Published 1st Aug 1792 by Harrison & C.º Nº 18 Paternoster Row London.

STREATHAM PARK

BOSWELL IN THE COSTUME OF A CORSICAN CHIEF
AT THE SHAKESPEARE JUBILEE, 1769

Boswell was generally pleased with himself when he came to London this September. He was a rising advocate, a recognized author, and now he was about to take an important step in life. He was eager to have Johnson philosophize upon the subject of marriage; he was also hopeful that he could persuade the distinguished editor of Shakespeare [44] to accompany him to the Jubilee at Stratford — much talked of at the moment and appropriate, for the master plan was a creation of Johnson's ex-pupil, David Garrick.[45] (Festivities were to include a ball, at which Boswell intended to wear his dress of a Corsican chief.)[46]

Boswell called upon Johnson as soon as he arrived in London and was disappointed to be told that his mentor was in Brighton with the Thrales. Johnson had no mind to go to Stratford, no desire to play second fiddle to his one-time student. Garrick had asked him to write the *Ode to Shakespeare* which he was going to recite at the opening of the new Town Hall, the high point of the ceremonies. Johnson flatly refused; he took no interest in the Jubilee, he ignored it completely — a pity, for if Johnson had lent his powerful assistance, Shakespeare's Jubilee might have been a worthier tribute. As it was, Johnson had no connection with the celebration; the only trace of him to be found in Stratford in September 1769 was a line of verse from his Drury Lane Prologue [47] on "Shakespeare Ribbands" worn by many of the visitors.

---

judgment, for Peggie, though warm and physically attractive, was far less beautiful than other ladies he had considered, and she was exceedingly reticent, not dazzling as others had been, and she was certainly poorer — £1000 was her total fortune. But Peggie Montgomerie had qualities which were unique: patience, complete understanding, and sympathy. She had intelligence and good sense, delightful humor and an unfailing, telling, mordant wit. She gave him confidence, and comfort and devotion. Her greatest wish now (and always) was for his happiness.

[44] *The Plays of William Shakespeare*, in Eight Volumes, with the Corrections and Illustrations of Various Commentators; To which are added Notes by Sam. Johnson. London: J. and R. Tonson. 1765.

[45] David Garrick (1717–1779), the most celebrated actor of the day, had been one of the few students who had attended Johnson's ill-fated school at Edial in 1736. Johnson and Garrick had come down to London together the following year to try their fortunes.

[46] He did, and in his Journal for 7 September 1769 reported: "My Corsican dress attracted every body." *Boswell Papers*, VIII, 100–101.

12 September: a drawing was made by Mr. Wale of Boswell in this costume. *Ibid.*, 107.

23 September: Mr. Miller engraved a print of the same. *Ibid.*, 127.

[47] "Each change of *many-colour'd* life he drew." *Life*, II, 69.

Boswell was sorry that Johnson would not accompany him to Stratford; and after he returned, was further disappointed to find him still in Brighton. He wrote to Johnson that he was eager "to have as much of his conversation as [he] could before engaging in a state of life which would probably keep [him] more in Scotland." [48] Johnson did not reply, and in an attempt to ascertain his plans, Boswell dispatched his first letter to Mrs. Thrale. He did not spell her name correctly, but 18th century spelling was something of an individual matter as the characters in this story show — Johnson had written both "Trails" and "Thrail's" in the first January of his acquaintance.[49]

Boswell's letter was confident and easy: if Johnson would not come to London, he would "come" to Brighton. That is what Boswell had in mind to say, but he changed "come" to "wait upon," a tactful change, for the phrase indicated a single demand upon the prospective hostess.

[page 1]

Oxford
5 Sept[r] 1769.

Madam.

I presume to trouble you with a few lines, which I am not afraid to do, when I recollect the polite and obliging manner with which you was pleased to behave to me, when I had the honour to pass a little time with you before M[r] Johnson's Court. I told you, Madam, that you and I were rivals for that great man. You would take him to the country, when I was anxious to keep him in town. But as I believe you to be a generous rival, I beg you may do me the favour to put M[r] Johnson in mind to write to me. After much inconstancy I am fixed in my choice of a wife & am to be married when I return to Scotland.
Before

[page 2]

Before entering on that important state to happiness or misery, I am anxious to hear the Oracle, and therefore have written to M[r] Johnson to let me know if he can be soon in London, because if he cannot, I will ⟨come⟩ wait upon him at Brighthelmston. To you, Madam, my enthusiasm will not appear extravagant. I hope you will excuse this trouble, and will believe me to be very respectfully
   Madam
      your most obedient

[48] *Life*, II, 68.
[49] Johnson's 1765–1784 Diary. MS:Hyde. Text in *Samuel Johnson Diaries, Prayers, and Annals*, Edited by E. L. McAdam, Jr., with Donald and Mary Hyde (New Haven: Yale University Press, 1958), pp. 84, 88.

humble servant
James Boswell.
P.S. I am so far on my road to Shakespeare's Jubilee; but shall be at M̲ͬ Dilly's Bookseller in London, on Saturday.[50]

———

[Addressed:]
  To
    M̲ͬˢ Thraile
      Brighthelmston

It is interesting that at their first encounter in the coach, and again in this letter, Boswell said that he and Mrs. Thrale were "rivals for that great man." The word "rivals" was used lightly, and in a kindly sense, "a generous rival," but the fact of its initial use, its remembrance, and repetition, has definite psychological significance.

Mrs. Thrale did not have to persuade Johnson to write: Boswell's news was sufficiently important to provoke a quick reply from the "Oracle" himself.[51] He said he would return to London in about a fortnight, so Boswell decided not to "wait upon" him in Brighton.

After Johnson's return to town, the two met frequently,[52] and on the 30th of September, as Boswell was to write years later in the manuscript of the *Life*,[53] Johnson "delivered me" a card from Mrs. Thrale. "Dr. Johnson had probably praised me," he explained, and the outcome was an invitation to Streatham. The card "in the fair handwriting of that Lady," he said he had preserved "as [his] first ticket to a great deal of most agreeable society." The invitation was quoted in the manuscript, but both the comment and the note were later deleted. The "ticket," however, has survived.

[In Boswell's hand] First Card from the Thrale Family
30 Septr. 1769.
M̲ͬ and M̲ͬˢ Thrale present their best Compliments to M̲ͬ Boswell, and should think themselves highly favour'd in his Company to Dinner at Stretham [sic] any day he shall think fit to appoint.
30: Sep: [54]

The manuscript passage in the *Life* describing Boswell's first visit to the Thrales was not changed greatly in the printed text. Streatham was

[50] MS. Letter: Hyde.
[51] Johnson to Boswell, 9 September 1769. Letter #222. *Letters*, I, 230–231.
[52] *Life*, II, 71.
[53] MS. *Life*: Yale (Papers Apart 349).
[54] MS. Card: Hyde.

a charming house, six miles from London, with "every circumstance that can make society pleasing" [changed from "valuable" in the manuscript]. The *Life* comment that Johnson was "looked up to with an awe, tempered by affection, and seemed to be equally the care of his host and hostess" was only slightly changed from the manuscript text in which Johnson was first said "to be equally venerated by his host and hostess in their different ways." Both texts concluded with "I rejoiced at seeing him so happy." [55] The description of the evening is not detailed, and one reason for this is given in a note on the subject: "1769 . . . *This* autumn, I was invited to Streatham & went 6 Octr — dined & past the evening. I am not sure if I returned to town that night (Be not too minute)." [56]

A month later, when Boswell was about to set off for Scotland and his wedding, he begged Johnson for a farewell meeting. Johnson replied: "it will less incommode you to spend your night here, than me to come to town. I wish to see you, and am ordered by the lady of this house to invite you hither." [57] Boswell was detained in town too late to go on the 9th, but came to Streatham early in the morning of November 10th. Mr. Thrale further impressed him with his friendliness and Mrs. Thrale with her liveliness, also her courage in argument with Johnson. To his great satisfaction Johnson accompanied him back to London to see him off for Scotland.[58]

On November 25th Boswell married his cousin, Margaret Montgomerie. Domestic life and legal business kept him from London for the next three years, during which time he did not write to the Thrales, and his correspondence with Johnson all but ceased.

1772

On the 3rd of March 1772 Boswell wrote to Johnson [59] that he would soon be arriving in London to defend the appeal of a Scottish schoolmaster ("deprived of his office for being somewhat severe in

[55] MS. *Life*: Yale (Papers Apart 349). *Life*, II, 77.

[56] *Life* materials. Yale (M153, p. 3).

[57] Johnson to Boswell, 9 November 1769. Letter #225. *Letters*, I, 232.

[58] *Life*, II, 111.

[59] Boswell to Johnson, 3 March 1772. MS. Letter: Hyde. Partial text in *Life*, II, 144–145. Full text in *Letters of James Boswell*, Collected and edited by Chauncey Brewster Tinker, 2 v. (Oxford: Clarendon Press, 1924), I, 185–187. Hereafter referred to as *Tinker Boswell Letters*.

First Card from the Thrale Family
30 Septr. 1769.

Mr: and Mrs Thrale present their best
Compliments to Mr: Boswell, and should
think themselves highly favour'd in his
Company to Dinner at Streatham any day
he shall think fit to appoint.

30.. Sept:

MRS. THRALE TO BOSWELL
30 SEPTEMBER 1769

Four Oaks Farm

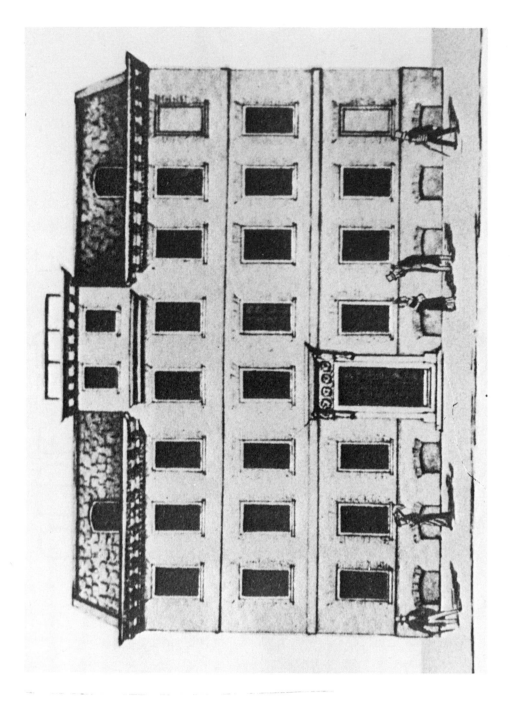

THE THRALE HOUSE
AT THE BREWERY, 1833

the chastisement of his scholars"). Boswell was pleased that this provided an opportunity to meet with Johnson, giving "a renewal of that spirit which your presence allways gives me, and which makes me a better and happier man." He hoped "at length to fix our voyage to the Hebrides," the excursion which they had been discussing since the year of their first meeting. A courtesy at the end of the letter (not published in the *Life*) was, "I beg you may make my best compliments to Mr. Thrale's family . . ."

Johnson replied on March 15th, delighted that his friend was "coming so soon to town." He expatiated upon the law case but did not mention the proposed tour to the Hebrides. Responding to Boswell's message for the Thrales, he wrote, on his own and without warrant from the lady, "Mrs. Thrale loves you." [60]

Boswell came to London in the late afternoon of March 19th and called at Johnson's Court. He recorded in his Journal (though not in the *Life*) that his friend was not at home but with the Thrales in Southwark.[61] By the 21st, however, Johnson was back and gave his visitor an affectionate welcome. They saw much of each other from then until mid-May, when Boswell returned to Scotland. During this time, Boswell forwarded his project of a tour to the Hebrides, and he laid the groundwork for something else. He recorded in his Journal for the 31st of March:

I have a constant plan to write the Life of Mʳ Johnson. I have not told him of it yet; nor do I know if I should tell him. [Sentence deleted] I said that if it was not troublesome and presuming too much I would beg of [changed to "request"] him to tell me all the little circumstances of his life, what schools he attended, when he came to Oxford, when he came to London etc, etc. He did not disapprove of my curiosity as to these particulars; but said 'They'll come out by degrees as we talk together.' [62]

Re-working this passage for the published account, Boswell does not mention the fact that Johnson had no knowledge of the plan, nor his quandary — whether or not to tell him. He simply introduces the second part of the Journal entry by saying "if it was not troublesome

[60] Johnson to Boswell, 15 March 1772. Letter #274. *Letters*, I, 276. See also Mrs. Thrale's marginal note, "Not I. I never lov'd him," in Boswell's *Life of Johnson* (with marginal annotations by Mrs. Thrale Piozzi; The Limited Editions Club; London: Curwen Press, 1938), I, 465. Hereafter referred to as *Life Limited Edition*.

[61] *Boswell Papers*, IX, 16 (19 March 1772).

[62] Boswell Journal in Notebook. Yale (Notebook 24, p. 126). Later edited as MS. *Life*: *Life*, II, 166.

and presuming too much . . ." after bringing up the subject of biography through Goldsmith's *Life of Parnell*.[63] The interesting thing to remember is that in the spring of 1772 Johnson had not yet been told of Boswell's "constant plan."

Boswell did not have much opportunity to study his subject at the Thrales on this visit to London, but he was graciously received whenever he wished to come to them. He was twice at their house with Johnson [64] and, before leaving London, came to call. This was a congenial occasion, and Mrs. Thrale expressed the hope that Mrs. Boswell would accompany her husband to London the next year.[65] The Thrales would have something important to show them, for major renovations were going forward at Streatham — a new library room was being created. Johnson was guiding the selection of books and the celebrated Sir Joshua Reynolds [66] was working on portraits for the room: Thrale would be above the door, Mrs. Thrale and Queeney above the fireplace mantel, and the portraits of other friends would hang over the bookcases around the wall.[67]

It was a warm parting between Boswell and the Thrales, and the prospects of a solid friendship seemed quite possible. Johnson, who originally had not shown interest in bringing his friends together, was pleased with the present state of cordiality and, during the winter, in the postscript of a letter to Boswell, sent the message, "You continue to stand very high in the favour of Mrs. Thrale." [68]

1773

The spring of 1773 found Boswell again contemplating a trip to London and on March 19th, shortly before setting out, he wrote to

[63] *Life*, II, 166 (31 March 1772).

[64] *Boswell Papers*, IX, 256 (22 April 1772); *Ibid.*, 260 (28 April 1772): "Mrs. Thrale's, capital."

[65] "Gen[eral's] chariot took me Mrs. Thrale's. Much of John[son.] Kind invit[ation,] 'Wife, etc., next year'. Charming day." *Boswell Papers*, IX, 266 (11 May 1772).

[66] Sir Joshua Reynolds (1723–1792). This distinguished, charming, and popular artist had been brought into the Thrales' orbit by Johnson, and he was now very much at home with them. His own self-portrait would be included among the friends chosen for the library decoration.

[67] *Life*, IV, 158, n. 1. For furnishings: see *Catalogue of the Streatham Park, Surrey, Auction Sale. On the premises, Wednesday, 8 May 1816.*

[68] Johnson to Boswell, 24 February 1773. Letter #295. *Letters*, I, 304. Marginal comment in *Life Limited Edition*, II, 48: "Poor Mrs. Thrale was forced to say so in order to keep well with Johnson." (Date of letter is incorrectly given here.)

Johnson and Henry Thrale, according to his Letter Register.[69] The
location of his letter to Thrale is not known now, but it can be assumed
that it mentioned his imminent arrival; it probably also referred to
the kind invitation extended the previous year to Mrs. Boswell. She,
unfortunately, was not well enough to make the trip.

As it turned out, Mrs. Thrale would not have been able to offer
much hospitality, for a series of trials had beset her; Thrale had suffered
in the business crisis of 1772 and was still worried and morose. To
complicate matters he had suddenly become the center of a newspaper
scandal — amorous episodes of his past and gross present insinuations.[70]
Mrs. Thrale was startled by the revelations and genuinely wretched.
She had lost a child the past autumn and was now pregnant again;
though she felt far from well, she forced herself to come to the Borough
for part of every week to help straighten out matters at the brewery
and to see Johnson. The rest of the week Mrs. Thrale was at Streatham
nursing her mother, whom it was thought best to keep in the country.
Mrs. Salusbury was suffering from cancer of the breast and was in constant pain.

When Boswell arrived in London at the beginning of April, he
called late at Johnson's Court. His friend was still out for the evening
but he talked to Miss Williams until he came home. Because of the
Thrales' preoccupation, Boswell saw a great deal of Johnson during
this stay and made admirable progress with his collection of biographical details. Johnson gave him many more particulars of his
youth. "You shall have them all for two-pence," Johnson said, and
added, "I hope you shall know a great deal more of me before you
write my Life." [71] So, at least by April Johnson had been informed
of Boswell's "constant plan," and was not displeased with the project.
The two talked of many wide-ranging subjects, not the least of which
was the definite possibility of their excursion to the Hebrides this
summer. The idea fired Boswell's imagination, and it elated him to
think that while they were constant companions he would have the
opportunity for minute observation and deep probing, which he had
long envied Mrs. Thrale. Johnson was challenged by the idea, but
uncertain about the actual trip.

[69] Boswell's Letter Register: Yale (M253).
[70] *Clifford*, pp. 97–99.
[71] *Life*, II, 217 (13 April 1773).

On three occasions when Mrs. Thrale was in London, Johnson and Boswell came to Southwark. Boswell was good humored, confident, and easy, and Mrs. Thrale was very grateful for his attention to Johnson.

In May Boswell returned to Scotland and began to make plans for the journey. Johnson's health was a serious problem. He came down with a fever and, when this left him, a serious eye infection developed. He wanted to come to Streatham: "My eye is yet so dark that I could not read your note. I have had a poor darkling week . . . I wish you could fetch me . . . I long to be in my own room . . . I hope I shall not add much to your trouble, and will wish at least to give you some little solace or amusement. I long to be under your care." [72] By the first of June Johnson had been brought to Streatham, but he found it a sad, changed place; Mrs. Salusbury's condition was constantly worsening,[73] and her daughter found Johnson's presence a trial rather than a comfort. She gave careful attention to his eye, however, and there was marked improvement.

As Boswell continued with his plans for the Highland jaunt and pressed him to be definite, Mrs. Thrale abetted the scheme. She knew that her mother was dying, and Johnson's melancholy behavior and charges of neglect made things even harder for her. She sent a note to his room: "to struggle with the loss of one Friend . . . let me not put to hazard [the loss of another, whom] I esteem beyond Kingdoms, and value beyond the possession of them." She urged Johnson to go to the Hebrides: "Dissipation is to you a glorious Medicine, and I believe Mr. Boswell will be at last your best Physician." [74]

Boswell was not able to leave Edinburgh until the rising of the Court of Session in mid-August, too late for the best weather, though not, he was confident, too late to make the journey. Boswell had worried about Johnson's eye, but now by early July it was much improved. Boswell had also received the good news that their friend, Robert Chambers, the law professor whom they had seen five years before in Oxford, would accompany Johnson as far north as New-

---

[72] Johnson to Mrs. Thrale, 29 May 1773. MS. Letter: Mrs. Maas. Letter #311.1. *Letters*, I, 331.

[73] Mrs. Salusbury died on 18 June 1773.

[74] Mrs. Thrale to Johnson, c. 30 May 1773. MS. Letter: Rylands Library, Manchester, England, Eng. MS. 539/30. Letter #311.1a. *Letters*, I, 332. This library hereafter referred to as Rylands.

castle. Boswell wanted nothing to go wrong; his proposed itinerary was ambitious, and his agitation was great. At the end of July, he wrote to Thrale, urging him and his wife to "launch" Johnson northward.

Edinburgh
29 July 1773.

Dear Sir.

It is a most fortunate circumstance that Mr Chambers comes north just now, as that will I hope insure me our friend Mr Johnson. But I must once more apply to you & Mrs Thrale to *launch* him from London, as I called it. He will return to you with a cargo of at least some *curious* things, if not with *valuable* ones. You can scarcely imagine how great joy I feel in the prospect of his coming. You will excuse me for troubling you with the enclosed to him. I offer my best compliments to Mrs Thrale, and ever am with very sincere regard,

Dear Sir your obliged humble servant
James Boswell.[75]

––––––

To
Henry Thrale Esq.
Member of Parliament
Southwark
London

Johnson was "launched" and arrived in Edinburgh on August 14th. He took an immediate liking to Mrs. Boswell, a fine, sensible woman. She did not reciprocate his warmth (though she moved out of her own room to accommodate the celebrated visitor). She found him troublesome, he kept irregular hours, and had uncouth habits. She also felt Johnson had too great an influence over her husband,[76] always taking him away — they too were rivals for his attention. Mrs. Boswell thought the present trip unnecessary and viewed the entire expedition with uneasiness. She bade the travelers farewell on the 18th of August with reluctance. She certainly had cause for alarm, but providence was kind and though they encountered poor weather and a certain number of mishaps, the trip was a celebrated success. Johnson, despite

[75] MS. Letter: Rylands, Eng.MS.542/1.

[76] Boswell said (*Life*, II, 269, n. 1): "She once in a little warmth, made, with more point than justice, this remark upon that subject: 'I have seen many a bear led by a man; but I never before saw a man led by a bear.'"

the fact that he was about to be sixty-four, and had not been well, was equal to vigorous exertion; several times he sustained hardships more easily than his stronger thirty-three year old companion. Johnson's pleasure in Boswell's company was keen and, as always, he delighted in seeing new sights and gathering new ideas. For Boswell, the trip was the realization of a romantic dream — to observe the Rambler in Scotland. "If I survive him," Boswell wrote in his Diary, "I shall be one who shall most faithfully do honour to his memory." [77] Johnson, who was enjoying Boswell's Journal as they traveled, read this passage, approved it, and gave his future biographer further details of his early years.

He pleased Boswell by telling him that he planned to publish an account of their journey when he returned home. Johnson was keeping no regular diary to guide him, though he was writing a book of remarks (which has not survived); also, to help with the project, he was sending long journal letters to Mrs. Thrale. Boswell "wondered to see him write so much so easily" to her.[78] These letters are interesting in content and they show how much the Thrales were in Johnson's thoughts and how much he missed them. Boswell himself was fully aware of his companion's high regard for the Thrales. For example: at Tobermory, when Boswell said, "we shall see Dr. Maclean, who has written the history of the Macleans," Johnson replied, "I'd rather hear the history of the Thrales." [79] And at Fort Augustus he rebuked Boswell for speaking of Mrs. Thrale with levity. Boswell had said playfully that he was thinking of writing "an Epistle to [Johnson] *on his return from Scotland*, in the style of Mrs. Gulliver to Captain Lemuel Gulliver"; Johnson had "laughed and asked in whose name I'd write it. I said Mrs. Thrale's. He was angry and said, 'Sir, if you have any sense of decency or delicacy, you won't do that.'" [80] And at Inverary, when Johnson and Boswell drank whisky ("Come, let me know what it is that makes a Scotsman happy") Boswell "proposed Mrs. Thrale should be our toast. He would not have *her* drank in whisky" and proposed some insular lady instead.[81]

---

[77] Boswell's *Journal of a Tour to the Hebrides with Samuel Johnson, LL.D.*, Edited by Frederick A. Pottle and Charles H. Bennett (New York: Viking Press, 1936), p. 300. Hereafter referred to as *Hebrides.*

[78] *Life*, V, 110.

[79] *Hebrides*, p. 302.

[80] *Ibid.*, p. 105.

[81] *Ibid.*, pp. 348–349.

When Boswell begged a copy of the "very pretty" Ode Johnson had written Mrs. Thrale from Skye, he was told, " 'I'd as soon give you my ears.' But he said I might get it from her if she pleased." [82]

The only communication from the Thrales to Boswell during the tour was a brief note from Thrale in August, enclosing a letter to Johnson. This note has not been located but it was acknowledged by Boswell in his letter to Thrale of November 22nd, at the conclusion of the jaunt. Boswell wrote with evident satisfaction; the journey had been successful. He imagined that Johnson's letters to them had given "a pretty full account" and he hoped they would prod him on to prepare a manuscript for publication.

One of the interesting features of the tour was the strengthening of the bond between Johnson and Boswell. Traveling is a severe test and frequently produces the opposite result, but in their case it created a firmer tie. Johnson found Boswell even better natured and possessed of stronger faculties and discernment than he had realized. For the first time their friendship became a mature one; he accepted Boswell as a man of responsibility and was delighted to see him in his natural surroundings, particularly pleased to find that he was welcomed everywhere with respect.

At the end of the tour Boswell brought Johnson to Auchinleck (2 to 8 November 1773). There, after a few days, the celebrated "collision" between Johnson and Boswell's father took place. [83] Still, when the distinguished guest departed, "notwithstanding the altercation that had passed" the old Baron "was very civil to Dr. Johnson, and politely attended him to the post-chaise" [84] which conveyed the two travellers to Boswell's house in Edinburgh. All was serene on this return visit there (10 to 20 November), though Mrs. Boswell must have suffered more acutely from the presence of the celebrated visitor than Lord Auchinleck had. There were constant levees "from ten o'clock till one or two," a steady stream of callers "of very different characters and descriptions." Boswell escaped these receptions because he was attending the Court of Session; it was his wife who devoted "the greater part of the morning to the endless task of pouring out tea for my friend and his visitors." [85] Docile, long-suffering, instinctively

[82] *Ibid.*, p. 136.
[83] *Ibid.*, p. 375.
[84] *Life*, V, 384–385.
[85] *Ibid.*, 395.

polite, and doubtless devoutly thankful for the travelers' safe return from the wilds of the Hebrides, Mrs. Boswell stayed at the tea-table without complaint.

On the 20th of November Boswell accompanied Johnson to Hawthornden, Cranston, and Blackshiels. At the last town, on the morning of Monday, November 22nd, Boswell put his illustrious friend aboard the coach for Newcastle and took his leave. Returning to Edinburgh, he wrote to Thrale later on the same day.

[page 1]

Edinburgh
22 Nov.ʳ 1773.

Dear Sir.

I had the pleasure to receive a few lines from you in August when you enclosed a letter to Mʳ Johnson under cover to me. Since that time our much respected friend and I have had a long and very curious tour of which his letters have I suppose given you and Mʳˢ Thrale a pretty full account. The World however I hope will have a still fuller account from him. I hope you and Mʳˢ Thrale will not be wanting in keeping [him] in mind of the expectations which he has raised. He & I were last night at an Inn fourteen miles on his road to London, where I took leave of him this morning, & saw him into the Fly.

He

[page 2]

He will arrive in London on friday night, if no bad accident happens. I take the liberty to trouble you with a letter from an old acquaintance to Mʳˢ Williams, which I forgot to send by Mʳ Johnson. You will be so good as deliver it to him, or send it to his house. I shall be anxious till I hear of his safe arrival. I flatter myself that he shall have no cause to repent of his northern expedition. I offer my best compliments to Mʳˢ Thrale, and am with very sincere esteem   Dear Sir
          Your obliged and
          most obedient humble servant
               James Boswell.[86]

Johnson, upon his return to the Thrales, recovered his letters to them and began serious work on his *Journey to the Western Islands of Scotland*, one consequence of which was that Boswell had the pleasure of more frequent correspondence with him.

[86] MS. Letter: Hyde.

1774

In the beginning of 1774 Johnson wrote impatiently, "You must make haste and gather me all you can, and do it quickly, or I will and shall do without it."[87] Boswell, as commanded, sent some material which was useful, but Johnson depended in the main upon the long diary letters which he had written to the Thrales while on the trip. Boswell would have had more connection with the book if he had been able to come to London, but when the time arrived for his customary Easter visit, he had no ready money; and his wife, who was expecting a child in May, was not eager to let him go. Johnson sided strongly with Mrs. Boswell and counselled him to stay at home; Boswell regretfully abandoned the journey. He neither read nor discussed the manuscript with Johnson before publication.

Boswell continued, however, to send packets of material through Thrale and he also tried to plan a later visit. On May 13th he wrote to Thrale that he was glad Johnson's manuscript was "well advanced" and he wondered about the family's proposed excursion to Italy. This was the country, above all, which Johnson wished to visit. He had told Boswell about the Thrales' plan and how greatly he anticipated being a member of the party. Was the trip to take place in the spring, Boswell asked. If so, he might try to visit Streatham in the autumn.

[page 1]

Edinburgh
13 May 1774.

Dear Sir.

I know not if I should make an apology for troubling you with so many packets to our friend Mr Johnson. I believe you are very willing to take trouble either on his account or mine. But at present [yo]u are troubled for the benefit of the Publick. I rejoice to hear that his Northern Tour is well advanced. As I am not to have the pleasure of being under your hospitable roof this spring, it would be kind if you would favour me with a few lines informing

me

[page 2]

me how you all are, and how Mr Johnson is.

Poor Goldsmith will be much missed at your Literary Parties. The news of his death came upon me very suddenly and affected me more than any thing that has happened of a long time.

---

[87] Johnson to Boswell, 29 January 1774. Letter #343. *Letters*, I, 394.

I hope to be with you before you set out on your tour to Italy, of which Mͬ Johnson talked to me. If you are to go early in the spring before I can get to London, I may perhaps take a trip to Stretham [*sic*] in autumn. I offer my best compliments to Mͬˢ Thrale with whom I long to compare notes as to Mͬ Johnson's Northern tour, and I am with most sincere esteem

        my Dear Sir

          your obliged humble

            servant

              James Boswell.[88]

———

To

   Henry Thrale Esq. M.P.

      Southwark

        London

Henry Thrale did not respond. In early July [89] he and Mrs. Thrale took their eldest daughter, Queeney, and Johnson to Wales. For Johnson this was very different from his trip to the Hebrides the year before; that had been a long-planned and imaginative expedition in which a single companion dedicated himself to the great man's pleasure and lionization. The purpose of the Welsh trip was business (property which Mrs. Thrale had inherited from her uncle, Sir Thomas Salusbury).[90] Johnson was simply accompanying the family, seeing his hostess' much loved, ancestral Vale of Clwyd, meeting many relations, and trying to be helpful. There was little novelty to stimulate his powers. He did, however, keep a journal of the trip, and so did Mrs. Thrale.

Johnson wrote to Boswell on the eve of departure,[91] simply saying, "I am going into Wales to-morrow." He gave no details, and did not name his traveling companions (though Boswell could be presumed to associate Wales with Mrs. Thrale). Johnson gave no addresses where he might be reached and he did not write to Boswell again until he returned. Then, he dismissed the trip in one short paragraph, without mention of the Thrales: ". . . Wales is so little different from England, that it offers nothing to the speculation of the traveller." [92] Most of his letter was given over to other matters, including the manner

[88] MS. Letter: Harvard.
[89] *Life*, III, 453.
[90] *Clifford*, pp. 106, 113.
[91] Johnson to Boswell, 4 July 1774. Letter #357, *Letters* I, 409.
[92] Johnson to Boswell, 1 October 1774. Letter #360. *Letters*, I, 412.

in which complimentary copies of his Hebrides book should be distributed. "I wish you could have read the book before it was printed, but our distance does not easily permit it."

Boswell's hope of being at Streatham in the autumn came to nothing.

1775

Boswell did not make a trip to London until the spring of 1775; this was a propitious time and one of his happiest visits. Johnson's *Journey to the Western Islands of Scotland* had been published and enthusiastically received.[93] It was discussed everywhere, and Boswell was delighted that in this shared adventure the public recognized his close friendship with Johnson.

Boswell arrived on March 21st and, following his usual pattern, called at once upon his friend, whom he was pleased to find at home. Johnson was, however, going to the Thrales in the afternoon but he asked Boswell to go with him to Southwark. Boswell agreed, and had an enjoyable visit with Mrs. Thrale, Johnson, Giuseppe Baretti,[94] and Peter Garrick, the actor's eldest brother.[95]

The Thrales showed considerable regard for Boswell. Within a week Thrale offered him "a general invitation to dine when not otherwise engaged as [Johnson] was to be much there." Boswell recorded

[93] *A Journey to the Western Islands of Scotland.* London: for W. Strahan and T. Cadell. 1775.

[94] Giuseppe Baretti (1719–1789). This talented and impetuous scholar had been introduced to the Thrales by Johnson, his steadfast friend. He seemed the ideal person to give Queeney instruction in Italian. Baretti had had considerable reputation as a writer in Italy before a controversial piece of satire had forced him to leave Turin and seek employment elsewhere. He had come to London and opened a school for the teaching of Italian; he also published an *Introduction to the Italian Language*, and a book about the lives and works of the principal writers in Italy, and produced an authoritative *Italian and English Dictionary*.

Baretti agreed to teach Queeney, and came to live with the Thrales in 1773. A sympathetic accord soon developed between teacher and pupil; the other Thrale girls also liked Baretti. He was extremely indulgent — no disciplinarian. Mrs. Thrale, on the other hand, believed that physical punishment was often necessary to assure obedience; she and Baretti were at swords' points on all matters concerning the children.

About fifteen months after the visit mentioned here, Baretti, in a frenzy of anger, walked out of the house without taking any leave whatsoever. In later years Thrale would still offer him hospitality as a visitor, and he would sometimes come despite his hatred of Mrs. Thrale.

[95] *Boswell Papers*, X, 136 (21 March 1775).

in his Journal, "This was exceedingly kind, and I valued both the kindness and the advantage of it, as one values an *useful* dish or vase of *fine* metal, (a bad simile enough, I fear)." [96] He commented justly on his cool appraisal, but though his simile was crass, he did appreciate Thrale's welcome, and he responded well to Thrale himself, "his manly, true [E]nglish heartiness." [97] At five, the usual dinner time, the family, including Johnson and Baretti, sat down to a plain and plentiful meal. When Boswell complimented his host upon a delightful French liqueur, Thrale said he had a dozen bottles of it and would reserve them all for Boswell, bringing out a bottle only when he was with them.[98]

A few days later, on April 1st, Johnson made two engagements to dine, one with Boswell, the second with other friends. Thrale, in an effort to extricate Johnson, sent a card to Boswell, inviting them both to Southwark. Johnson did not come, but Boswell walked over London Bridge to the Thrales', the first time he had been there for a meal alone, a significant development; but it was disappointing that Johnson could not have been a member of the party, for only that morning he had received his Doctor of Laws diploma from Oxford [99] — talk on the subject merited a record. Boswell, nevertheless, enjoyed the evening, even without Johnson's company. Thrale was particularly attentive, not only bringing out the special liqueur but, when the company went to tea, drawing him apart to talk. This gave Boswell an

[96] *Ibid.*, 158 (28 March 1775).

[97] *Idem.*

[98] *Ibid.*, 159 (28 March 1775).

Mrs. Thrale also made Boswell a present sometime during this year: a copy of Johnson's Latin verses (and her English imitation) of "In Theatro." "One Night in Feb:1771. or later in the Spring — Oratorio Season I made Mr Johnson go with me to one," she wrote in *Thraliana*, I, 213. They sat in a side box at Covent Garden, according to *Anecdotes*, 72. Soon she noticed that Dr. Johnson had "left off listening to the Musick but said little, so [she] thought he was minding it: when [they] came home however he repeated [to her] the following Verses which he had been composing at the Play house it seems."

The lines are written on a tiny piece of paper 4 7/8 by 3 1/8 inches, with Boswell's annotation: "Mrs. Thrale gave me this. 1775" On the verso is Mrs. Thrale's English imitation, with an added Boswell annotation. The literary activity of all three is shown on this small card. (MS: "In Theatro": Harvard).

Two years later Mrs. Thrale would give Boswell another Johnson verse, and again Boswell would annotate it. (15 August 1777 — MS. Letter enclosure: Hyde).

[99] "He did not vaunt of his new dignity, but I understood he was highly pleased with it." *Boswell Papers*, X, 170 (1 April 1775).

HENRY THRALE
BY SIR JOSHUA REYNOLDS

Four Oaks Farm

MRS. THRALE AND QUEENEY
BY SIR JOSHUA REYNOLDS

opportunity to pose his troublesome problem (discussed with many other friends) — should he or should he not come to the English bar? Thrale took a friendly interest in the matter and was "rather *for*" it.

A few days later, Boswell, after a riotous night, steadied himself with coffee and two "basons" of soup and walked over London Bridge. By chance he met Thrale in his coach. He talked briefly with him, then continued on to see Mrs. Thrale at the Southwark house. They chatted about various subjects, including Johnson, and when the time came for her engagement in London, she took him in her coach to his lodgings.[100]

During this period of frequent and pleasant meetings Thrale told Boswell something which electrified him, ". . . there is a Book of *Johnsoniana* kept in their Family, in which all Mr. Johnson's sayings and all they can collect about him is put down." Boswell noted in his Journal, "I must try to get this *Thralian* Miscellany to assist me in writing Mr. Johnson's Life, if Mrs. Thrale does not intend to do it herself. I suppose there will be many written." [101]

After the Thrales moved to the country for the summer, and before he returned to Scotland, Boswell went to Streatham. It was on the 16th of May,[102] an anniversary of Johnson's and Boswell's meeting, and surely an appropiate time for the rivals to discuss their great man. This they did, to their mutual enjoyment and to his displeasure, real or feigned.

Very likely with the "Thralian Miscellany" in mind, and with the hope of further convincing his hostess that he was "as Johnsonian" as she was, and to let her sample his style — Boswell brought along his manuscript Journal of the Hebridean jaunt. He probably read passages from the three pocket volumes to the assembled company as he had to his literary banker friend, Sir William Forbes, the previous January in Edinburgh. Forbes had been "much enter-

---

[100] *Ibid.*, 187 (5 April 1775).

[101] Reported in *Boswell Papers* (**X**, 200), but not in the *Life*. Thrale's reference to the "Thralian Miscellany" was probably to Mrs. Thrale's early Journal in which she had been recording Johnsoniana since the late 1760's. It is possible, however, that Thrale referred to another collection of which there is no trace, that reported by the newspapers in January 1785, "an octavo, full of blank paper" left in a "common room" for "every person in the family to note each remarkable saying of [the] Doctor." *Clifford*, p. 124.

[102] Mrs. Thrale's letter to Boswell, Thursday, 18 May 1775, gives the date as "last Tuesday."

tained." [103] So of course had Johnson been, when he read extensively in the Journal during the tour itself. Boswell could not refrain from including some of his companion's enthusiastic remarks when the book came to be published, such as this: "I take great delight in reading it . . . You improve; it grows better and better . . . It might be printed, were the subject fit for printing." [104]

At the end of the Streatham evening Boswell left his Journal with Mrs. Thrale, as he had also done with Forbes, so that she might read more fully. Boswell's departure for Scotland was imminent, however, and she was forced to read with haste. The books were very, very small, the writing cramped, the pages overcrowded — she reached only as far as the travelers' arrival on the Isle of Coll [105] before she was obliged to return the little books, almost blinded.

> Streatham
> Thursday 18: May
> 1775.

Sir

I return you a thousand Thanks for your entertaining Manuscript and hope it will not be *very* long before we shall have an Opportunity of conversing freely about our Friend's Excellencies without offending him as on last Tuesday Evening — Your Journal has almost blinded me, and I can but just see to tell you how earnestly I wish you a happy meeting with your family, and with what sincere Esteem I have the honour to be
> Sir
> Your most Obedient Servant
> Hester :L: Thrale.

————

> To
> James Boswell Esq[r]
> Gerrard Street
> Soho.

[At right angles to address, in Boswell's hand: "M[rs] Thrale after having read a great part of my Journal of a Tour to the Hebrides."] [106]

Her note of thanks is interesting, and remarkable for its brevity.

[103] *Boswell Papers*, X, 75 (1 January 1775).
[104] *Life*, V, 226–227.
[105] Enclosure in Boswell's letter to Malone, 3 April 1786. (Letter and enclosure: Hyde.)
[106] MS. Letter: Yale (C2265).

Perhaps, as she wrote, the strain of reading prevented a longer letter, but her "thousand Thanks for your entertaining Manuscript" is a polite cliché that says very little. She made no personal comment, no criticism, gave no thoughful praise. The restraint of the letter is not typical of Mrs. Thrale. She is usually more effusive, leaving no empty pages; here, she seems on guard, careful to avoid any statement of opinion or commitment. She used the word "Manuscript" and this is important, for, like Johnson and Forbes, she considered what she had read a personal diary. None of them treated the manuscript Journal as they would have treated a published book.

Johnson was curious about her reaction, and wrote: "I am not sorry that you read Boswel's journal. Is it not a merry piece?" [107] She did not answer, and the next month he wrote: "You never told me, and I omitted to enquire, how you were entertained by Boswel's Journal." [108] Despite her lack of answer, Johnson, writing to Boswell in August said: "Mrs. Thrale was so entertained by your *Journal* that she almost read herself blind." And he added, again on his own, "She has a great regard for you." [109]

The next month, when Johnson wrote to Boswell, he said (the letter is not printed in full in the *Life*): ". . . I shall not very soon write again, for I am to set out to-morrow on another journey." After a marked deletion, "Your friends are all well at Streatham." [110] This was misleading, for the Thrales and their eldest daughter, Queeney, were again his traveling companions. The trip to Italy was still postponed, but the Thrales were now taking Johnson to France. In the letter (from the text printed in the *Life*) there was no itinerary, no remark on the significance of the journey, no suggestion indeed that Johnson was leaving England.

According to his Letter Register, Boswell wrote to Thrale in London on September 30th [111] but soon thereafter he was told that the

---

[107] Johnson to Mrs. Thrale, 22 May 1775. MS. Letter: Hyde. Letter #395. *Letters*, II, 31–32. "Boswel's Journal" is inked out, but restored by Samuel Lysons.

[108] Johnson to Mrs. Thrale, 11 June 1775. MS. Letter: Hon. John Freemantle. Letter #405. *Letters*, II, 43. "Boswel's Journal" is deleted, but restored by Lysons.

[109] Johnson to Boswell, 27 August 1775. Letter #431. *Letters*, II, 83. Mrs. Thrale's comment in *Life Limited Edition*, II, 183 (on reading herself blind) was "That is true"; (on regard for Boswell) "not I — never had: I thought him a clever & a comical Fellow."

[110] Johnson to Boswell, 14 September 1775. Letter #435. *Letters*, II, 86.

[111] Location of the letter unknown. Boswell's Letter Register. Yale (M253).

Thrales were in France, and that Johnson was with them. By the second week of October he urgently wished to reach Johnson to announce a significant event, the birth of his son and heir on the 9th of the month, but he had to wait until he knew that Thrale had returned to Parliament; then, he assumed, Johnson would be home as well. He wrote on October 24th, telling the important news, and he commented goodnaturedly on the trip:

> Shall we have *A Journey to Paris* from you in the winter? You will, I hope, at any rate be kind enough to give me some account of your French travels very soon, for I am very impatient. What a different scene have you viewed this autumn, from that which you viewed in autumn 1773! [112]

Johnson responded on the 16th of November, congratulating Boswell on the birth of Alexander, "the young Laird." He said little about the French journey, no more than he had said about the Welsh journey — again a single, short paragraph, which, as before, included a gracious comparison to their own trip, "Paris is, indeed, a place very different from the Hebrides, but it is to a hasty traveller not so fertile of novelty, nor affords so many opportunities of remark." [113] It is interesting that when traveling with Boswell, Johnson kept no diary [114] but wrote constantly to the Thrales; when traveling with them, both in Wales and in France, he kept a diary and did not write to Boswell.

Boswell now sent two letters to Johnson, on the 5th of December and on the 18th. Receiving no reply, he was worried that Johnson was offended with him, or ill. According to his Letter Register, [115] Boswell also wrote to Thrale on the 18th for news of Johnson. The location of this letter is not known, but Johnson referred to it in his reassuring answer on the 23rd of December: "Mr. Thrale would have written to you if I had omitted; he sends his compliments, and wishes to see you." [116] They were on cordial terms.

Indeed, in 1775 all seemed to be well between Boswell and Mrs. Thrale, but something had happened in this year that would later cause serious trouble. The guarded, innocuous note which Mrs. Thrale

[112] Boswell to Johnson, 24 October 1775, *Life*, II, 386. *Tinker Boswell Letters*, I, 243–244.

[113] Johnson to Boswell, 16 November 1775. Letter #439. *Letters*, II, 89.

[114] On the tour to the Hebrides, as mentioned before, Johnson kept a "Book of Remarks," but this has never been recovered.

[115] Boswell's Letter Register. Yale (M253).

[116] Johnson to Boswell, 23 December 1775. Letter #446. *Letters*, II, 94.

had written, thanking Boswell for letting her read the small pocket notebooks of his Tour would — ironically, ten years later — be held as evidence against her, and fan the flames of their public quarrel.

CHAPTER II

RESTRAINT

1776 through 1781

1776

Early in March, the long-planned trip to Italy was finally material-
izing. Johnson wrote to Boswell that he would be leaving with the
Thrales during the first part of April. If Boswell wished to see him,
he must come to London at once. Boswell obligingly departed in haste
and arrived in London late on the night of March 15th. Early next
morning, when he presented himself at Johnson's Court, he found that
his friend had moved to Bolt Court; upon going there, he discovered, as
so often before, that Johnson was not at home but with the Thrales,
fortunately in Southwark. He took a boat, and when he came to the
house, found Johnson at breakfast with Mrs. Thrale. He was heartily
welcomed by them both, and soon by Thrale as well. The reception
was cordial. "Mrs. Thrale and I looked to each other while [Johnson]
talked . . . and our looks expressed our congenial admiration of
him." [1] This Boswell recorded in his Journal, but in the *Life* added
the word "affection" to admiration, also his own impression, "I shall
ever recollect this scene with great pleasure," and her remark, "There
are many . . . who admire and respect Mr. Johnson; but you and I
love him." [2] It was a happy occasion, Johnson elated about Italy, the
Thrales solicitous for his enjoyment, and Boswell pleased to be asked
by Johnson to accompany him on a round of farewell visits to old
friends. They would go to Oxford to visit Dr. Adams, [3] Master of

[1] *Boswell Papers*, XI, 134 (16 March 1776). MS. *Life*, p. 497: Arthur A. Houghton, Jr.
[2] *Life*, II, 427. This passage was on the verso of MS. *Life*, p. 496, which has not
been recovered.
[3] Dr. William Adams (1706–1789). Johnson met Adams while at Oxford, and
shortly thereafter he was doubtless pleased to see Adams replace William Jorden as
a Pembroke tutor (1734). Adams later took holy orders but returned to Oxford in
1775 to become Master of Pembroke.
He was to receive Johnson with warm hospitality on numerous occasions. Twice,
this March 1776 and in June 1784, Boswell was also a member of the party.

MRS. THRALE'S BREAKFAST TABLE

FROM A DRAWING BY ISAAC CRUIKSHANK

THE THRALE BREWERY AROUND 1820
BY DEAN WOLSTENHOLME, THE YOUNGER

Four Oaks Farm

Pembroke College; on to Birmingham to see Edmund Hector,[4] whom Johnson had known since grammar-school days; then to Lichfield to see Johnson's step-daughter, Lucy Porter[5] and many others; and finally to Ashbourne to enjoy the abundant hospitality of Dr. Taylor.[6] As Johnson and Mrs. Thrale and Boswell talked of their plans with animation and pleasure, they little imagined the destruction of their hopes within the next few days.

[4] Edmund Hector (1708–1794) attended the Lichfield Grammar School with Johnson and around 1729 became a surgeon in Birmingham. Johnson, after leaving Oxford, lived in Birmingham for about a year and a half. It was a difficult period in Johnson's life and Hector showed him great kindness. (It may well have been Hector who introduced him to Harry and Tetty Porter.) Johnson kept this important early friendship in good repair throughout his life, visiting Hector in Birmingham on at least six occasions between 1772 and 1784.

[5] Lucy Porter (1715–1786). After her mother left Edial to join Johnson in London in 1737, Lucy went to Lichfield; until Johnson's mother died in 1759, Lucy lived with her there and took care of her.

Three years after this, Lucy's brother, Henry Jervis Porter, a Captain in the Royal Navy, died, leaving her some £10,000. With part of this money she built a "stately house," and it was here that Johnson stayed when in Lichfield by himself. "She had never been in London," Boswell remarked in the *Life* (II, 462), and he also said that Johnson "had a parental tenderness for her," but Lucy, though she reverenced her step-father, showed little affection for him and was often hardly civil.

Boswell described her in 1776 as "an old maid, with much simplicity of manner" (*Life*, II, 462). Anna Seward, the Lichfield poetess, told Boswell some years later that Johnson had courted Lucy before he courted her mother (*Life*, I, 92, n. 2); but despite the fact that the ages of the three involved would make this plausible, it does not appear to have been so — Tetty was the one who had tenderness and a romantic spirit.

[6] Dr. John Taylor (1711–1788) was one of Johnson's earliest friends. They had gone to the Lichfield Grammar School together and later Taylor followed to Oxford. He would have matriculated at Pembroke College but, dissuaded by Johnson's report of the ignorance of his tutor, William Jorden, went instead to Christ Church.

After brief practice as an attorney, Taylor was ordained in the Church of England, and at one time was Chaplain to the Duke of Devonshire. Taylor accumulated an extraordinary number of preferments, to which duties he paid very little attention. With large resources, both official and private, he lived at his family residence in Ashbourne, scarcely in the style of a country parson — he was commonly known as "the King of Ashbourne."

Johnson, who visited Taylor with regularity, had deep affection for him and considered him a sensible man with a strong mind. While enjoying Ashbourne hospitality, Johnson was glad to turn his hand to sermons for Taylor, just as he had written law lectures for his host Robert Chambers in Oxford, and as he produced election pieces for Thrale whenever requested.

Taylor owned the finest breed of milch-cows in Derbyshire, perhaps in England. In Johnson's letters to Mrs. Thrale "the great bull" was a subject of light amusement. Ten years later "the great bull" was to serve Boswell for a crude and heavy jest.

After pleasant visits in the first two cities, Johnson and Boswell had come to Lichfield, and there the latter was busy collecting youthful anecdotes about his friend. At breakfast on the 25th of April, Johnson received a letter from Thrale's clerk which agitated him very much. When he had finished reading, he exclaimed: "One of the most dreadful things that has happened in my time." [7] Boswell thought from the phrase "*my time*" that it must be a public event, the assassination of the King, or a gunpowder plot, or another fire of London. When Johnson finally told him that young Harry, the Thrales' only son, had died very suddenly (probably from appendicitis), Boswell, though he knew this nine-year-old boy to be a remarkably bright, appealing, and promising young lad, thought of the event for a moment with relief, as personal and comparatively unimportant. Johnson's shock continued and Boswell endeavored to be sympathetic; he also carefully observed the great man's reaction to personal tragedy.

Johnson insisted that they make only a brief stop at Ashbourne and then return to London; for, as he wrote to Mrs. Thrale: "in a distress which can be so little relieved, nothing remains for a friend but to come and partake it." [8] They arrived in London on the 29th; Boswell stopped to pick up his mail at Charles and Edward Dillys', the publishers and booksellers in the Poultry, and Johnson hastened on to the Thrales.

Boswell read through his mail and drafted a letter to Mrs. Thrale on the blank pages of an almanac. It is interesting to see his natural fluency choked by the difficulties so many others find in writing a condolence message. The strong Johnsonian feeling of the letter is also worth noting.

To Mrs Thrale

Dear Madam.

⟨I hope it will not be considered as officious intrusion⟩ Allow me to assure you & Mr Thrale that I very sincerely / ⟨lament⟩ / ⟨sympathise with you in⟩ / regret / your present ⟨great⟩ affliction and ⟨that I⟩ very sincerely wish ⟨that⟩ it were in my power to alleviate it. ⟨You have now with you and⟩ Were you as sure as I am of my concern for you I doubt not that it would be ⟨a small⟩ some relief. You have now with you Dr Johnson whose friendship is the ⟨great-

[7] *Life*, II, 468. The printed text dealing with the death of young Harry Thrale varies but slightly from the manuscript. (MS. *Life*, pp. 540–545: Arthur A. Houghton, Jr.)

[8] Johnson to Mrs. Thrale, 25 March 1776. MS. Letter: Hyde. Letter #465. *Letters*, II, 117–118.

est⟩ most effectual consolation under heaven. I wish not to intrude upon you; but ⟨whenever you I am informed that⟩ as soon as you let me know that ⟨it⟩ / my presence / will not be troublesome ⟨to you⟩, I shall hasten to your house, where as I have shared much happiness I would willingly ⟨take a share of mourning⟩ bear a part in mourning

> I ever am
> Madam
> your obliged
> humble servant [9]

Boswell copied the draft, affixed a black seal to his letter, and posted it to Southwark.

Dear Madam.

Allow me to assure you and Mʳ Thrale that I very sincerely regret your present affliction, and very sincerely wish it were in my power to alleviate it. Were you as sure as I am of my concern for you, I doubt not that it would be some relief. You have now with you Dʳ Johnson, whose friendship is the most effectual consolation under heaven. I wish not to intrude upon you; but as soon as you let me know that my presence will not be troublesome, I shall hasten to your house, where as I have shared much happiness, I would willingly bear a part in mourning.

> I ever am
> Madam
> your obliged humble servant
> James Boswell.[10]

Mʳ Dillys in
the Poultry
Friday 29 March
  1776.

To
  Mʳˢ Thrale
  at Henry Thrale's Esq.
    Southwark

Meanwhile, as Johnson approached the Southwark house, he was astonished to find a coach waiting at the door to take Mrs. Thrale and Queeney and Baretti to Bath. Queeney was sick. Mrs. Thrale was distraught; she had only a few words with Johnson. Thrale was absorbed in his own grief and did not want company. Johnson, who had made a great effort to give comfort, was surprised and hurt not to be needed, but he was philosopher enough to accept any actions of be-

[9] MS. Draft: Hyde.
[10] MS. Letter: Hyde.

reavement with understanding. He went off sorrowfully to his own house.[11]

Here, Boswell found him that afternoon, in ill humor but loyal to the Thrales. Boswell was angry at the indifference they had shown; his opinion of them was lowered and he also resented Johnson's mild acceptance. He was relieved on one point; they still planned to make the trip to Italy, and he knew how much this meant to Johnson. But later, as Boswell thought about the trip, it seemed but another instance of Johnson's total dependence, and he wrote critically in his Journal: "After all, though his intimacy in Thrale's family has done him much good, I could wish that he had been independent of it. He would have had more dignity." [12]

Mrs. Thrale did not answer Boswell's note directly, but writing Johnson from Bath on April 1st gave this message: "Shall I beg you to tell Mr. Boswell that I feel myself but too much affected by his Friendship; Yours has long been the best Cordial to my Heart, it is now almost the only one." [13]

The days that followed found Boswell restless, the Thrales numb and inactive, and Johnson extremely depressed. Boswell began drinking heavily and seeking pleasure with ladies of the street; these "conquests" became a constant subject of his conversation, eventually annoying to Johnson.

On Good Friday, April 5th, about a week after Boswell and Johnson had returned from their interrupted trip, Thrale came to Johnson's house. Boswell thought him composed despite his grief; Thrale spent most of the day in their company and in the evening all three went to church.

On Easter Sunday Boswell sat by Thrale at St. Paul's. Mrs. Thrale and Queeney, now well again, were back from Bath and also there, as was Johnson. Boswell observed that Mrs. Thrale was "in tender grief." She said to him, "What we have been now about is the true comfort." [14]

[11] "This was not the Attention to *Imlack* which might have been expected," Boswell commented in his Journal. *Boswell Papers*, XI, 212 (recorded the day after, 30 March 1767).

[12] *Idem.*

[13] Mrs. Thrale to Johnson, 1 April 1776. MS. Letter: Rylands, Eng.MS.539/51. Letter #467a. *Letters*, II, 121.

[14] *Boswell Papers*, XI, 232 (7 April 1776).

The following Wednesday Boswell was asked with Johnson to dine at the Thrales. Johnson did not care whether Boswell came or not. He had lost respect for him because of his wayward behavior and had talked to him severely. Boswell, worried that Johnson might treat him coldly in front of the Thrales, stopped at his house early on Wednesday to deliver a letter of philosophic self-defence, but his mentor had already gone to Southwark. Boswell followed and during the dinner was a model of decorum — he drank only water — though Thrale offered champagne which he had brought from Paris. Boswell found a chance to talk to Johnson apart and somewhat reinstated himself in his friend's opinion. Sadly, Johnson told him that the Thrales had abandoned the trip to Italy. Feeling Johnson's disappointment, Boswell argued that "an Italian journey would do Mr. and Mrs. Thrale good. 'No, Sir,' said Dr. Johnson, 'while grief is fresh, every attempt to [alleviate it is futile].' "[15] He checked his own disappointment, and philosophically accepted the Thrales' decision. There was some talk of the excursion taking place at a later date, but Johnson sensed that the hope he had cherished so long for a classical tour would probably never materialize, and it never did.

Within a few days the Thrales took Johnson to Bath, a poor substitute, but he went willingly, eager to do anything helpful. It was vexing for Boswell, having Johnson go away, and he suggested that he also come to Bath — he had never been there. Johnson encouraged the plan and on April 26th Boswell arrived for a four-day visit. He did not stay at the Thrales' house, but they were all much together, and the Thrales took pains to make Boswell's stay enjoyable. They saw to it that he met people in the Pump Room and introduced him to dancing partners. It was kind hospitality, difficult at the time to give.

Boswell returned to London after his long weekend and remained there until May 16th. It seems strange that he wrote no letter of thanks, particularly in view of the circumstances, and also Mrs. Thrale's request to hear from him when he was home,[16] but May passed and most of June. Then, it was Mrs. Thrale who wrote, to introduce a traveler, a short, formal letter, undertaken on the part of William Seward, a mutual friend, interested in literary matters. She wrote, she said, at the order of her husband, who was busy.

[15] *Ibid.*, 233 (10 April 1776). Two pages have been torn out of the Journal at this point.

[16] Letter of Boswell to Mrs. Thrale, 30 August 1776, printed below, pp. 42–43.

Streatham
20: June
1776.

Sir

Our worthy & amiable Friend Mʳ Seward has desired a recommendatory Letter to you for a Gentleman who he says is deserving of your Attention, & will be made happy by your Acquaintance: He is Son to Admiral Boscawen, is himself a Land Officer, and goes next Week to Edinburgh on a recruiting Party. Mʳ Thrale orders me to write as he is very busy, & I am really not displeased to have this opportunity of enquiring how you found your Family after the little absence which they probably thought a long one.

Doctor Johnson has once or twice expressed a little anxiety lest all should not be well, as you seldom fail writing; we will however hope the best. It is now I think more than Time to apologize for this Liberty which I yet flatter myself will be easily forgiven — as you perfectly well know the real Esteem with which I am

Sir
Your most Obedient
and faithful Servant
Hester : L: Thrale.

Mʳ Thrale sends you his Compliments.[17]

———

[Address]
    James Boswell Esqʳ
      Edinburgh

Mrs. Thrale had mentioned Johnson's anxiety; it was well founded, for Boswell was not well; a heavy melancholy had settled over him after his return from London, for the trip, which he had undertaken with enthusiasm, had turned out to be a dismal failure. He had not shone as he had the year before; he had been wild and irresponsible and had lost stature in Johnson's eyes. At home, he felt worthless and insignificant. It was hard for him to work and he found no pleasure in company.

Captain Boscawen was the second traveler this summer for whom the Thrales had provided an introduction, and presumably he was for a while in the country recruiting and did not immediately deliver this letter. For the moment Boswell was giving his attention to the earlier visitor, Count Manucci, whom he himself had met at the Thrales and liked. Manucci was a Florentine, an officer of cavalry in the Im-

---

[17] MS. Letter: Yale (C2266).

perial Service, a man of great charm and good humor. But despite his being "knowing and affable" Boswell was not enjoying the visit. He wrote in his Journal that his depression was so great that there was more burden than pleasure in the Count's company,[18] when he came on the 14th of July for breakfast and returned for supper. A few days later the Count was badly hurt in a fall from his horse, and Boswell was attentive, calling upon him at his lodgings on the 19th.[19] As soon as Manucci was well enough to go out, he came twice again for supper, and later wrote to Thrale of Boswell's kindness. Thrale promptly sent a letter to Boswell thanking him, an open, hearty letter; its postscript shows why Thrale was loved for his generosity.

> Streatham.
> 25: July 1776.
>
> Dear Sir
>
> The Civilities you have shewn to Count Mannucci have impressed him very deeply, & require my best Acknowledgments: if he is not yet well enough to be set out for London, you will be so good as give him the enclosed in Answer to his own ludicrous Account of the Accident.
>
> Our Friend Dr Johnson gets rid of his Gout gradually, He thinks himself now quite free. You will be pleased to accept my Wife's Com:^s & Thanks for the obliging Manner in which you received & excused her Letter concerning Mr Boscawen. I am every day more & more my dear Sir
> Your faithful & obliged Servant
> H Thrale
>
> turn over.
>
> If Count Mannucci wants Money to continue his Journey — let me beg of you to supply him & draw upon me.[20]

———

To
　　James Boswell Esqr
　　　　at
　　　　　　Edinburgh
　　HFreeThrale

On July 30th, the day the Count returned to London, Boswell went to the Edinburgh Ranelagh, and there by chance ran into Captain Boscawen.[21] He asked him to dine two days later, and recorded the

[18] *Boswell Papers*, XII, 16 (14 July 1776).
[19] *Ibid.*, 17 (19 July 1776).
[20] MS. Letter: Yale (C2988).
[21] *Boswell Papers*, XII, 19 (30 July 1776).

dinner guests in his Journal, though he gave no details of the party.[22] Despite the fact that Boswell was suffering from one of his darkest periods of melancholia this summer, he was able to fulfill his obligations to the Thrales.

In the latter part of August Boswell struggled to make himself more active. During the months of miserable, listless torpor, he had been dilatory about many things. He felt guilty that he had not written to Johnson, nor to the Thrales,[23] and on August 30th he resolutely wrote both letters, "which did me good." [24]

The letter to Mrs. Thrale was written with care. He first apologized for his apparent thanklessness (but assured her of his constant regard); he was ashamed to hear from her before writing, but explicit that he had done something for Captain Boscawen. He then gave a word about his wife, who was not well and was expecting a child; he wished that their two families might meet. After this, he turned to haunting Johnsonian subjects, again begging a copy of the "Ode" Johnson had written to her in Skye; and, with his biography always in mind, politely wheedling, he asked her to send him some of the Johnsonian sayings she had collected, advising her also how best to record. His passage on the death of the philosopher, David Hume, was suggestive: he hoped for Johnson's comment. Finally, in an effort to please, he concluded the letter on a spiritual note.

> Edinburgh
> Madam.   30 August 1776.
> When I parted from you at Bath, after passing a very calm agreable evening under the shade of our venerable Friend, you kindly desired to hear from me after I got home. I am ashamed that I did not embrace the earliest opportunity of testifying my sense of your goodness. I am still more ashamed that I have had the honour to receive an obliging though short Epistle from you, by Captain Boscawen, and I have not yet acknowledged the favour. Be pleased, Dear Madam, to forgive me, and to accept of my sincerest thanks for all the obligations you have conferred upon me. Though I have not expressed my gratitude, I have very constantly, and very warmly felt it. A clock may go very well, though it does not strike. Excuse such a mechanical allusion.
>
> Captain

[page 2]

Captain Boscawen favoured us with his company one day at dinner. He

[22] *Ibid.*, 20 (1 August 1776).
[23] *Ibid.*, 32 (23 August 1776).
[24] *Ibid.*, 35 (30 August 1776).

has not called since, and I imagine is in the country recruiting. Any person whom you recommend to me shall be sure of receiving all the civilities that I can shew.

My wife and children were all in good health when I returned to them from my last excursion in England. My wife has been complaining for a fortnight of a cough & pain in her breast, which cannot but alarm her as several of her family have died of consumptions which begin with these symptoms. But I am hopeful she has only a common cold. She is far gone with child. You may imagine what fears sometimes distress me. I am delighted with my children; I wish much that your family & mine could meet.

May

[page 3]

May I beg leave Madam to put you in mind of your promise to send me a copy of Dr Johnson's Ode to you, which he read to me, in the Island of Rasay. I already engaged not to circulate it.

It would be very kind if you would take the trouble to transmit to me sometimes a few of his admirable sayings, which you collect. May I beg of you to mark them down as soon as you can. You know what he says in his *Journey* of dilatory notation. You & I shall make up a Great Treasure between us.

Our only literary news here is the death of David Hume, if that should be called so. It has shocked me to think of his persisting in Infidelity. Gray in one of the letters published by Mason represents Hume as a child. I cannot agree with him. Hume had certainly considerable abilities. My notion is that he had by long study in one view, brought a stupor upon his mind as to futurity. He had pored upon the earth, till he could not look up to heaven. He was like one of the Bramins who, we are told, by a rigid perseverance in maintaining a certain posture, became unable to change it. Or may we not with propriety compare him to the woman in the Gospel, who was bowed down, and could in no wise lift herself up, till healed by our Saviour who described her as one "whom Satan hath bound lo these eighteen years." Hume told me about six weeks before his death, that he had been steady in his then sentiments, above forty years. I should like to hear Dr Johnson upon this.

What a blessing is it to have a constant faith in the Christian Revelation! This I am persuaded depends much upon our own pious endeavours; and I am of Dr Johnson's opinion that those who write against Religion ought not to be treated with gentleness. I beg leave to offer my compliments to Miss Thrale and I am Dear Madam

your obliged humble servant
James Boswell.[25]

Mrs. Thrale was not moved by Boswell's letter; she put it away unanswered. In September, a few weeks before her thirteenth wedding

[25] MS. Letter: National Library of Scotland. Copy in hand of John Lawrie, heading in Boswell's hand: Yale (L1072).

anniversary, Thrale gave her six handsome quarto blank books, in calf covers with red labels bearing "the pompous Title of Thraliana." [26] Now, her "Miscellany," her record of Johnson's sayings, would be contained in volumes worthy of their importance. She continued to collect her "treasure."

1777

This year began dismally for Boswell. His wife's health was worse and he feared she was consumptive (this was the fact, but he refused to accept it for several years). The child, about to be born when he wrote to Mrs. Thrale, had come in the autumn: David, a sickly infant, who died in March of this year. These family distresses and serious financial problems precluded any visit to London. Boswell wrote Johnson suggesting a meeting in the north, perhaps Carlisle, where he had business to take care of, and by way of inducement, he reminded his friend that the Carlisle cathedral was the only one in England he had not seen.[27]

In late June Johnson replied: Carlisle was too far — perhaps Manchester; they would write about it further. He then asked Boswell if he would look out for William Seward, the friend who had urged an introduction for Captain Boscawen the year before. Johnson wrote that Seward was setting out for Edinburgh, "enkindled by our travels, with a curiosity to see the Highlands." [28] Seward was a man of thirty, exceedingly intelligent, polite and agreeable if he chose, but more apt to be critical and abrupt; many people did not find him appealing, but at this time he was a great favorite at Streatham.

He arrived in Edinburgh on July 10th and presented himself to Boswell, who was in a more sociable mood than he had been the summer before; indeed, not having been able to go to London, he was extremely eager to see a member of the literary circle. He took Seward under his wing, introduced him to several friends, and for the fortnight of his visit to Edinburgh entertained him constantly.

Boswell's kindness, far beyond the call of duty, was soon reported by Seward, and Mrs. Thrale wrote a note of appreciation, short, but with the warmth typical of her letters to other friends, though not to

[26] *Thraliana*, I, 1.

[27] Boswell proposed this meeting in his letter of 4 April 1777, and repeated the suggestion in that of 9 June. *Tinker Boswell Letters*, I, 259–260; 261–265.

[28] Johnson to Boswell, 28 June 1777. Letter #524. *Letters*, II, 181.

THE THRALE HOUSE IN BRIGHTON
WATERCOLOR
Four Oaks Farm

Ode from Skie by Dr Sam: Johnson

Sermo terras, ubi nuda rupe
Saxeas miscet nebulis ruinas
Torva ubi rident steriles coloni
    Rura labores.

Pervagor gentes, hominum ferorum
Vita ubi nullo decorata cultu
Squallet informis, tigurique fumis
    Foeda latescit.

Inter Erroris salebrosa longi,
Inter ignota strepitus loquela
Quot modis mecum, quid agat requiro
    Thralia dulcis!

Seu Viri curas, pia nupta mulcet,
Seu fovet Mater sobolem benigna
Sive cum Libris novitate pascet
    Sedula mentem.

Sit memor nostri, fideiq. merces,
Stet fides constans, meritoque blandum,
Thralia discant resonare Nomen
    Littora Sciae.

Scriptum in Skia Sep: 6: 1773.

This is in Mr. Thrale's handwriting. She sent it to me. But she has written rupe instead of rupes

"ODE FROM SKIE BY DR. SAM: JOHNSON"
IN HAND OF MRS. THRALE, ANNOTATED BY BOSWELL
Four Oaks Farm

Boswell. She did not refer to the important subject of Johnson "treasure," broached in his letter of twelve months before, but she did enclose the requested copy of Johnson's "Ode from Skye."

Streatham
15: Aug: 1777.

Dear Sir

I have a thousand Obligations to acknowledge, and your kind Attention to Mr Seward whom you made very happy crowns them all. The inclosed Verses are so flattering that I am almost as much ashamed to copy them out & send them you, as I was at first proud to receive them, but you have long wished for them and here they are.   Accept all our best Compliments from the hand of

Sir
Your most faithful
and obedient servant
Hester : L : Thrale.[29]

———

To
    James Boswell Esqr
        Edinburgh
HfreeThrale

Three weeks before this letter was sent, Johnson had continued the subject of a possible meeting with Boswell, writing: "I shall perhaps come to Carlisle another year; but my money has not held out so well as it used to do. I shall go to Ashbourne, and I propose to make Dr. Taylor invite you . . . the Thrales are well." [30] Boswell agreed to this suggestion and by the end of the month Johnson was on his way, though without much enthusiasm. He wrote to Thrale from Oxford: "I know not whether I shall go forward without some regret. I cannot break my promise to Boswel[l] and the rest; but I have a good mind to come back again." [31] Mrs. Thrale answered with a sprightly letter, ending: [32] "I shall be sorry for Mr. Boswell if you don't see him — but I don't value Mrs. Aston of Stowe Hill." [33]

[29] MS. Letter: Hyde.

[30] Johnson to Boswell, 22 July 1777. Letter #528. *Letters*, II, 183.

[31] Johnson to Thrale, from Oxford, 31 July 1777. MS. Letter: Historical Society of Pennsylvania. Letter #532. *Letters*, II, 187.

[32] Mrs. Thrale to Johnson, 2 August 1777. MS. Letter: Rylands, Eng.MS.540/66. Letter #532a. *Letters*, II, 188.

[33] Elizabeth Aston (1708–1785) was one of the numerous members of the Aston

Boswell's departure from Scotland was delayed by a visit from his cousin, Godfrey Bosville, his "Yorkshire Chief." Johnson accepted this interruption philosophically, writing him not to disturb himself about postponing the meeting: "I hope we shall have many . . . We have both endured greater evils, and have greater evils to expect." [34] To Mrs. Thrale he wrote on the same day, "Bozzy, you know makes a huge bustle about all his own motions, and all mine." [35]

Almost a month later, Johnson, now in Ashbourne, was still hoping for a meeting; he wrote to Boswell that "the Thrales, little and great, are all well, and purpose to go to [Brighton] at Michaelmas. They will invite me to go with them, and perhaps I may go . . ." [36]

On the 14th of September Boswell finally arrived in Ashbourne, "brisk and lively" and his ten days' visit with Johnson was highly satisfactory. Dr. Taylor provided all creature comforts, and the guests were left without responsibility, able to enjoy the inexhaustible play of mind and spirit. As Mrs. Thrale wrote to the absent member of her household: "Mr. Boswell will make Ashbourne alive better than three Hautboys & the Harpsichord," but she reminded him, "you have Friends at Streatham who love you more than many a Man is loved by his Wife & Children." [37]

Two days later, with a slightly acid touch, she began her letter with a subject that would seem to have been discussed often between them: "I am glad Mr. Boswell is with you — nothing that you say for this Week at least will be lost to Posterity . . . Give a thousand Compliments to Mr. Boswell . . . Mr. Seward & Mr. Thrale call to me from the Lawn to send their Compliments to you & to Mr. Boswell." [38]

On the last night of the Ashbourne visit, Boswell said he was afraid

---

family in Lichfield, known to Johnson since his youth. Mrs. Thrale's asperity would have been more appropriately directed to the deceased Molly Aston Brodie, "a beauty and a scholar," of whom Tetty was jealous, with "no reason," Johnson said. "The ladies never loved Molly Aston." *Anecdotes*, p. 158.

[34] Johnson to Boswell, from Oxford, 4 August 1777. Letter #534. *Letters*, II, 189.

[35] Johnson to Mrs. Thrale, 4 August 1777. MS. Letter: Hyde. Letter #533. *Letters*, II, 189.

[36] Johnson to Boswell, from Ashbourne, 1 September 1777. Letter #541. *Letters*, II, 199.

[37] Mrs. Thrale to Johnson, 16 September 1777. MS. Letter: Rylands, Eng.MS.540/71. Letter #547a. *Letters*, II, 207.

[38] Mrs. Thrale to Johnson, 18 September 1777. MS. Letter: Rylands, Eng. MS.540/72. Letter #548a. *Letters*, II, 209.

he kept his friend "too late up. 'No,' said he, 'I don't care though I sit up *all night* with you.' This was spirited in one of 68." [39]

Boswell departed from Ashbourne on September 24th, but not without the help of Mr. Thrale. "Boswell has spent more money than he expected," Johnson wrote to Mrs. Thrale on the 20th, "and I must supply him with part of his expences home. I have not much with me, and beg Master to send me by the next post a note of ten pounds, which I will punctually return." [40] Once again, Thrale straightened out a financial problem, this time for Boswell's benefit.

1778

Boswell had not been in London since 1776 and he had a strong desire to make a visit this spring; but there were difficulties, the most serious of which was his wife's health. She had been confined to the house for three months when he wrote in January. Johnson, a strong believer that change of scene benefited health, urged him to bring Mrs. Boswell to London:

London is a good air for ladies; and if you bring her hither, I will do for her what she did for me — I will retire from my apartments, for her accommodation. Behave kindly to her, and keep her cheerful. [41]

By early spring Mrs. Boswell was somewhat better, as was always the case when she was having a child, but this fact made her dread more than ever the rigors of a London visit. She urged Boswell to go alone, and with reluctance, he consented.

He arrived on the evening of March 17th and, as on earlier occasions, hurried to Johnson's house, only to be told by Francis Barber that he "was at Streatham with Mr. and Mrs. Thrale. This both pleased me and disappointed me. I was glad he was so well as to be in the country. But I felt a want in not seeing him immediately as I had expected." [42] Boswell ran into him the next day by chance at Dr. Taylor's house in Westminster,[43] Johnson having come up to London for a few hours. Boswell received a kind but preoccupied embrace.

[39] *Boswell Papers*, XIII, 60 (23 September 1777).

[40] Johnson to Mrs. Thrale, 20 September 1777. MS. Letter: Hyde. Letter #549. *Letters*, II, 210.

[41] Johnson to Boswell, 24 January 1778. Letter #568. *Letters*, II, 239.

[42] *Boswell Papers*, XIII, 107 (17 March 1778).

[43] *Ibid.*, 109 (18 March 1778). One of Dr. Taylor's preferments was St. Margaret's, Westminster.

Two days later he had an unexpected and pleasant half hour with the great man at Bolt Court,[44] but these glimpses were far from satisfying, and he wrote in desperation, complaining that a week's separation, when they were so close, was as hard as a year's at a distance. The result was an invitation from the Thrales.

Boswell's entries in his Journal at this period show a continuing regard for Mrs. Thrale. Later, when writing the *Life*, in a hostile mood, he developed certain scenes not recorded, though perhaps suggested by his Diary, and he transposed certain conversations, thus creating a different picture. For instance, on his visit to Streatham on March 30th, he complained, in the *Life*, of Mrs. Thrale's inaccuracy. Before dinner, he said, he repeated a ridiculous story told him by "an old man." Mrs. Thrale soon alluded to the "story told . . . by the old *woman*." Boswell took the "opportunity, in the presence of Johnson, of shewing this lively lady how ready she was, unintentionally, to deviate from exact authenticity of narration."[45] Nothing is said of this in the Journal — simply, "Fine Mrs. Thrale."[46]

In his Journal for April 7th, 1778, Boswell did refer to Mrs. Thrale's inaccuracy; conversation between the two in the coach going to Streatham:

[44] *Ibid.*, 112 (20 March 1778). Boswell noted in his Journal that the room he had had in Johnson's house when he was last in London was now occupied by a Mrs. Desmoulins. She was the indigent daughter of Johnson's godfather, Dr. Swynfen, and years before she had been a companion to Tetty Johnson. Sharing the room with Mrs. Desmoulins was Poll Carmichael, "a stupid slut," whom Johnson at first hoped to improve, but he soon despaired of doing so. The blind Miss Williams, the destitute Dr. Levett, and Francis Barber, the black servant, were the other inmates; "discord and discontent reign in my humble habitation," Johnson wrote Mrs. Thrale, "Mr. Levet[t] and Mrs. Desmoulins have vowed eternal hate" (Johnson to Mrs. Thrale, 16 October 1779. MS. Letter: Hyde. Letter #633. *Letters*, II, 308). Again, he wrote Mrs. Thrale, "We have much malice, but no michief. Levet[t] is rather a friend to Williams, because he hates Desmoulins more, a thing that he should hate more than Desmoulins is not to be found" (Johnson to Mrs. Thrale, 7 November 1779. MS. Letter: Hyde. Letter #644. *Letters*, II, 322).

When asked how he could bear to be surrounded by such quarrelsome and undeserving people, Johnson answered: "If I did not assist them, no one else would, and they must be lost for want." Arthur Murphy, *Life of Johnson*, p. 146. Quoted in *Life*, III, Appendix D, 463.

[45] *Life*, III, 226.

[46] Boswell Journal, 30 March 1778. Yale (MS. J55). Also *Boswell in Extremes* (1776–1778 Journal), ed. Charles McC. Weis and Frederick A. Pottle (Yale Research Edition; McGraw-Hill: New York, 1970), p. 230. Hereafter referred to as *Boswell in Extremes*.

We talked of Mrs. Thrale's laxity of narrative, inattention to truth, and he said, "I'm as much vexed at the ease with which she hears it mentioned to her as at the thing itself. I told her, 'Madam, you are contented to hear every day said to you what the highest of mankind have died rather than bear.' You know, Sir, the highest of mankind have died rather than bear to be told they tell a lie." [47]

In the *Life* he does not name the lady; Johnson talked to him "with serious concern of a certain female friend's 'laxity of narration, and inattention to truth.'" The rest of the quotation was much as it had been in the Journal, though at the end he added that Johnson said, "Do talk to her of it: I am weary." [48]

"Pride" was another charge which Boswell made against Mrs. Thrale in the *Life*, and, as before, he used Johnson for the accuser. On April 18th, 1778, when Boswell visited Johnson at his house, he noticed for the first time that the drawing room was "very genteelly fitted up." When he remarked upon it, Johnson replied: "Mrs. Thrale sneered when I talked of my having asked you and your lady to live at my house. I was obliged to tell her, that you would be in as respectable a situation in my house as in hers. Sir, the insolence of wealth will creep out." [49] In his Journal record of this conversation, Boswell defended Mrs. Thrale at this point, "She is a good woman," though he did add, "But she has a little of both of the insolence of wealth and of the conceit of parts." [50]

The day before this conversation took place, Boswell's Letter Register shows that he wrote to Mrs. Thrale and that he received her reply on the 21st. Neither letter has been recovered, but from the Register we know that the exchange concerned a dinner invitation to Boswell and General Paoli. [51]

---

[47] *Boswell in Extremes*, p. 246.

[48] *Life*, III, 243 (7 April 1778). In the Journal, after recording conversation in the coach: "Arrived at Thrale's, sweet place." *Boswell in Extremes*, p. 249.

Going home in the coach, Johnson had a compliment for Boswell, rather than a criticism: "'You make yourself agreeable wherever you go. Whoever has seen you once wishes to see you again' . . . BOSWELL. 'You and I do quite well to travel together. The composition just fits. I love to be under some restraint, some awe, and you're as easy with me as with anybody.'" *Ibid.*, p. 250.

[49] *Life*, III, 316.

[50] *Boswell in Extremes*, p. 301.

[51] Boswell's Letter Register at Yale (M254) shows that he sent a letter to Mrs. Thrale, 17 April 1778 (changed from 18): "Mrs. Thrale that Gen. Paoli & I will dine at Streatham any day next week after monday." Boswell received an answer on

On the 12th of May Boswell called at the House of Commons for Thrale: "not there." [52] Hoping to get a chaise or a coach to Streatham he walked over Westminster Bridge, and then:

had ambition to walk it out. Did so, with gay vigour. Stopped at barber's at Streatham. Shaved, clean shirt, wig powdered. Arrived, dinner half done, but in time enough. Had good fricassee and mushrooms, etc.[53]

He told Johnson after dinner that he had been with Lord March- mont,[54] who had agreed to help the Doctor with the Life of Pope; he had fixed an interview for the next day. Johnson was infuriated by this meddlesome kindness and exclaimed, "I shall not be in town to- morrow. I don't care to know about Pope." In the *Life*, Mrs. Thrale was "(surprized as I was, and a little angry)." In both accounts she said virtually the same thing: " 'I suppose, Sir, he thought that as you are to write Pope's life, you'd wish to know about him.' JOHNSON. 'Why, wish. If it rained knowledge, I'd hold out my hand. But I would not trouble myself to go for it.' This was really a mortifying disappointment." [55] The last sentence Boswell omitted in the *Life*, substituting, "Mr. Thrale was uneasy at his unaccountable caprice." [56] In both accounts Johnson stood firm; he would not listen.

Boswell stayed on at Streatham and the atmosphere became more pleasant. That night, according to his Journal, "walked round his field with Mr. Thrale in perfect good spirits. Then coffee and tea." [57] After Mrs. Thrale had gone to bed, Johnson and Boswell talked about virtue and the influence of character upon the success of life. Boswell "had biscuits and lemonade, and was very cheerful." [58]

At twelve we went upstairs . . . Found in my room several books in a press in the wall, and some of *Taxation no Tyranny* with corrections *by his own*

---

21 April 1778: "Mrs. Thrale that they will be happy to see General Paoli & me at Streatham next thursday or Friday." (For Paoli, see note 74 below.) To give some idea of the volume of Boswell's correspondence: at the end of 1778, he had sent 200 letters, besides those to his wife, and he had received 186, besides those from his wife.

[52] *Boswell in Extremes*, p. 338.

[53] Yale MS. J55 and *Boswell in Extremes*, p. 338.

[54] Hugh Hume Campbell, 3rd Earl of Marchmont (1708–1794), Keeper of the Great Seal of Scotland. He had been an intimate friend of the poet, Alexander Pope (1688–1744), and one of his executors.

[55] *Boswell in Extremes*, p. 338.

[56] *Life*, III, 345.

[57] *Boswell in Extremes*, p. 340.

[58] *Ibid.*, p. 344.

hand, and a paragraph I believe delete. This I treasured up, for it was a frag-
ment remaining from waste paper, as it seemed.[59] Went to bed with that comfortable association of ideas which I have in the bedroom at Streatham since
I lay in it in autumn 1769, when I was going to be married. Thanked GOD
I had such a wife and children.[60]

There is no Journal for May 13th, but the *Life* records an agreeable
breakfast. Mrs. Thrale, informed by Boswell of the night's discussion,
took issue with Johnson's opinion on the influence of character.[61]
A messenger had been dispatched the previous day, with a polite card
written by Boswell, saying that the Doctor could not now wait on Lord
Marchmont, but would hope to "do himself the honour . . . at another time." [62] Boswell stayed at Streatham all the 13th, and Johnson
"talked a great deal, in a very good humour." [63]

This was the last meeting of the year between Boswell and the
Thrales. According to contemporary evidence he continued to think
well of her; and by the same token she considered him an agreeable
companion. This is shown by his marks in a tabulation which Mrs.
Thrale drew up for her own amusement during the summer.[64] She
rated a number of friends (and her husband) in respect to certain qualities, "20" being the perfect score for each category. Boswell shared
with Dr. Burney [65] and Lord Sandys [66] the honors for the highest
score (19) in "Good Humor," a category in which her husband received "5," Johnson "0," and Queeney also "0." Boswell received "10"

[59] These pages of "Proof Copy" of *Taxation no Tyranny* marked by Johnson,
and with notation by Boswell: Hyde.

[60] *Boswell in Extremes*, p. 344.

[61] *Life*, III, 350.

[62] *Ibid.*, 345.

[63] *Ibid.*, 351.

[64] *Thraliana*, I, 329–330.

[65] Dr. Charles Burney (1726–1814) was the distinguished musical writer, head of
a talented family, and, though shy, a social favorite. Dr. Burney was the subject of
one of the Reynolds portraits in the library at Streatham, and when Mrs. Thrale
came to write a verse for each picture, she said of Burney: "Every Power to please —
every Talent to shine." See *Thraliana*, I, 137, for further praise. Dr. Burney began
giving music lessons to Queeney in December 1776 — a project not without problems. Dr. Johnson was somewhat more successful instructing Queeney in Latin.

[66] Edwin Sandys, 2nd Baron of Ombersley (1726–1797) had long been a close
friend of the Thrales. His portrait was also in the library. According to his verse,
this nobleman was "sunk" and the scholar "obscur'd" by the "Oppression for Forty
long Years" of parents and wife (MS. Portrait Verses: Hyde). For Mrs. Thrale's
writing of the verses, see below, p. 58.

in both "General Knowledge" and "Person and Voice." Contrasted
with this, was Johnson's "20" in "General Knowledge" and "0" in
"Person and Voice." Thrale rated "9" in the former and "18" in the
latter; no one surpassed her husband in "Person and Voice" and only
Garrick was equal to him. Boswell received "5" in "Religion,"
"Morality," and "Scholarship," strong categories for Johnson, who was
perfection in the first two and "19" in the last. Thrale held his ground
in the first two with "18" and "17" but was only "9" in "Scholarship."
In "Wit" Boswell scored "7" and in "Humor" (which surely included
the ability to laugh at one's self) Boswell was given "3," his lowest
mark. Thrale received "0" in both.[67]

1779

Boswell's first communication with the Thrales in this year was
unfortunate. He wrote to Thrale on the 22nd of January and, though
the present location of the letter is not known, his Letter Register
gives this information, to: "Henry Thrale Esq: freindly compliments — How is Dr. Johnson? Has he ever been to visit Lord Marchmont?" Boswell wrote to Johnson the same day, retaining a copy.
In his Letter Register, he noted: "Dr. Samuel Johnson that I am exceedingly well, & the better of drinking wine sometimes. Begging
to have as my new years Gift his letter to Lord Chesterfield [68] which
he at length *promised* to send me etc. etc. etc." With his Johnsonian
Collection in mind, he also wrote to Francis Barber, "reminding him
to preserve . . . the M. S. and Proof sheets of his Master's Prefaces
Biographical & Critical to the English Poets." [69]

Thrale did not answer Boswell's letter and when Johnson finally
replied on March 13th, he began in annoyance:

[67] *Thraliana*, I, 329–330.

[68] Philip Dormer Stanhope, 4th Earl of Chesterfield (1694–1773) had believed
himself to be Johnson's patron at the time of the great project of the *Dictionary of
the English Language*, but as the two folio volumes neared publication, he was
told: "Seven years, My Lord, have now past since I waited in your outward
Rooms or was repulsed from your Door . . . Is not a Patron, My Lord, one who
looks with unconcern on a Man struggling for Life in the water and when he has
reached ground encumbers him with help." Johnson to the Earl of Chesterfield,
7 February 1755. MS. Letter: untraced, but MS. copies survive. Letter #61.
Letters, I, 64.

This celebrated letter was much admired by Johnson's friends — and it was also
admired by Lord Chesterfield, who would, upon occasion, read it aloud to visitors.

[69] Boswell's Letter Register: Yale (M254).

Why should you take such delight to make a bustle, to write to Mr. Thrale [70] that I am negligent, and to Francis to do what is so very unnecessary. Thrale, you may be sure, cared not about it; and I shall spare Francis the trouble, by ordering a set both of the Lives and Poets to dear Mrs. Boswell, in acknowledgement of her marmalade. [71]

This letter crossed Boswell on the road to London, where he arrived on the 15th of March. Next morning when he went to Bolt Court, he was informed that Johnson was well but not yet up. [72] Grateful for good news of his health, Boswell went off for a while and returned to find Johnson at breakfast; Mrs. Desmoulins and Dr. Levett were with him, also a clergyman who had brought his poems for Johnson to read. Boswell was disappointed by the casualness of his welcome, and Johnson soon began to complain about his bothering Thrale. He was, indeed, still angry, but in time, as on many other occasions, he forgave Boswell and good relations were re-established.

They both went to Streatham on the 19th of March; [73] and on the 6th of April Boswell: "Posted to General's, [74] and away to Streatham." There, a spirited discussion took place. " 'I w[oul]d not be Burke,' [75] said She against me. JOHNSON. 'No, you w[oul]d gain nothing but breeches.' She said well she would be Pascal [the French philosopher]." [76]

[70] Boswell had written Johnson again on 2 February, and on the 23rd complained "of his silence, as I had heard he was ill, and had written to Mr. Thrale, for information concerning him." Footnote 1 to Johnson's letter to Boswell, 13 March 1779. Letter #607. *Letters*, II, 282.

[71] Johnson to Boswell, 13 March 1779. Location as above.

[72] *Boswell Papers*, XIII, 210 (16 March 1779).

[73] *Life*, III, 377.

[74] Pasquale Paoli (1725–1807), Corsican patriot and general, who fought for the independence of his country, first against Genoa and then against France. Boswell had visited him in 1765, during the conflict, and on returning to England had dedicated his *Corsica* to Paoli. After the surrender to France in 1769, Paoli came as a refugee to London. Boswell soon saw to it that he met Johnson and others of the circle; Paoli formed warm friendships with many of these men.

[75] Edmund Burke (1729–1797). This celebrated statesman became a friend of the Thrales through Johnson, who had the deepest admiration for him despite his opposite political views; he called him "an extraordinary man" (*Life*, II, 450), "one of the most luminous minds of the present age" (*Life*, I, 471). Once at Reynolds' house Johnson touched him on the shoulder and said, "le grand Burke" (*Life*, IV, 20, n. 1).

He was an original member of the Club. The Thrales, saluting him in their own way, had his portrait painted for their collection of friends in the library at Streatham.

[76] *Boswell Papers*, XIII, 216 (6 April 1779).

May the 1st was a rewarding day for Boswell. In the morning Johnson came to him from Streatham and together they proceeded to Lord Marchmont's in Curzon Street. Marchmont met them at the door of his library. He was exceedingly polite and Johnson was exceedingly courteous. For about two hours anecdotes of Pope were discussed, to Johnson's benefit. When they left, Boswell said he would have been vexed if Johnson had failed to come, to which Johnson replied, "Sir, . . . I would rather have given twenty pounds than not have come." [77] The two went on to Streatham to dine, a pleasant occasion in contrast to the angry scene of the year before. This time there was happy accord all round and the Thrales complimented Boswell upon his perseverance.

About the 3rd of May Boswell started out for Scotland,[78] and there was no further opportunity to see the Thrales; they themselves departed for Brighton late in the month, taking their three eldest daughters and a close new friend — Fanny Burney.[79] In Brighton they were joined by Arthur Murphy, and all were occupied in reading *The Witlings*, a play which Fanny was writing.[80] Johnson had shown no enthusiasm in being a member of the party and had taken this opportunity to make a visit to Lichfield and Ashbourne. From the former place he wrote to Mrs. Thrale about the few activities of nine days:

This is the course of my life. You do not think it much makes me forget

[77] *Life*, III, 392. No Journal entry for this date.

[78] Boswell left London late in the evening of 3 May or early on the morning of the 4th. *Boswell Papers*, XIII, 236.

[79] Fanny Burney (1752–1840) was the daughter of Dr. Charles Burney, the eminent musician and author, one of the close members of the Streatham circle. Fanny had largely educated herself, reading in her father's extensive library, and meeting the leading musicians, authors, and actors of the day in the drawing room. Her passion for "scribbling," as her stepmother termed it, found expression in a diary (begun in 1768 and continued for 72 years!); also in a novel, written secretly and published anonymously the year before, 1778, *Evelina, or, A Young Lady's Entrance into the World.*

Evelina made Fanny an instant celebrity in the literary world. She was soon brought to Streatham and this, she recorded in her Diary, was "the most consequential day I have spent since my birth." The initial visit was succeeded by many others, and in a short time she became the darling of both Johnson and Mrs. Thrale — she also became a close friend of the reserved Queeney Thrale.

[80] Fanny had undertaken the play at the suggestion of Mrs. Thrale, and Arthur Murphy had offered his help as a play-carpenter. *The Witlings* was a comedy about the Blue Stocking Ladies. Fanny's friends encouraged her with the project in Brighton, but her beloved adviser, "Daddy" Crisp, and her own father soon thereafter dissuaded her from becoming a dramatist.

Streatham. However it is good to wander a little, lest one should dream that all the world was Streatham, of which one may venture to say *None but itself can be its parallel.* [81]

The Thrales had returned to Streatham by the 1st of June and a week later, it became a far from happy place. Thrale suffered an apoplectic stroke, and for a while was deprived of both reason and speech. Johnson at first was not aware of the seriousness of the attack, believing it to be "not apoplectical, but hysterical, and therefore not dangerous to life." He did, however, think Mrs. Thrale's account of the illness was "very terrible" and wrote: "If I can comfort you, I will come to you." [82] Two days later, he wrote: "If my coming can either assist or divert, or be useful to any purpose, let me but know." [83] He also wrote a cheerful and encouraging letter to Thrale, wishing that he might "live long and happily, and long count [him] among those that love you best." [84]

Mrs. Thrale, nervous and distraught, resented Johnson's absence: "something always *does* happen . . . when you leave us for long"; [85] but she did not summon him. Soon Thrale was better and Johnson wrote to him again: "My wicked Mistress talks as if she thought it possible for me to be indifferent or negligent about your health or hers. If I could have done any good, I had not delayed an hour to come to you . . ." [86] To Mrs. Thrale, he wrote: "You really do not use me well . . . There is nobody left for me to care about but you and my Master . . ." [87] Mrs. Thrale apologized: "You have been exceedingly kind, and I have been exceedingly cross; & now my Master is got well, & my Wrath over, I ask your Pardon sincerely." [88]

[81] Johnson to Mrs. Thrale, 29 May 1779. MS. Letter: Hyde. Letter #616. *Letters*, II, 289.

[82] Johnson to Mrs. Thrale, 12 June 1779. MS. Letter: Hyde. Letter #617. *Letters*, II, 290.

[83] Johnson to Mrs. Thrale, 14 June 1779. MS. Letter: Hyde. Letter #618. *Letters*, II, 291.

[84] Johnson to Thrale, c. 18 June (misdated 15 July) 1779. MS. Letter: Hyde. Letter #619. *Letters*, II, 293.

[85] Mrs. Thrale to Johnson, 17 June 1779. MS. Letter: Rylands, Eng.MS.540/90. Letter #620a. *Letters*, II, 294.

[86] Johnson to Thrale, from Lichfield, 23 June 1779. MS. Letter: Herman W. Liebert. Letter #622. *Letters*, II, 296.

[87] Johnson to Mrs. Thrale, 24 June 1779. MS. Letter: last location known to me: Sotheby Sale, 15 February 1926, Lot 42. Letter #623. *Letters*, II, 297.

[88] Mrs. Thrale to Johnson, 24 June 1779. MS. Letter: Rylands, Eng.MS.540/91. Letter #623a. *Letters*, II, 297.

Actually, it was as well that Johnson was away at the moment of crisis, for Thrale's doctors were attentive, and William Seward stood a helpful watch with Mrs. Thrale; Johnson would only have created confusion. He did return to London at the end of June and at that time Mrs. Thrale realized that her pleasure in his company was not the same as it had been — nor would it ever be again. Once Thrale was ill and she had to face domestic uncertainties alone, the presence of Johnson, also ailing and complaining, was no longer a delight but an added burden. In August she suffered a miscarriage and was very ill herself.

Boswell made an unusual second visit to London this year, arriving on the 4th of October, but there was no chance for him to enjoy the company of the Thrales; Mrs. Thrale was making arrangements to take her husband, now convalescing, to Brighton. Exercise and sociability were prescribed by the doctors, a doubtful prescription, though Johnson concurred in it. Immediately upon Boswell's arrival, Johnson asked him to go to Southwark to see his Master, "to watch all appearances with close attention, and bring [him] his observations." Johnson believed in the validity of a candid first impression. "At his return [Boswell reported] that without previous intelligence he should not have discovered that Mr. Thrale had been lately ill." [89]

This was the only glimpse Boswell had of either of the Thrales on his short October visit, but as Johnson did not follow his family to Brighton, Boswell was able to enjoy his company to the full, before returning to Scotland on the 18th. The following day Johnson wrote to Taylor in Ashbourne; he did not mention Boswell, but he explained why he had not accompanied the Thrales to the seaside:

[Thrale] rides very vigourously, and runs much into company, and is very angry if it be thought that any thing ails him. Mrs. Thrale thinks him for the present in no danger. I had no mind to go with them, for I have had what [Brighton] can give, and I know not they much wanted me. [90]

1780

This was a year in which Boswell and Mrs. Thrale were mainly pre-

[89] Johnson to Mrs. Thrale, 5 October 1779. MS. Letter: last location known to me: Francis Edwards Catalogue, December 1918, Item 301. Letter #630. *Letters*, II, 305.

[90] Johnson to Mrs. Thrale, 19 October 1779. MS. Letter: New York Public Library. Letter #635. *Letters*, II, 309.

occupied with their own troubles. Boswell was badly in debt; his wife was again having a child; and his father's health was failing. He saw no hope of a visit to London.

With Mrs. Thrale, every movement was dictated by her husband's illness. They spent a miserable winter in Southwark. Sick, fearful, and depressed, Thrale's personality changed, he was no longer the sensible, kind person whom both his wife and Johnson had depended upon so heavily. He became indifferent to his family and to his business. He ate to excess. His actions were unpredictable and frightening.

The doctors' earlier advice, urging greater exercise and activity, was reversed; they now cautioned Thrale to eat little, to rest, and be quiet. This was what Mrs. Thrale had been begging for some time, but Thrale was headstrong and heedless. He suffered another dangerous attack on February 21st, but rallied and plunged again into senseless activity. In April Mrs. Thrale took the family to Bath; a round of gaiety ensued of which he was the center, though Mrs. Thrale herself was made much of by Mrs. Montagu,[91] queen of the Blue Stocking Ladies, who was also making a stay in Bath and who created a social circle wherever she was. Mrs. Thrale had brought Fanny Burney to be with the family: she was more helpful than Johnson and more agreeable in company. So for the third time when he wanted to be a comfort in a moment of crisis, Mrs. Thrale drew away — there was not an extra room for him in the house, she said. The truth was that she now found him a difficult old man and his presence only increased her troubles. Johnson was never to comprehend this change in their relationship. He worked along on his *Lives of the Poets*, and patiently waited to be summoned to Bath, which he liked better than Brighton. His constant letters to Mrs. Thrale gave unwelcome news of his poor health and of the tense political situation in London. He could not understand why she did not send for him.

In the end, he sent for her — to campaign for her husband — since Thrale was unable to support his own interests, a "little bustle, and a

---

[91] Elizabeth Robinson Montagu (1720–1800) was an author and leader of society. Born into wealth and given every advantage, the precocious Miss Robinson grew into a high-spirited and most accomplished young woman. She married Edward Montagu, a serious man of great wealth, older by many years. He admired and indulged her, and from 1750 onwards the Montagus' house on Hill Street became the center of intellect and fashion in London. Her evening assemblies were known as "conversation parties"; here, discussion on literary topics was preferred (and no card playing was allowed). To these assemblies the term "Blue Stocking" was first applied.

little ostentation will put a stop to clamours, and whispers, and suspicions of your friends, and calumnies of your opponents." [92] Mrs. Thrale drove to London on May 9th with Fanny Burney, and for a week plunged herself into strenuous election activities; then she returned to Bath.

Very shortly thereafter the Gordon riots broke out, a series of outrageous attacks upon Catholic citizens by a Protestant mob led by Lord George Gordon. The cause of fury was the relaxation of the severe penal provisions against Catholics. The house of the magistrate, Sir John Fielding, was pulled down and his goods burnt in the street. The house of Lord Mansfield, the eminent jurist, was burned with all his furniture, books, and papers. Catholic chapels were destroyed, Papist shops looted, prisons burned and prisoners freed — Newgate, the Fleet, Clerkenwell, Bridewell. Suddenly, riots flared up in Bath, and a rumor circulated there that Thrale was a Papist. In great alarm, on the night of June 10th, Mrs. Thrale took her family to Brighton, and as soon as her household was re-established there, she returned to Southwark; Johnson joined her at once. The brewery had barely escaped destruction. The mob had actually forced its way into the premises, but John Perkins, Thrale's manager, had the courage and presence of mind to treat with the rioters, offering them free beer and food, and while they drank and ate, Sir Philip Jennings-Clerke, M.P. and family friend, hurried off to summon troops. As a reward for Perkins' service and bravery, Mrs. Thrale presented him with two hundred guineas and gave his wife a silver urn. [93]

After a quick trip to Streatham, Mrs. Thrale returned to Brighton, where she took care of her sick husband and enjoyed the company of her little girls. Fanny Burney did not wish to return to Brighton, and though Mrs. Thrale missed her company, she kept herself amused with a literary project, completing the verses she had started some while before, characterizations for the Reynolds portraits of friends, which decorated the walls of the Streatham library. [94]

[92] Johnson to Mrs. Thrale, 8 May 1780. MS. Letter: Sir Samuel Scott. Letter #665. *Letters*, II, 354.

[93] Gordon riot account in *Life*, III, 427–433, and *Clifford*, p. 185.

[94] The verses described the portraits in this order:
1. Lord Sandys "appears first, at the head of the Tribe."
2. George Lyttelton (first Baron), "Next him on the Right hand."
3. and 4. — double picture: Mrs. Thrale and Queeney.

There was another interest also; she was enjoying the entertainment of "the great Italian Singer," Gabriel Piozzi,[95] who was in Brighton, he said, to recover his voice. This seemed to her past belief for as she wrote in *Thraliana*: "his Singing surpasses every body's for Taste, Tenderness, and true Elegance; his Hand on the Forte Piano too is so soft, so sweet, so delicate, every Tone goes to one's heart . . ."[96] She was determined that this delightful artist should give voice instruction to Queeney — a project which Gabriel Piozzi undertook soon after the Thrales returned to London.

They were forced to return when Parliament was dissolved on September 1st, for against all advice, Thrale was determined to stand again for the Borough. Once he was seen by the voters, his physical incapacity was obvious; he looked and acted like a dying man. The news spread quickly and when the polling day came, he was rightfully and heavily defeated.

During this anxious time Boswell had again been pressing Johnson to meet him somewhere in the north of England, not to let the year go by without an interview, but Johnson was unresponsive; his first

-----

5. Arthur Murphy, in whom "Learning turns Frolic with Humour his Guide."
6. Oliver Goldsmith, "a Poet so polish'd, so paltry a Fellow."
7. Sir Joshua Reynolds, of whom "all Good should be said, & no harm."
8. Sir Robert Chambers, his "soft Character sweetly display'd."
9. David Garrick, his "lov'd Features our Mem'ry may trace."
10. Henry Thrale:
    "See Thrale from Intruders defending his *Door*,
    While he wishes his House should with People run o'er."
11. Giuseppe Baretti "hangs next, by his Frowns you may know him."
12. Dr. Charles Burney, in "happy contrast," a favorite of all.
13. Edmund Burke. See "bright Intelligence beam from his Face."
14. Dr. Samuel Johnson, "Gigantic in Knowledge, in Virtue, in Strength."
— MS. of Mrs. Piozzi's Portrait Verses: Hyde.

[95] Gabriel Piozzi (1740–1809) was six months older than Mrs. Thrale. He had been born in Quinzano in the Venetian State, of upper-middle-class parents. He was one of fourteen children and it was intended that he enter the priesthood, but his passion for music and his desire to try his talents made him run away to Milan. There, he became the protégé and friend of the Marquis D'Araciel.

Piozzi had established a considerable reputation as a singer and composer by the time he came to London in 1776. Here, he gave concerts and was a fashionable vocal teacher. He was hospitably received by many, in particular, the Burneys. Mrs. Thrale had first heard him sing at their house in St. Martin Street in the winter of 1778. *Clifford*, p. 188, and *Thraliana*, I, 448, n.7.

[96] *Thraliana*, I, 452.

loyalty was to the Thrales and he would not commit himself. Finally, on the 17th of October, he wrote to Boswell that there was no hope of a meeting this autumn; he had at last been invited to join his family in Brighton. "I do not much like the place, but yet I shall go, and stay while my stay is desired." [97] The reunion was a sad one. In less than a month the household followed Thrale's doctor back to London.

1781

Thrale fought his illness stubbornly, struggling to remain the genial host, to be in company, to be active; but even in the middle of a sentence, his head would drop forward and he would drowse off to sleep. He tried to conduct business at the brewery but was incapable of giving orders. Mrs. Thrale and Johnson helped as much as they could but, as she said, affairs went on "perversely." [98]

Thrale was still determined to make the trip to Italy — was it to please Johnson? The prospect, which Mrs. Thrale had once happily anticipated, she now began to dread.

. . . how shall we drag him thither? A Man who cannot keep awake four Hours at a Stroke . . . Well! this will indeed be a Tryal of one's Patience; & who must go with us on this Expedition? Mr. Johnson! he will indeed be the only happy Person of the party: he values nothing under heaven but his own Mind, which is a Spark *from* Heaven; & *that* will be invigorated by the addition of new Ideas — if Mr. Thrale dies on the Road, Johnson will console himself by learning *how it is* to travel with a Corpse . . .[99]

The children were to be left behind, but Baretti, Mrs. Thrale regretfully admitted, would have to be a member of the party:

. . . there is no Man who has so much of *every* Language, & can manage so well with Johnson; & is so tidy on the Road, so active too to obtain good Accommodations. He is the man in the World I think whom I most abhor, and who hates, & professes to hate *me* the most; but what does that signifie? he will be careful of Mr Thrale & Hester [Queeney] whom he *does* love — and he won't strangle *me* I suppose: it will be very convenient to have him — somebody we must have; Croza would court our Daughter, & Piozzi could not talk to Johnson, nor I suppose do one any Good, but sing to one: — & how should we sing *Songs in a strange Land?* Baretti must be the Man, & I will beg it of him as a favour — Oh the Triumph he will have! & the Lyes that he will tell!

[97] Johnson to Boswell, 17 October 1780. Letter #708. *Letters*, II, 406.
[98] *Thraliana*, I, 486 (18 March 1781).
[99] *Ibid.*, 487.

If I dye abroad I shall leave all my Papers in Charge with Fanny Burney . . .[100]

The day after she recorded these thoughts in *Thraliana*, Boswell arrived in London — March 19th. He called at Bolt Court that day, and again on the next. Johnson was away from home on both occasions, but later on the 20th, unexpectedly, walking along Fleet Street, he ran into his friend; they greeted each other with fervor, Boswell saying, "This is strange, for us to meet in this way." Johnson "carried me into Falcon Court and asked me kindly after my family . . . 'I love you better than ever I did,' "[101] said Johnson, and he promised Boswell that he would stay home the following afternoon for a long and proper visit.

Shortly after this chance meeting Johnson saw Thrale and told him of Boswell's being in London. Thrale, in boisterous spirits, would take no refusal — the two must dine next day at Grosvenor Square, where he had taken a house for the winter.[102] At Thrale's bidding, Johnson wrote out an invitation:

Mr Thrale desires the favour of Mr Boswels company to dinner, to day, at four.
    Wednesday.
Mr Johnson will be at Mr Thrale's.[103]

Boswell received the message and followed instructions, doubtless amused at the thought of the Great Lexicographer now having a special apartment reserved for his use in the most fashionable part of London.[104]

---

[100] *Idem.*

[101] *Boswell Papers*, XIV, 171.

[102] Boswell remarked in the *Life*, IV, 72, that he supposed the move to Grosvenor Square had been "by the solicitation of Mrs. Thrale" to be in the center of the social world. Her response to this in *Life Limited Edition*, III, 183, was (with an underline of her name): "spiteful again; he went by Direction of his Physicians [Lucas Pepys and Sir Richard Jebb] where they could easiest attend to him."

[103] MS. card: Hyde. This was very likely the card which Boswell enclosed in his letter to the Rev. John Fawcett, 12 October 1792. "To make amends" for his delay in writing, Boswell said he was sending "a small piece of the handwriting of my illustrious friend." On the card, in Boswell's hand, is: "This is a piece of the handwriting of Dr. Samuel Johnson. James Boswell." See *Waingrow*, p. 494 and n.1.

[104] On this subject, the Blue Stocking writer, Hannah More, commented: "Think of Johnson's having apartments in Grosvenor-square! but he says it is not half so convenient as Bolt-court." Hannah More, *Memoirs*, I, 207, and *Life*, IV, 72, n. 1.

Boswell recorded in his Journal: "Dined at Mr. Thrale's whom I found not at all well.[105] He introduced to me Mr. Crutchley,[106] who he said was his best friend. I was hearty here; but Dr. Johnson, finding that I was not at General Paoli's, supposed I did not get the card to dine; and so polite and attentive was he that he went home, as he had engaged to be there." [107] After Boswell left Grosvenor Square, he went to Bolt Court and there found Johnson with Miss Williams — still waiting for him. The three talked for a while, then Johnson led his visitor up to his own room for further talk. When Boswell left, he was given "a deal of the original *Copy* of his *Lives of the Poets* which had been kept for [him]." [108]

The next day, March 22nd, both Johnson and Boswell dined at Grosvenor Square; Dr. Burney and Fanny were also there.[109] Thrale told Boswell with some zest to note a change in the Doctor's habits: that he would "have the pleasure to see [Johnson] drink wine again, for he had lately returned to it." Boswell now observed, as Johnson

poured a quantity of it into a large glass, and swallowed it greedily. Every thing about his character and manners was forcible and violent; there never was any moderation; many a day did he fast, many a year did he refrain from wine; but when he did eat, it was voraciously; when he did drink wine, it was copiously. He could practice abstinence, but not temperance.

Mrs. Thrale and I had a dispute, whether Shakespeare or Milton had drawn the most admirable picture of a man. I was for Shakespeare; Mrs. Thrale for Milton; and after a fair hearing, Johnson decided for my opinion.[110]

[105] *Boswell Papers*, XIV, 171 (21 March 1781). In the *Life*, IV, 72, Boswell wrote that he found Thrale "now very ill . . . I was sorry to see him sadly changed in his appearance."

[106] Jeremiah Crutchley (1745–1805). This sickly, enigmatic young man was often said to be Thrale's natural son. *Autobiography, Letters and Literary Remains of Mrs. Piozzi (Thrale)*, Edited by A. Hayward (London: Longman, Green, Longman, and Roberts, 1861), I, 144. (Hereafter referred to as *Hayward*.) Mrs. Thrale thought so. His later fondness for Queeney, and hers for him, were to give Mrs. Thrale grave concern.

[107] *Boswell Papers*, XIV, 171–172 (21 March 1781).

[108] *Ibid.*, 172.

[109] *Idem.*

[110] *Life*, IV, 72–73. Mrs. Thrale's comments in *Life Limited Edition*, III, 184, were — on the drinking of wine: "copiously" underlined "and pour'd Capillaire into it." "Capillaire" is defined in the *O.E.D.* as "a syrup flavoured with orange-flower water," and Johnson's practice is cited.

On Milton: "Milton kept his Head closer to the *Man*; Shakespeare was more excursive; he heaped on Ornaments. — after all, *his* is a more *Dramatic*, — Milton's a more *Epic* Description. *Both* were *best* as the Children say."

On the 24th Boswell called upon the Thrales and found William
Seward with them; [111] on the 26th he had both dinner and supper —
"nobody there." [112] On the 28th he had tea — with Mrs. Thrale and
Johnson, Queeney, and Jeremiah Crutchley. [113] On the 29th, "I think
I dined today at Mr. Thrales." [114] On Saturday the 31st, the Thrales
gave a large party, a "rout," and Boswell felt free to ask that a friend
of his be invited. [115] It was a gay occasion on the surface, but under-
neath there was a sense of impending danger. Mrs. Thrale's exaggerated vivacity covered nervousness and fear, and Thrale's behavior was
alarming to all who watched him; his boisterousness was gone, he was
wholly lethargic, interested in nothing, he slept through most of the
party.

Next day, Sunday, April 1st, Mrs. Thrale heard "the Bishop of
Peterborough preach at May Fair Chapel," and she wrote in *Thraliana*,
"though the Sermon had nothing in it particularly pathetic, I could not
keep my Tears within my Eyes." [116] In the evening, when she returned "to the Square" from Lady Rothes's, [117] she found Sir John
Lade, [118] Johnson, and Boswell with her husband.

Boswell had come without being specifically invited, but since 1775
he had had "a kindly general invitation to dinner and supper. I said
I had a silver ticket. 'A gold ticket' said worthy Thrale." [119] This
sally was a particular show of animation; most of the time Thrale was
listless and inattentive, not joining in with the argument about the

[111] *Boswell Papers*, XIV, 173 (24 March 1781).
[112] *Ibid.*, 174 (26 March 1781).
[113] *Ibid.*, 175 (28 March 1781).
[114] *Ibid.*, 178 (29 March 1781).
[115] *Ibid.*, 181 (31 March 1781).
[116] *Thraliana*, I, 488.
[117] Jane Elizabeth, Countess of Rothes, wife of Lucas Pepys, one of Thrale's
physicians.
[118] Sir John Lade (1759–1838) was Thrale's nephew, "a mere fashionable non-
entity . . . a Centaur" (*Boswell Papers*, XIV, 187). Sir John would later become
an intimate of the Prince of Wales through his prowess in horsemanship. It was to
Lade that Johnson had addressed the "short song of congratulation" the year before,
"Long-expected one and twenty." Thrale thought Fanny Burney would make him
a good wife. But Johnson told him, when they discussed the general subject of
marriage: "I would advise no man to marry, Sir, who is not likely to propagate
understanding." Hayward notes that Lade "married a woman of the town, became
a celebrated member of the Four-in-Hand Club, and contrived to waste the whole
of a fine fortune before he died." *Life*, IV, 412, n. 1.
[119] *Boswell Papers*, XIV, 184 (1 April 1781).

American war, criticism of men of fortune, discussion of the guest Boswell had brought to the "rout," talk of Seward's inaccuracies (in his presence),[120] and of Mrs. Thrale's garrulity (in her presence). "She is the first woman in the World," Johnson said. "Could she but restrain that wicked tongue of her's, she would be the only Woman in the World. Could she but command that little whirligig." [121]

John Perkins, the brewery manager, and Sir Philip Jennings-Clerke had been there for dinner. Sir Philip was the person who had summoned the troops to save the brewery during the Gordon riots the year before. John Lade, William Seward, and Henry Smith, a cousin of Thrale's, had come in later.

Next day, Monday, April 2nd, fear was felt for Thrale. One of his doctors, Sir Richard Jebb, was at dinner, also Johnson and Baretti. Mrs. Thrale wrote in her Journal that her husband:

. . . eat voraciously — *so* voraciously — that encouraged by Jebb & Pepys who had charged me so to do — I checked him rather severely, & Mr Johnson added these remarkable Words. Sir — after the Denunciation of your Physicians this Morning, such eating is little better than Suicide. he did not however desist . . .[122]

But Boswell saw Thrale on Monday evening, "at which time he was not thought to be in immediate danger." [123]

The next day, Tuesday, April 3rd, Mrs. Thrale was busy "going and coming," seeing the landscape artist, John Webber's drawings of the South Seas, and greeting the "numberless *Blues*" who attended the exhibition; but she had "lowspirited Terrors" about her husband, though he had not "one Symptom worse than he had had for Months." [124] When she came home to dress, "Piozzi — who was always admitted to the Toilette, & sate in the next Room teaching

---

[120] Seward had said that when he was in Edinburgh "he had seen three Volumes in folio of Dr. Johnson's sayings collected by me. 'Nay,' said I, 'I must put you right, as I am very exact in authenticity. You could not see folio volumes of his sayings, for I have none. You may have seen Octavos and quartos. Now,' said I, 'this is inattention which one should guard against.' 'Sir,' said the Doctor, 'it is a want of concern about veracity. He does not know that he saw any volumes. If he had seen 'em, he could have remembered their size.'" *Boswell Papers*, XIV, 187–188.

[121] *Ibid.*, 186.

[122] *Thraliana*, I, 488.

[123] *Life*, IV, 84. There is no Journal entry for 2 April 1781.

[124] *Thraliana*, I, 488.

[Queeney] to sing" lamented that he had a prior engagement and could not attend the reception the Thrales had planned for "the Indian Ambassadors" the following night, April 4th. Mrs. Thrale suddenly burst into tears, startling Piozzi. She regained her poise, but when a letter was delivered from Lucas Pepys:

I burst out o'crying again, read the Letter to Piozzi who could not understand it, & threw myself into an Agony, saying I was sure Mr. Thrale would dye. The tenderhearted Italian was affected, bid me not despair so, but recollect some precepts he had heard Dr. Johnson give me one Day; & then turn'd to me with a good deal of Expression in his Manner, rather too much — it affected me. — and sung Rasserena il tuo bel Ciglio &c &c [125]

Then Thrale came home; he had been out in his carriage, inviting more guests to the reception. He was in exceedingly high spirits and "delighted to think what a Show we should make. He eat however more than enormously; — six things the Day before, & eight on this Day, with Strong Beer in *such* Quantities! the very Servants were frighted, & when Pepys came in the Evening he said this could not last — either there must be *legal* Restraint or certain Death." [126]

Later, when Mrs. Thrale went to look for her husband, she found him sitting on his bed, with his legs up; and still a few minutes later Queeney found him on the floor. Pepys and Jebb were sent for, and Queeney located Jeremiah Crutchley (he was already on hand for the party next day). One fit of violent apoplexy followed another — into the night. Jebb, "seeing Death certain, quitted the House without even prescribing; Pepys did all that could be done, & Johnson who was sent for at 11 o'Clock never left him, for while breath remain'd *he* still hoped. I ventured in once, & saw them cutting his Clothes off to bleed him, but I saw no more." [127]

Thrale died early on the morning of April 4th; Johnson, feeling the last flutter of his pulse, was desolated. [128] Mrs. Thrale, in a state of ner-

---

[125] *Ibid.*, 489. "I suppose (says Mrs Byron who saw & heard him,) that you *Know* that Man is in Love with You. I am replied I, too miserable to care *who* is in Love wth me. *She remembers it.*" *Idem*, n. 2.

[126] *Ibid.*, 489.

[127] *Ibid.*, 490.

[128] Johnson records in his Diary that Thrale died about "five (I think)." He looked "for the last time upon the face that for fifteen years had never been turned upon me but with respect or benignity. Farewel[l]." *Johnson Diaries* (note 245 below), p. 304 (entry for 14 April 1781).

vous prostration, fled with Queeney to Brighton. Thrale was buried at Streatham on April 11th.[129]

With unseemly haste the London wits began discussing the future prospects of the rich, attractive widow, and it was not long before her name was linked to Johnson's. Boswell did not try to protect her feelings, quite the reverse. It is hard to believe what he did, knowing that he had accepted Thrale's hospitality to the very end, also knowing the respect he had for Johnson's dignity when he shared it by reflection — but now, in boisterous spirits, he took little heed of either Mrs. Thrale's feelings or of Johnson's anger. Eight days after Thrale's death (one day after his funeral) he diffused gaiety by composing a "Song [on Dr. Johnson and Mrs Thrale]." This epithalamium he wrote on two sheets of paper, while at Sir Joshua Reynolds' house.[130] Soon, he was rendering his "Song" at various gatherings. He became obsessed with the idea of the match and even discussed it in Johnson's house on April 15th with Dr. Scott, the international lawyer. They "agreed that it was possible Mrs. Thrale might marry Dr. John[son], and [they] both wished it much." [131]

Boswell was in an ebullient mood all during April. "I catched fire," he wrote one correspondent.[132] On the 22nd, in "extraordinary spirits,"

[129] Johnson wrote in his Diary: ". . . with him were buried many of my hopes and pleasures." *Samuel Johnson Diaries, Prayers, and Annals,* Edited by E. L. McAdam, Jr., with Donald and Mary Hyde (New Haven: Yale University Press, 1958), p. 304 (13 April 1781). Hereafter referred to as *Johnson Diaries.*

Thrale's will, dated 17 March 1781, left Streatham to Mrs. Thrale for life; its contents were hers unconditionally.

The executors were: Thrale's widow; Johnson; Jeremiah Crutchley; John Cator (1730–1806), a timber merchant and friend; and Henry Smith (1756?–1789), a cousin of Thrale's.

The executors were also named guardians of the Thrale daughters.

[130] *Boswell Papers,* XIV, 196 (12 April 1781), and Yale (M302). Text in Appendix.

The next month (8 May 1781) Boswell brought Johnson and Wilkes together for the second time. It was at Dilly's house. (*Life,* IV, 101 ff.) There Wilkes put Boswell *"in fear* of Dr. Johnson's anger" (*Tinker Boswell Letters,* II, 314. Boswell to Wilkes, 14 February 1783). The cause was "a certain epithalamium." Boswell must have "a pleasant apology" or "there must be an end to a certain classical and gay connection." Boswell to Wilkes, 26 March 1783. *Ibid.,* 315.

[131] *Boswell Papers,* XIV, 198 (15 April 1781).

Another suitor, though not causing the discussion that Johnson did, was Sir Philip Jennings-Clerke. By May he was making love to Mrs. Thrale "quite openly & seriously; says he shall marry me for that his Wife is Ill." *Thraliana,* I, 538.

[132] Boswell to Margaret Cunynghame Stuart, [16 April 1781]. Yale (L1202).

SIR LUCAS PEPYS
BY HENRY EDRIDGE

BOSWELL'S "SONG" ON DR. JOHNSON AND MRS. THRALE
Reproduced by permission of the
Yale University Library

as he phrased it, he made a drunken spectacle of himself at Miss Monckton's,[133] while Johnson struggled to keep him quiet. He paid no condolence call upon Mrs. Thrale, nor did he write a proper letter of sympathy, as he had at the time of young Harry Thrale's death, but on the 26th sent a curious letter. He hoped that she "will beleive he feels all he ought to." This must surely mean his sympathy for the death of her husband; by adding to the same sentence, "though his gayety of fancy is not to be subdued," the full meaning can only be: though he sympathized with her, he could not prevent his imagination from gaily playing with her future.

Mr Boswell presents his best compliments to Mrs Thrale. Hopes she will beleive he feels all he ought to do, though his gayety of fancy is not to be subdued. Begs to know how she does, and if in any thing he can prove his sincere regard for her. He returns to General Paoli's Southaudley Street on Saturday.

Richmond
Thursday 26 April 1781 [134]
To
    Mrs Thrale
      Streatham

Boswell's note indicates that he feared Mrs. Thrale might know of his *jeu d'esprit*, and to protect himself, he wrote a limited apology. Fanny Burney reported such a jest when she wrote to Streatham: "I have heard some verses . . . about you & Dr. Johnson! such as you so well foretold." [135]

Boswell's "sportive lay" [136] was rough repayment to Mrs. Thrale for years of courtesy and kindness.

----

[133] The Hon. Mary Monckton, an enchanting Blue Stocking, who later became the Countess of Cork and Orrery. Description of Boswell's behavior at her house, *Life*, IV, 109–110.

[134] MS. Letter: Rylands, Eng.MS.542/2. Copy in Boswell's hand: Yale (L1073).

[135] *Clifford*, p. 199.

[136] See Plate XIV, stanza 4.

CHAPTER III

ESTRANGEMENT

1782 through 1786

1782

For Boswell and Mrs. Thrale 1782 was a crucial year, a turning point in their lives. At forty-two, Boswell, the heir, finally became Laird of Auchinleck; at forty-one, Mrs. Thrale, the widow, fell in love.

As the year opened, Boswell faced many anxieties. He was in financial difficulties and not well; his wife, it could no longer be denied, had consumption, and in an advanced state. She was alarmed herself; Boswell was distraught and also apprehensive about the possibility of being left with five children. In January, when his father's health was failing rapidly, he received an affectionate letter from Johnson, but it only increased his worries, for it was another report of sickness and depression,[1] and though Boswell wanted to come to London, he could not at the moment think of making the trip. On March 18th, according to his Letter Register, Boswell wrote to Johnson, saying that he might be coming to London this spring. In the Letter Register is also the note that he had written to "Mrs. Thrale desireous that our acquaintance may continue — Begging to hear particularly of Dr. Johnson."[2]

Boswell's retained draft of this letter shows that he had difficulty in trying to re-establish a tone of easy relationship, after his lapse of the year before. He now attempted to express proper sympathy for her husband's death, even though it was almost a year after the event. On the subject of Johnson, he was on surer ground. He reminded her of the bond of affection they shared, and earnestly begged news of Johnson's health. The matter of literary assistance, though not forgotten, was wisely not mentioned.

---

[1] Johnson to Boswell, 5 January 1782. Letter #756. *Letters*, II, 455–456.
[2] Boswell's Letter Register. Yale (M254).

Edinburgh

Dear Madam. 19 March 1782.

I was very sorry to /leave England/ ⟨go to Scotland⟩, without /waiting upon/ ⟨having the pleasure of seeing⟩ you, after the loss of Mᚱ Thrale, whom I had much reason to value. But, I was told it was not proper ⟨to wait upon you⟩ till I /should/ receive⟨d⟩ a message; and none came, while I remained in London.

May I now presume to inquire how you are, and to express my wish for /the/ continu⟨ing⟩/ance of/ an acquaintance to which I am indebted for a great deal of happiness.

The last letter which I had from Dᚱ Johnson gave me an anxious concern for, it informed me that his health had been tottering — and two months have since elapsed without my hearing from him. You have pleased me, Madam, more than

once

[page 2]

once by saying that however he may be respected and admired by others, you and I are distinguished for also loving him. I trust this similarity with which I am flattered, will induce you to ⟨w⟩ let me know particularly about him. He himself is never /minute/ ⟨particular⟩ enough.

Whether I shall have the pleasure of being in London this spring ⟨I cannot⟩ I do not yet know. There is a struggle between my wishes and my embarrassments   Perhaps Dᚱ Johnson may determine.

I beg you may present my ⟨best⟩ compliments to Miss Thrale

I have the honour to be
Dear Madam
your most obedient
humble servant [3]

Mrs. Thrale did not reply at once, and on March 28th Johnson himself wrote to Boswell. He gave a dissertation upon the evils and miseries of poverty and bluntly told Boswell to stay at home. As for his health, Johnson said, he had suffered from a cold, but by bleeding had recovered.[4]

Johnson did not write again and on May 13th Mrs. Thrale made a token reply to Boswell's letter of two months before. She answered his request for news of Johnson with brevity. She made no acknowledgment of his inquiry of how she herself was, nor did she comment upon his hopes for continued friendship. There was only one personal mention, perhaps protective, in case Boswell had heard of her strained relationship with Johnson (they had quarrelled in April); she assured

---

[3] MS. Letter: Sotheby's, 2 June 1908, Lot 768. MS. Draft: Hyde.
[4] Johnson to Boswell, 28 March 1782. Letter #775. *Letters*, II, 474-475.

him that their dear friend was with her at Streatham, receiving every comfort and kindness.

Streatham
13: May 1782.

Sir

You wrote to me some Time ago, & begged an Acc.ᵗ of our dear D.ʳ Johnson's Health; I have waited for a better till I am weary, & now must send you a bad one. He has lost no fewer than 50 ounces of Blood within this last week, 100 since this Year began; & though the Symptoms are relieved by this practice, the Disease — a Cough & difficulty of Breathing — is not removed. He is at my House now: and enjoys I hope every Consolation in the power of
> Dear Sir
> > Your Obedient
> > and faithful Serv.ᵗ
> > H:L:Thrale [5]

Boswell was away when her letter arrived but, as soon as he received it, he hastened to send a cordial reply. The coolness of her note did not dampen his spirits. What was important was that she had written; it gave him hope that he might be able to establish a regular correspondence. Boswell asked if she would let him know "once a week" how Johnson did (with practicality and consideration, he said "by a single line"). This was an effective approach.

Edinburgh
25 May 1782.

Dear Madam.

Having gone upon a Ramble into the country, the letters which came to me in my absence, were kept at my house here till my return, which has occasioned my not receiving till long after its date, your letter of the 13.ᵗʰ current.

The Account which it gives me of D.ʳ Johnson alarms me to the heart; and you whose veneration and affection for him are in unison with mine, will conceive what I feel. It distresses me that I submitted to his forcible, but too cool advice not to come to London this spring. For now my practice as a Lawyer in the Court of Session must detain me here

till

[page 2]

till August, when I am resolved to be with him, God willing.

In the mean time, it will be doing me a kindness, which I shall most gratefully acknowledge, if you will be pleased once a week to let me know by a single line how he recovers. I avoid strong expressions. I only refer you to

[5] MS. Letter: Hyde.

yourself to judge of me. I ardently wish for any opportunity to prove with how much regard I have the honour to be My Dear Madam

                your much obliged
                    humble servant
                        James Boswell.[6]

To
      Mrs Thrale
          Streatham
          Surry

In a little over a week Mrs. Thrale wrote a brief, not very encouraging report: Sir Richard Jebb, one of Thrale's doctors, was in charge; Johnson's own physician and devoted friend, Thomas Lawrence, was more seriously ill than Johnson. Mrs. Thrale's letter has considerable interest between the lines. She makes no allusion to the important event of three days before, the sale of the brewery to Thrale's manager, John Perkins, Sylvanus Bevan, and David and Robert Barclay. Though Mrs. Thrale was glad to lose the "Golden Millstone from [her] Neck,"[7] Johnson was disappointed. He had enjoyed his brief business career. Mrs. Thrale's news that Johnson soon was going to Oxford conceals the fact that this was a trip he did not have any desire to make. Despite the tension and argument, Johnson wanted to be at home with his Mistress but she was tired of his burdensome company and barking cough, and urged him to seek improvement elsewhere. Her enthusiastic postscript to Boswell, that she was glad he was coming to London in August was sincere.

                                  3: June 1782.

Sir

I am sorry my Letter alarmed you so, for I did not mean that it should; I cannot however promise you chearful Accounts of our valuable Friend's Health: Sir Richard Jebb attends him, Dr Lawrence is in the last Stage of Life. —You will however think better of Dr Johnson, when I tell you he means to go to Oxford soon by way of changing the Air for his Cough.

                I have the honour to be
                    Dear Mr Boswell's most
                      faithful humble Servt
                          H:L:Thrale

[6] MS. Letter and John Lawrie MS. Copy: Hyde.

[7] So Mrs. Thrale wrote Mrs. Lambart on the same day she wrote Boswell. From now on she would "float once more on the Current of Life like my Neighbours — I long to salute You in my restored Character of a Gentlewoman." *Clifford*, p. 202.

I am glad you are to come in August.[8]
James Boswell Esq
⟨Edinburgh⟩
[Forwarded by Lawrie]
        Vally field by
        Dumfermline

A month later, Mrs. Thrale sent another few lines to Boswell. Johnson had made only a short visit to Oxford, June 10th–19th,[9] and was
now back at Streatham.

Streatham
4: July 1782.

Dear Sir
    As I once wrote you an alarming Letter, let me now write you a consolatory
one: M.r Johnson came home from Oxford so much mended we were all
amazed, & he continues very much recovered indeed — You will I hope find
him quite well, tho' the Pulse is intermittent & irregular. I am sorry to hear
M.rs Boswell is indisposed, & hasten to relieve your Mind of all the Anxiety I
can; being with great Esteem   Sir
                Your most Obed.t & faithful
                    Serv.t
                        H: L: Thrale.[10]

        James Boswell Esq
            Edinburgh

For several weeks the Boswell household had been in a miserable
state. He himself had influenza and his wife was suffering from swelling, sweats, and shooting pains. She had coughed up a great deal of
blood. Now, however, she was a little better.

    On July 8th, the day of Boswell's own recovery, when he shaved
and dressed and went out for the first time since his illness,[11] he received this letter from Mrs. Thrale. He replied on the instant, writing
with care, and feeling. He told her of the joy her good news had
given him, dramatically adding that he had kissed the signature of her
note. He appreciated the happy hours she had given him in the past
and anticipated the letters she would write in the future. He urged
that they be "at more length," and hoped that they would be filled
with anecdotes "of our illustrious Imlac." He also complimented her

    [8] MS. Letter: Hyde.
    [9] *Life*, IV, 151, n. 2.
    [10] MS. Letter: Hyde.
    [11] *Boswell Papers*, XV, 95–96 (8 July 1782). Boswell had come down with in-
fluenza on the 19th of June.

upon the ease with which she wrote, certainly not demonstrated by her forced communications with him.

(To Mrˢ Thrale)   Edin. 9 July 1782.

Dear Madam

Last nights post brought me your kind Letter informing me of Dr Johnson's being so much better, since his jaunt to Oxford. It is needless to tell you what joy it gave me. I kissed the Subscription H.L. Thrale with fervency The good news elated me; and I was at the same time pleasingly interested by the tender wish which you express to releive my anxiety as much as you can. My Dear Madam, from the day that I first had the pleasure to meet you, when I jumpt into your Coach, not I hope from impudence, but from that agreeable kind of attraction which makes one forget ceremony, I have invariably thought of you with admiration & gratitude Were I to make out a chronological account of all the happy hours which I owe to you I should appear under great debt, & debt of a peculiar nature, for, a generous mind cannot be discharged of it by

the

[page 2]

the Creditor.

May I presume still more upon your kindness, and beg that you may write to me at more length. I do not mean to put you to a great deal of trouble. But you write so easily that you might by a small expence of time give me much pleasure. Anecdotes of our literary or gay friends but particularly of our illustrious Imlac would delight me.

I hope you have not adopted a notion which I once heard Dr Johnson mention, that for fear of tempting to publication it was his study to write letters as ill, I think, or as dryly or jejunely I am not sure of the very phrase but it meant as insipidly as he could. He said this last year at Mr Dillys in company

with

[page 3]

with Mr Wilkes if I am not mistaken. — I suggested to him that his writing so would most certainly make his letters be preserved and published; for, it would be a choice curiosity to see Dr Johnson write ill.

         "Behold a miracle instead of wit
         "See two dull lines by Stanhopes pencil writ."

My wife is a good deal better though still sadly distressed. But I flatter myself that the symptoms of that dismal disease a Consumption are disappearing. I experience a comfort after my late apprehensions, which raises my Soul in pious thoughts. I have the honour to be My Dear Madam Your much obliged, faithfull humble servant.[12]

Boswell's new approach, with added gallantries which he felt her present independence permitted, was ineffective.

[12] MS. Letter was W. K. Bixby; present location not known. Lawrie MS. Copy: Hyde.

Mrs. Thrale did not respond; she was neither flattered nor interested. She was harassed by her own problems — financial and emotional. Her income was now greatly reduced, and she had failed in the Welsh property suit against Lady Salusbury, the widow of her uncle.[13] Thrale and his lawyers had been able to delay this action for several years, but now the blow had fallen and the only course of action was to reach a settlement. This was finally agreed upon, but the question of how to raise the money remained; economy measures were certainly indicated. Mrs. Thrale decided to give up having a London house and to let Streatham Park for three years. She would further economize by taking the three older girls, Queeney, Sophy, and Susan, to Italy. There, money would go further, and the cultural benefits of travel and study of the language would be thrown into the bargain. Queeney's music master, Gabriel Piozzi, would guide the party.

The problem of Johnson caused Mrs. Thrale considerable anguish. She well knew how he had longed to go, and how stoically he had borne the various postponements of the trip. All his friends were aware of his cherished dream of a classical expedition, and she realized that she would be sharply criticized if she left him behind. Yet his precarious health would make an intolerable burden, and there was real danger in taking him. An impossible dilemma. On the 22nd of August Mrs. Thrale "mustered up" her resolution and told him of her "Necessity of changing a Way of Life [she] had long been displeased with," [14] (phraseology which implies more than financial distress). A stay in Italy, she told Johnson, would be a wise and prudent solution for her problems. To her surprise, Johnson agreed with her, saying he "thought well of the Project & wished [her] to put it early in Execution." [15] She could hardly believe his reaction, and it was even harder to credit what Queeney told her later, that he would not have joined the party, even if he had been asked.[16]

The enormous relief of knowing positively that Johnson would not

[13] Lady Salusbury strove to collect the money paid almost thirty years before by her husband, Sir Thomas, to save Bach-y-Graig, the estate of his brother, John Salusbury (Hester Thrale's father). Sir Thomas did not intend his niece to assume this debt; but his widow was not of that mind and possessed a document to prove the debt. *Clifford*, p. 211.

[14] *Thraliana*, I, 540.

[15] *Idem.*

[16] *Idem.* In contrast to Mrs. Thrale's long entry in her Diary for Thursday, August 22nd, Johnson simply recorded in his: "Mrs. Thrale told me her design of going abroad." *Johnson Diaries*, p. 325.

come allowed Mrs. Thrale the feminine privilege of feeling irritation at his indifference. She wrote in *Thraliana*:

I fancied Mr Johnson could not have existed without me forsooth, as we have now lived together above 18 years, & I have so fondled and waited on him in Sickness & in Health — Not a bit on't! he feels nothing in parting with me, nothing in the least; but thinks it a prudent Scheme, & goes to his Book as usual.[17]

If Mrs. Thrale had put herself in Johnson's place, she would have realized that no other reaction on his part was possible. He had now reached the sad moment when age and infirmity mean that life must almost stand still. At this point a man can complain or accept, or even with spirit he can talk about the future — but no matter which way he views things, his activity has virtually ceased, and will cease altogether if much exertion is demanded. In Johnson's case, he faced the issue squarely. He knew that a quiet trip to Italy would still be possible, if it were planned especially around him, but to be a sixth wheel in such a long, rigorous journey as Mrs. Thrale planned was impossible. Johnson knew his days of distant rambles with young companions were over.

Mrs. Thrale did not appreciate the fact that Johnson turned back "to his Book" to ease the heartache; he did not appreciate the fact that *her* heart controlled the unmentioned and strongest reason for going to Italy — to be shown this country and its classical treasures by Piozzi "has long been my dearest wish." [18] This gentle, soft-spoken man had become an increasingly important and helpful person in the masterless household. Mrs. Thrale was constantly in his company, she depended upon him, enjoyed him, admired him; in fact now, a year after Thrale's death, she admitted to herself that she was in love with him — romantically in love for the first time in her life. She was forty-one years old, the perilous time when a woman realizes that she has her final chance of a new, full life. She wanted to marry Piozzi, and she knew she must marry quickly if she were to have a child by him — and this she wanted very much. She could not continue to nurse Johnson — he might live another ten years. She must decide. Such a marriage, she knew, would provoke a public scandal. She knew how London society would treat her. What to do? The summer was an unhappy time of soul-searching, uncertainty, and vacillation.

[17] *Thraliana*, I, 540–541.
[18] *Ibid.*, 540.

It was an unhappy summer for Boswell as well. He was not able to come to London in August as he had hoped he might, because his father's illness became critical, and on the 30th of that month Lord Auchinleck died. It was an unthinkable time for Boswell to leave home, yet he was determined to consult Johnson about his new responsibilities, "Dr. J[ohnson]'s wisdom was highly requisite," [19] he recorded in his Journal. On the 24th of September Boswell set out for London, but on the road next day was brought word that his wife had "had a violent fit of spitting of blood. [He] rode home in agitation." [20] A few days later, he was still undecided whether or not he should go to London, but on the 27th he received a letter from his mentor "which settled [him] not to go." [21] Johnson said firmly to stay home, watch over his wife, and take care of his new duties as Laird of Auchinleck.[22] Boswell consoled himself with a gesture of sentiment, beginning his "Book of Company," [23] his register of guests at Auchinleck, on his celebrated friend's birthday. In writing to Johnson on the 1st of October, he said in a postscript: "Pray present my best compliments to Mrs. Thrale. Do not think it a wild imagination that I may one day have the pleasure of seeing her here." [24]

As for a final visit to Streatham, Boswell's opportunity no longer existed. Arrangements were being made to lease the property to Lord Shelburne for three years. Early in October preparations and packing were going forward. Johnson dined for the last time and read for the last time in the library, and on October 6th he made his pathetic farewell to the home where his happiest days had been spent. He offered a prayer, "with humble and sincere thankfulness [remembering] the comforts and conveniences . . . enjoyed at this place" and expressing the hope that he might "resign them with holy submission." [25]

Mrs. Thrale did not view the relinquishment of Streatham Park with the same despondency. For her, the house had lost its attraction;

[19] *Boswell Papers*, XV, 125 (24 September 1782).

[20] *Idem* (25 September 1782).

[21] *Idem* (27 September 1782).

[22] Johnson to John Taylor, 3 October 1782. MS. Letter: New York Public Library. Letter #807. *Letters*, II, 509.

[23] MS. "Book of Company at Auchinleck": Hyde.

[24] Boswell to Johnson, 1 October 1782. MS. Letter: Yale (L673). *Boswell Papers*, XV, 251.

[25] *Johnson Diaries*, p. 338.

without Thrale it was too difficult and too expensive to run, and her interests were now centered in Piozzi. Johnson, though aware of the Italian's constant presence and Mrs. Thrale's attentions to him, in contrast to her neglect of himself, refused to acknowledge that he was a threat to the family. And the London papers still proclaimed that Johnson was the foremost suitor for the widow's hand. If Boswell had seen *The Morning Post* of October 15th, he would have read that a treaty of marriage was "on tap" between Dr. Johnson and Mrs. Thrale. On the 18th this newspaper, carrying the impudence still further, described the coming event. Boswell would have been delighted to have been so prophetic.

After leaving Streatham, Mrs. Thrale took the children to Brighton. Johnson was asked to join them and he did, though, as said before, he heartily disliked this resort. He suffered existence there in a terrible humor, so rude to everyone that he was omitted from all invitations. Fanny Burney joined the party within a few days and tried to make the situation happier, without success. She herself was soon shocked and miserable, for Mrs. Thrale confided to her and to Queeney that she loved Piozzi and wanted to marry him. This prospect was horrifying to them both, and they offered every objection: Fanny pleaded with her and Queeney refused to give her consent. Mrs. Thrale was tortured with indecision: should she give up Piozzi as they urged? Would she be able to? Might Queeney possibly be more understanding when spring came, the time set for going to Italy? She hardly knew what to do, but finally decided to take a house in Argyll Street for the winter. Toward the end of November the family returned to London.

On the 7th of December Johnson wrote to Boswell that "Mrs. Thrale and the three Misses" were now installed. He too had a room in the Argyll Street house, and a semblance of the old closeness was maintained, but Johnson was not with Mrs. Thrale as often as before; he wrote to her frequently from Bolt Court, feeling neglected and abused. In the letter of December 7th to Boswell, his old friend wrote sadly: "At your long silence I am rather angry . . . [you cannot] suspect after so many years of friendship, that when I do not write to you, I forget you. Put all such useless jealousies out of your head . . ." [26]

[26] Johnson to Boswell, 7 December 1782. Letter #815. *Letters*, II, 518.

Boswell had his wife write Johnson a letter expressing "the agreeable hopes of seeing [him] in Scotland again." [27] Boswell also wrote to Mrs. Thrale, saying that he was relieved she had not already gone abroad, and that he hoped to see her when he came to London in the spring. He again asked for news of Johnson, "from time to time," he suggested in a less demanding way than formerly.

Edinburgh

Dear Madam. 20 Decr. 1782.

It is strange that I am not yet old enough not to give credit to what I read in the newspapers. I did beleive that you was gone or just going abroad; and I was selfish enough to be sorry for it. But a letter from our most respected Freind Dr Johnson has informed me that you and three Misses are in Argyll Street. I hope to have the pleasure of finding you there in March. In the mean time, may I again intreat to hear from you how Dr Johnson does, from time to time. I express myself inelegantly. But I trust you think me worthy of that attention; and I know I am grateful for your goodness.

Every body here is running after Cecilia; and I am vain of telling that I have had the pleasure of being frequently in Miss Burney's company at Mrs Thrale's.

I am Dear Madam
your obliged and faithful
humble servant
James Boswell. [28]

————

To

Mrs Thrale
London

Boswell was completely unaware of the drama in Mrs. Thrale's life.

1783

By January Mrs. Thrale's situation was approaching a crisis. Jeremiah Crutchley, who was not only an executor of Thrale's estate but also one of the guardians of the children, told her that she must give up all thought of the trip to Italy. Rumors, he said, were circulating that Piozzi, her ardent admirer, would be one of the party. Rumors, at last, concerned the right man. Crutchley and the other guardians, John Cator and Henry Smith, would not permit the children to leave England in the company of Piozzi. Mrs. Thrale's hopes that the passage of time would bring acceptance and sympathy had not been realized. Everyone opposed Piozzi.

[27] Margaret Boswell to Johnson, 20 December 1782. *Life*, IV, 157.
[28] MS. Letter and Copy in Boswell's hand: Hyde.

By the end of January Mrs. Thrale regretfully abandoned her plans for Italy, and in response to Queeney's charge that the Italian music-master would bring ruin to the family, she finally sacrificed her own happiness, and gave Queeney her promise that she would not marry him. Piozzi returned all her mother's letters to Queeney, and began his slow preparations for leaving England.[29]

Queeney, the ambitious and talented young Miss of eighteen, now expected that the household would return to normal, and that her mother would, for a change, consider the wishes and pleasures of her daughters. This, Mrs. Thrale firmly refused to do. Exhausted and heartbroken, she could no longer bear the sight of critical friends — nor of London itself. She took a small house in Bath; there she hoped to live quietly and economically and in some measure to regain her health and peace of mind. By the middle of March, when she was preparing to leave London with Queeney, Susan, and Sophy, Boswell arrived. No one had informed him of Mrs. Thrale's infatuation, and though Johnson now openly criticized her behavior, he did not fully enlighten him, nor could Johnson have done so, for he still refused to believe that Piozzi was a serious threat. Thus, even in May, after having been in London for some time and having seen Mrs. Thrale before her departure, Boswell still clung to his notion of her possible marriage to Johnson. On May 17th he recorded that at Bolt Court Johnson said:

"I'll shew you what I have for some time concealed" (or refrained, or some such word). ⟨He⟩ took out a letter from a drawer. "There's a letter from Mrs. Thrale which you may read." I imagined upon my honour it was some TENDER epistle; something of love, perhaps of marriage. But it was ⟨wri⟩ting him that if he chose to scold me, ⟨I⟩ had one night come to her house . . .[30]

Tantalizingly, the Journal breaks off at this point. What was the incident? Did it refer to the limited apology which Boswell wrote soon after Thrale's death?[31] Probably not, for the phrase in that note, "gayety of fancy," implies a mental exertion, a written or re-cited jeu d'esprit: Boswell's "Song" on Dr. Johnson and Mrs. Thrale would fit the definition perfectly. He would have been more apt to

[29] *Autobiography, Letters and Literary Remains of Mrs. Piozzi (Thrale)*, 2 vols. Edited by A. Hayward (London: Longman, Green, Longman, and Roberts, 1861), II, 52. Hereafter this is referred to as *Hayward*.
[30] *Boswell Papers*, XV, 226 (17 May 1783).
[31] Boswell to Mrs. Thrale, 26 April 1781. See p. 67 above.

use the phrase "gayety of spirits" to describe the action suggested in his Journal — misbehavior when invited to her house or a brash, noisy intrusion, uninvited and tipsy, late at night. If such an encounter took place, it must have been *before* Thrale's death, for according to Boswell's Journal for the 21st of March 1783, this was the first time he had seen Mrs. Thrale since her husband's death.[32]

In this year, 1783, Boswell arrived in London on the evening of March 20th. The following morning he called at Bolt Court, and there he was told, as upon so many previous occasions, that Johnson was with the Thrales. He went to the house in Argyll Street and was shown at once to Johnson's room. He "was disagreably surprised to find him looking very pale, and afflicted with a difficulty of breathing."[33] Johnson sent word to Mrs. Thrale that Boswell was with him:

She came, and I saluted her with gladness. I had not seen her since Mr. Thrale's death till now. She promised me a copy of the verses on Levet. She asked me to stay dinner. We had no company but her three eldest daughters. She said she was very glad I was come, for she was going to Bath and should have been uneasy to leave Dr. Johnson till I came. He had told me of her going to Bath, and said they had driven her out of London by attacks upon her which She had provoked by attacking every body.[34]

Boswell found Johnson still at Mrs. Thrale's on the following day, but planning to return to Bolt Court in the afternoon. As the three talked together, Boswell, in his new role of Scottish laird, imagined that Mrs. Thrale appreciated him more, and that Johnson felt greater affection for him. Both reactions were true, but not for the reasons he supposed. Johnson was demonstrative because he felt Mrs. Thrale's neglect; she was responsive because she was relieving herself of responsibility. When Boswell said goodbye, with the conventional wishes that she have a good journey, a pleasant stay in Bath, and that they might meet again soon, all seemed probable enough — but Boswell and Mrs. Thrale were never to lay eyes on each other after Friday the 21st of March, 1783.

[32] *Boswell Papers,* XV, 174 (21 March 1783).

[33] *Ibid.,* 173.

[34] *Ibid.,* 174 (21 March 1783). On the subject of Bath, there is a MS. note by Boswell (Hyde): "Dr. Johnson said of Mrs. Thrale I am glad She is gone to Bath to some place where her head may cool. Sir they have fairly driven her from London. Sir she has made innumerable enemies by her tongue. *L*[angton] said to me *who* has helped her to it. — D[r] J–n said I. — He knocks them on the head and she cuts their throats. They butcher it fairly between them."

As it happened, Mrs. Thrale's departure for Bath was delayed, but the reason precluded any further meeting. Her two younger daughters, who were to stay behind at Mrs. Ray's school in Streatham, had both fallen ill: Cecilia, six, had whooping-cough, and Harriett, not quite five, had measles, swollen glands, and a cough. By April 5th they were somewhat improved, sufficiently, Mrs. Thrale thought, for her to set out on her journey. On that day, filled with anxiety, she parted from Johnson. "I was much moved," he wrote in his Diary. "I had some expostulations with her. She said that she was likewise affected. I commended the Thrales with great good will to God; may my petitions have been heard!" [35]

Johnson's "expostulations" were probably that Mrs. Thrale accept her widowhood philosophically, and live sensibly, no longer indulging in the romantic dreams and strange behavior which had damaged her reputation since Thrale's death. He was sure she would soon realize that her chief concern was her family — and this very definitely included himself. He made poignantly clear his need for her.

She was fully aware of his dependence and felt guilty, but she also felt sorry for herself. She sympathized with his infirmities and remembered with gratitude the pleasure and help he had once given her. She revered him as a father, but he was not going to control her life. She had given up love and happiness for the benefit of her daughters, but neither they, nor he, could expect a surrender beyond this. There would be no return to the old way of life.

Johnson had been completely unable to understand Mrs. Thrale's feelings after her husband's death. He was, of course, personally involved: jealous of all threats to his own security and claims of affection, and also fearful of his failing powers and loath to see any change. But it is curious that he could not have taken a wider view, because surely he must have remembered that when he was a young man, courting Mrs. Porter, his own position had been not unlike Piozzi's. Yet such a comparison never entered his head. Neither he nor the daughters understood Mrs. Thrale's actions, nor had any sympathy for her. They followed the usual pattern of old and young who find it impossible to visualize a middle-aged woman as a passionate being with rights of her own. To all of them, her pursuit of happiness was an undignified spectacle which they viewed with personal embarrassment — they could only see her in relation to themselves.

[35] *Johnson Diaries*, pp. 358–359 (5 April 1783).

So the parting between Dr. Johnson and Mrs. Thrale at Argyll Street on the 5th of April (less than a month after she had said good-bye to Boswell), was a strange farewell. Johnson had been close for so many years, a loved friend and counselor; they had shared inmost thoughts, but now there was no communication between them. They parted and, as far as is known, never saw each other again after this day.

On the next, April 6th, she made her final, agonizing parting from Piozzi,[36] and then she drove with Queeney, Susan, and Sophy to Bath. No peace and quiet was found there, for soon after their arrival alarming bulletins came from Streatham: "Terrible Accounts from poor Caecilia and Harriett; I fear those poor Babies will dye, notwithstanding the Efforts of Jebb & Pepys to relieve them . . ."[37] On the 18th of April a letter came from John Cator, saying that Harriett had died; a letter from Johnson next morning with the same report. Mrs. Thrale hurried back to Streatham, where she found, with some relief, that Cecilia was out of danger. She stayed only long enough to arrange for the burial of Harriett and the care of Cecilia, and then she returned to Bath. Seeing Johnson while she was at Streatham would only have added to her anguish; she did not summon him, and he did not force himself upon her. Piozzi was still in London, but she could not bear the pain of another farewell.[38] She saw only Sir Lucas Pepys for an hour and then returned to Bath, where she found the three eldest daughters "at their work and their drawings. I *think* they scarcely said 'How d'ye do? or how does Cecilia do?' and we went on together without either rough words or smooth ones."[39]

Boswell left for Scotland on the 30th day of May and a little over two weeks later, alone in London, Johnson suffered a severe stroke.[40] At first he was paralyzed and without the power of speech, but quite quickly he was able to form words — his understanding remained clear throughout. Mrs. Thrale did not come to London to nurse him, though he had great need of her help. The only person left in his

[36] When Piozzi agreed to leave England, he removed from the bank the savings of a lifetime; contrary to the canard that Mrs. Thrale paid him £800 a year while he was on the Continent, he at this moment gallantly lent her at least £1000 for her pressing current needs. *Clifford*, p. 219 and n. 1.

[37] *Thraliana*, I, 563.

[38] Piozzi waited at the front window of a public house all day to see Mrs. Thrale's coach pass to and from Streatham.

[39] *Hayward*, II, 53.

[40] On the 17th of June, 1783.

household to care for him was Francis Barber. Levett had died in January of 1782,[41] and his blind companion, Miss Williams, was now terminally ill herself.[42] Mrs. Desmoulins had gone away. The house daily became more disordered and dirty and desolate.

Time passed and Johnson's condition improved. Still, though letters were passing frequently between them, no invitations came from Mrs. Thrale to join the family in Bath. The year before she had sent Boswell short, "weekly" notes about Johnson's indifferent health; now that catastrophe had struck, she sent no word whatsoever, though she had full information of his condition from several sources.[43] Johnson himself wrote to her two days after his stroke, a remarkable letter on four folio pages, describing his attack minutely. His handwriting was unchanged, his mind unimpaired. The letter ended with pathos:

Let not all our endearment be forgotten, but let me have in this great distress your pity and your prayers. You see I yet turn to You with my complaints as a settled and unalienable friend, do not, do not drive me from You, for I have not deserved either neglect or hatred.[44]

Boswell had no knowledge of the stroke until Johnson himself reported it on July 3rd; the letter clearly showed that he was fending

[41] Robert Levet (1705–1782) had died of a sudden stroke in his sleep on 17 January 1782. He had been "eminently cheerful" the night before, Johnson wrote in a letter (*Life*, IV, 137). In another: "I suppose not one minute passed between health and death; so uncertain are human things." (*Life*, IV, 142).

[42] Anna Williams was to die on the 6th of September 1783, while Johnson was visiting William Bowles, near Salisbury. (See *Life*, IV, 235, n. 1.) Her death affected Johnson greatly for her firm presence in his household over the years had given him comfort. She was the kind of woman, he felt, that "every wise man will choose for his final and lasting companion in the languor of age, in the quiet of privacy, when he departs weary and disgusted from the ostentatious, the volatile and the vain." (*Life*, IV, 235, n. 2).

[43] Tom Davies, the bookseller, wrote to Mrs. Thrale on the 18th of June, the day after the stroke, trying to appeal to her sympathy: ". . . I have just now received a most affectionate note from him [Johnson] in answer to a letter of mine in which Mrs. Davies tender'd her services.

"He is really much to be pitied, He has no female friend in his House that can do him any service on this occasion — Mrs Du Moulin has left the House for what cause, I do not know, & I would not ask —

"I believe he does not wish this misfortune should be publickly known — I could not conceal it from you, but must entreat you not to hint from whence you obtained your information.

"Dr Johnson now speaks pretty plainly."
(This quotation is from *Life*, IV, Appendix J, p. 522. MS. Letter: Rylands.)

[44] Johnson to Mrs. Thrale, 19 June 1783. MS. Letter: Hyde. Letter #850. *Letters*, III, 35.

for himself. If he had been in Mrs. Thrale's household, Boswell would have demanded posthaste the full story of the seizure and constant bulletins, but now there was no point in writing to her since she had removed herself from the scene; indeed, she did not merit a letter; he could not understand her behavior.

Boswell deeply regretted the fact that he was not nearer, to be of assistance, or that he had not brought Johnson with him to Scotland at the end of May. He had asked him, before he left London, "to come to Auchinleck." Johnson had replied, " 'I cannot come this year. But when I grow better, as I hope I shall, I should gladly come. I should like to totter about your place, and live mostly on milk, and be taken care of by Mrs. Boswell. We're good freinds now, are we not?' I told him yes . . ." [45] Boswell was much disturbed by Johnson's plight.

Not so, Mrs. Thrale. There was no break in her cruel indifference; even when summer came, she did not suggest a visit with the family. For this solace, Johnson had to depend on others. In July he spent almost a fortnight in Rochester with his devoted old friend, Bennet Langton, and from August 28th to September 18th he visited a new friend, William Bowles,[46] a young man still in his twenties, recently made Sheriff of Wiltshire. Bowles received Johnson at Heale House with proper enthusiasm.[47] He wished to do everything he could to make the stay agreeable, and "meaning to gratifie him" even proposed going to Weymouth, where he had heard Mrs. Thrale was "for a few days." Bowles soon discovered that Johnson "had no great mind to see Mrs. Thrale." " 'Poor dear Mr. Thrale' were words often in his mouth." [48]

Though he did not go to her, Johnson continued to write to Mrs. Thrale constantly — disheartening letters, filled with complaints of his ill health and loneliness. She countered with reports of her own miseries, and these were not imaginary. She was suffering great emotional strain, and in November had a complete nervous collapse. Her physicians feared for the worst and believed that only the recall of

[45] *Boswell Papers*, XV, 233 (29 May 1783).

[46] William Bowles (1755–1826). *Life*, IV, 234, n. 2. In the next year, 1784, Johnson proposed Bowles for membership in The Club.

[47] Bowles carried his enthusiasm so far that he had his young friend, Gilbert Stuart, his exact contemporary, paint Johnson's portrait at Heale House.

[48] Memorandum from Bowles to Boswell. MS. Yale (M145). *Waingrow*, p. 251 and n. 42.

DR. JOHNSON

UNFINISHED PORTRAIT, PAINTED BY GILBERT STUART, WHEN JOHNSON
VISITED WILLIAM BOWLES, NEAR SALISBURY, IN SEPTEMBER 1783

Four Oaks Farm

GABRIEL PIOZZI
ARTIST UNKNOWN

Four Oaks Farm

Piozzi could save her life. Finally and very reluctantly Queeney gave her consent.

Johnson knew nothing of this decision and Boswell was still ignorant of Piozzi's importance. Boswell did not question what was the cause of her neglect of Johnson — he simply accepted it as showing her real colors — an unfaithful and heartless friend. He was the true friend. He felt exhilaration in the public demonstration of this. He regretted the fact that Johnson was not receiving every possible care, but he was, in his own way, glad that the break continued. Johnson indirectly assured him that the break indeed continued, complete and cruel, by saying in his letter the day before Christmas: ". . . sickness and solitude press me very heavily. I could bear sickness better, if I were relieved from solitude." [49]

1784

In this last year of Johnson's life, Mrs. Thrale made no attempt to reaccept him and relieve his suffering, but Boswell exerted himself in many helpful ways. It was clear to everyone that Johnson was failing.[50] He had been confined to his cheerless house since the middle of December. Francis Barber cared for him as he could, but Johnson longed for the attentiveness and the comfort he had known at the Thrales' house, and for the effortless company of his family. He found the calls of solicitous visitors only interruption and strain:

They come when I could sleep, or read, they stay till I am weary, they force me to attend when my mind calls for relaxation, and to speak when my powers will hardly actuate my tongue. The amusements and consolations of langour and depression are conferred by familiar and domestick companions . . . called at will . . . or dismissed . . . Such society I had with Levet and Williams, such I had — where I am never likely to have it more. [His correspondent, Mrs. Thrale, later noted: "Very true, it was at Streatham Park."] [51]

Johnson wanted to come home; he could not understand why Mrs. Thrale's bad health (which kept her at Bath, she said) continued so long. He had been conscious of Piozzi's strong attraction the year before but had faith that the virtues of her mind had now overcome

[49] Johnson to Boswell, 24 December 1783. Letter #920. *Letters*, III, 117.

[50] Johnson was suffering from a sarcocele, gout, asthma (emphysema), and dropsy — also kidney stones.

[51] Johnson to Mrs. Thrale, 27 December 1783. MS. Letter: Arthur A. Houghton, Jr. Letter #921. *Letters*, III, 118.

the frailties of her heart. "[W]hen sad fancies are excluded," he wrote, "health and peace will return together."[52] In another letter he advised her to give all her attention to her daughters, to "[s]ettle [her] thoughts and control [her] imagination, and think no more of Hesperian felicity."[53]

Mrs. Thrale had not written Johnson about the events of November; that Piozzi had been sent for, and that she had been anxiously awaiting the musician's return all winter. Now, as spring came and he did not appear, she became alarmed and her daughters became increasingly scornful. One of the humiliating aspects of the whole denigrating drama was that Mrs. Thrale had seemed from the start to have been the pursuer. It was now obvious, her children taunted, that Piozzi had no desire to return. The nearer truth is that he wanted to be sure of the reception he would receive. In late May he had the courage to leave Italy.

During the winter and spring Johnson wrote to Boswell (not so frequently as to Mrs. Thrale, but more frequently than usual) and he made clear his miserable situation. Boswell thought Mrs. Thrale's desertion was unpardonable, though he did not know the reason for her heartlessness. Still, he made not a single move to bring her back to Johnson. He wrote no pleading letter that she receive their revered friend in her household again and give him the tender care she had long supplied. The weekly bulletins he had begged from her two years before, he now requested from the person who did attend him, Francis Barber: "I am in very anxious concern about my much respected friend your Master . . . I will be obliged to you if you will once a week at least let me know with minute exactness how he is, who are with him and in what manner his time is employed."[54]

Boswell had been taking pains with Johnson's requests, consulting physicians about his case, and concerning himself with his comfort. Johnson wrote in February: "My nights are very sleepless and very tedious. And yet I am extremely afraid of dying . . . If my life is prolonged to autumn, I should be glad to try a warmer climate; though how to travel with a diseased body, without a companion to conduct

[52] Johnson to Mrs. Thrale, 21 January 1784. MS. Letter: Hyde. Letter #926. *Letters*, III, 125.

[53] Johnson to Mrs. Thrale, 26 April 1784. MS. Letter: Hyde. Letter #956. *Letters*, III, 160.

[54] Boswell to Francis Barber, 30 January 1784. MS. Letter: Yale (L27. See verso L635). *Waingrow*, p. 19.

me, and with very little money, I do not well see . . . Think for me what I can do." [55] Boswell applied to the Lord Chancellor, Baron Thurlow, to see if Johnson's pension might be increased to permit a winter abroad. This was Johnson's last hope of going to Italy [56] — Boswell tried — but in September the request was refused. [57]

Boswell again urged Johnson to come to Auchinleck, and induced his wife to write a letter of definite invitation. [58] He hoped with all his heart that the comfort of his house in Scotland and attention of the Boswell children would compensate for the loss of the Thrales — an attractive notion, it appealed to Boswell's imagination and to Johnson's as well, but the old man was too ill to consider such a visit seriously. Boswell soon realized that the greatest help he could render at the moment was to come to London, and this he promised to do.

The news buoyed Johnson's spirits. He was also feeling better physically for, as his doctors hoped, warm weather had brought improvement; his dropsy was virtually gone and his asthma was abated. He had hopes that his confinement to the house would soon be over and he looked forward to seeing Boswell; together they would enjoy old friends (it was too late now for new friendships). Boswell's visit unfortunately had to be postponed, for though he set out for London in mid-March, he heard on the road that Parliament had been dissolved, and he was forced to turn back to campaign as a candidate for Ayr. Johnson had not told Mrs. Thrale of Boswell's plans, but his letters to her, while he waited for his visitor, grew more cheerful. On April 21st he left his house, where he had been imprisoned for more than a third of the year, and went to St. Clement Danes in the Strand to give thanks for his "recovery." [59]

When Boswell finally arrived in London on May 5th he was relieved to find Johnson in better health than his letters had indicated, and he

[55] Johnson to Boswell, 11 February 1784. Letter #932. *Letters*, III, 133.

[56] The journey to Italy was not encouraged by Johnson's physicians, though an extraordinary show of affection was instanced by one of them, Dr. Brocklesby, who offered Johnson £100 a year for his life. "A grateful tear started into [Johnson's] eye, as he spoke this in a faultering tone." *Life*, IV, 338.

[57] *Life*, IV, 348–350.

[58] "When it will be fit for me to travel as far as Auchinleck, I am not able to guess; but such a letter as Mrs. Boswell's might draw any man, not wholly motionless, a great way." Johnson to Boswell, 18 March 1784. Letter #942. *Letters*, III, 142.

[59] Johnson to Mrs. Thrale, 21 April 1784. MS. Letter: Hyde. Letter #955. *Letters*, III, 158.

was overjoyed by the warmth of the welcome he received. During the next two months he felt closer to Johnson than ever before; he was winning possession from Mrs. Thrale — scarcely winning, for she had relinquished the prize — but her indifference made him no less proud of his triumph. Boswell felt a new responsibility and concern for Johnson's welfare, also perhaps the urgency to work on his biography while his subject was still alive. He at last made the momentous decision, the possibility so long considered — he would bring his family to live in London. Johnson had always strongly advised against this move; even now, he was opposed for Boswell's sake, and urged him to come only on certain conditions; but for his own sake, he was grateful that he would have his company.

Johnson wrote to Mrs. Thrale on May 31st and he mentioned Boswell's name for the first time in a long while. They were about to set off to visit Dr. Adams in Oxford,[60] he told her. He also said in the letter that the Boswell family would soon be coming to live in London, where Boswell would "try his fortune at the English Bar. Let us all wish him success." He concluded his letter by saying, "Think of me, if You can, with tenderness . . ."[61] This letter is interesting for the suggestion it gives that in the middle of the month, when Mrs. Thrale was in London for a week, staying with Fanny Burney and making preparations for Piozzi's arrival, she *may* have seen Johnson, for he says, "Why you expected me to be better than I am I cannot imagine; I am better than any that saw me in my il[l]ness ever expected to have seen me again."[62] One thing is certain: if Mrs. Thrale did have an interview with Johnson, she said nothing of her determination to marry Piozzi.

This intelligence she dispatched in a letter to Bolt Court on the 30th of June, the same day that Boswell parted there forever from his "revered Friend".[63] It was a form letter, sent to Johnson as an ex-

[60] This was the first jaunt Johnson had made since his illness, and both the journey and the visit went well. Johnson was in Oxford, which Boswell described as "that magnificent and venerable seat of Learning, Orthodoxy, and Toryism" (*Life*, IV, 285), from 3 to 19 June. Johnson was much satisfied with the polite hospitality of Adams and his daughter, and he enjoyed their agreeable circle of friends. His talk was as wide-ranging and powerful as ever.

[61] "A line follows, so heavily erased that I could make out nothing." R. W. Chapman, editor. Johnson to Mrs. Thrale, 31 May 1784. MS. Letter: R. W. Chapman credited Sir Charles Russell. Letter #963. *Letters*, III, 165.

[62] *Idem.*

[63] Wednesday, 30 June 1784. *Boswell Papers*, XVI, 52.

ecutor of Thrale's will and a guardian of his daughters; it acquainted
him with the fact that she was now alone in Bath, awaiting Piozzi's
return. Queeney, Susan, and Sophy preferred to be in Brighton with
a chaperone. Piozzi's arrival would soon be followed by their marriage. To this communication she added a personal note, begging his
forgiveness for concealing

a Connection which you must have heard of by many People, but I suppose
never believed. Indeed, my dear Sir, it was concealed only to spare us both
needless pain; I could not have borne to reject that Counsel it would have
killed me to take; and I only tell it you now, because all is *irrevocably settled*,
& out of your power to prevent.[64]

Johnson received this news with anguish and astonishment. He
wrote on the instant, imploring her to see him once more if the
ignominious marriage had not yet taken place.[65] She replied on the
4th of July that she desired "the conclusion of a Correspondence
which I can bear to continue no longer . . . till you have changed
your Opinion of Mr. Piozzi — let us converse no more. God bless
you!"[66]

Johnson responded philosophically, but in desolation.[67] On the 15th
of July (implying that she was already married, although the ceremony did not take place until the 23rd), she wrote, "Your last Letter
is sweetly kind . . ." She told him to have no fear, that her second
husband would "treat with long continued Respect & Tenderness the
Friend whom you once honoured with your Regard."[68] Johnson
did not answer this letter. With outrage and sorrow he tried to drive
from his mind all thoughts of the woman who for almost twenty years
had been so close a part of his life and contributed so much to his happiness. He burned all of her letters which he could find.[69]

If Boswell had remained in London another week, he would have

[64] Mrs. Thrale to Johnson, 30 June 1784. MS. Letter: Hyde. Letter #969a.
Letters, III, 172–173.

[65] Johnson to Mrs. Thrale, 2 July 1784. MS. Letter: Hyde. Letter #970. *Letters*, III, 174.

[66] Mrs. Thrale to Johnson, 4 July 1784. MS. Letter: Hyde. Letter #970.1a.
Letters, III, 175.

[67] Johnson to Mrs. Thrale, 8 July 1784. MS. Letter: Hyde. Letter #972. *Letters*,
III, 177.

[68] Mrs. Thrale to Johnson, 15 July 1784. MS. Letter: Rylands. Eng.MS.540/110.
Letter #978a. *Letters*, III, 184.

[69] "The last time Miss Burney saw Johnson, not three weeks before his death,
he told her that the day before he had seen Miss Thrale [Queeney]. 'I then said, —
"Do you ever, sir, hear from her mother?" "No," cried he, "nor write to her. I

witnessed the full impact that Mrs. Thrale's marriage had upon Johnson. As it was, the news reached him in Scotland. Now the reason for her desertion of Johnson was made clear; his reaction was final and complete disgust. That she should stoop to so low a connection made it impossible for him ever to write to her again on any subject. This feeling on his part was unfortunate (at least in his role of Biographer) because even a half-hearted letter of felicitation at this moment, any sign of friendship, would have been greatly appreciated. Such a letter would have been more persuasive than all his previous appeals. But Boswell would have nothing to do with the base Mrs. Piozzi.

Johnson, for the brief remainder of his life, turned to her rival. Letters to Boswell during the summer took on an added quality, something new — the personal touches that he had previously reserved for Mrs. Thrale: details of his health, remembrance of the past, terror for the future, pleas for affection and assurances of his own, "Write to me often . . . I consider your fidelity and tenderness as a great part of the comforts which are yet left me . . . Love me as well as you can." [70] Again: "I love you with great ardour and sincerity. Pay my respects to dear Mrs. Boswell, and teach the young ones to love me." [71] Letters were a cordial to Johnson and he was disappointed that Boswell did not write more frequently. Johnson complained of his silence when he wrote to him on the 3rd of November. He said that though he had been able to journey to Ashbourne and Lichfield,[72] he felt that he had lost ground very much:

My legs are extremely weak, and my breath very short, and the water is now encreasing upon me. In this uncomfortable state your letters used to relieve;

drive her quite from my mind. If I meet with one of her letters, I burn it instantly. I have burnt all I can find. I never speak of her, and I desire never to hear of her more. I drive her, as I said, wholly from my mind." ' " *Life*, IV, 339, n. 3.

[70] Johnson to Boswell, c. 5 August 1784. Letter #982. *Letters*, III, 188.

[71] Johnson to Boswell, c. 7 August 1784. Letter #982.1. *Letters*, III, 189.

[72] Johnson had spent the greater part of the summer "in quest of health" and in seeking the consolation of friends. "[T]hose whom I have left, have all contributed as they could to make my life more cheerful" (Letter to William Strahan, 30 September 1784. Original untraced. Letter #1016.1. *Letters*, III, 229).

Johnson had left London on 13 July for Lichfield; there he saw his step-daughter, Lucy Porter, Mrs. Aston, and other friends. From 20 July to 27 September he was with Dr. Taylor at Ashbourne. After leaving him, he made a second visit to Lichfield. He returned to London the middle of November. As he told Strahan, in this letter of 30 September: "Home has to a sick man a multitude of conveniences, and winter may be passed at London with more amusement and more assistance than at any other place."

what is the reason that I have them no longer? Are you sick, or are you sullen? [73]

Immediately upon receipt of this, Boswell answered, but with such a despairing letter that his wife would not let him send it. He did dispatch a letter on the 19th of November, and another thereafter, too late to be received.[74]

On December 13th, while Boswell was still making plans for his move to London, and the Piozzis were enjoying their wedding trip in Italy, Johnson died. Boswell received the news four days later in a note from Dr. Brocklesby. "I was stunned, and in a kind of amaze . . . My feeling was just one large expanse of Stupor." [75]

The following day Boswell had a letter from Mr. Dilly, his publisher, who "in the true spirit of *the trade* [wanted] to know if I could have an Octavo volume of 400 pages of [Johnson's] conversations ready by February." [76] Boswell replied that he must work on his materials slowly and deliberately. This determination cost him the title of official biographer. Sir John Hawkins,[77] Johnson's literary executor, a man who knew much about his subject's early life but did not write with Boswell's felicity, was given the honor, for he promised to bring out a *Life of Johnson* with dispatch, a promise that he kept.

[73] Johnson to Boswell, 3 November 1784, from Lichfield. Letter #1033. *Letters,* III, 245.

[74] See note 2 on Letter #1033 (Johnson to Boswell, 3 November 1784). *Letters,* II, 246.

[75] *Boswell Papers,* XVI, 65 (17 December 1784).

[76] *Ibid.,* 66 (18 December 1784). Boswell and Dilly had been in recent correspondence about a projected *Life of Johnson.* Boswell wrote to Dilly on 2 and 7 December, saying in the second letter that he had "a large Collection of Materials."

[77] Sir John Hawkins (1719–1789) became a friend when Johnson first came to London; both were writing for Edward Cave, publisher of *The Gentleman's Magazine.* Hawkins, disciplined and industrious, later apprenticed himself to an attorney, and in time became one himself. He further raised his fortunes by marrying an heiress, thereafter residing in Twickenham as well as in London. He continued his interest in literature and music. He also became a magistrate for Middlesex and was rewarded for his services in suppressing the Moorfield riots by being knighted in 1772.

Hawkins always remained a staunch friend to Johnson. He was close at hand during his last illness, and it was he who drew his will.

The choice of Hawkins as official biographer made one wonder about the book. His *General History of the Science and Practice of Music,* published in 1776, had been savagely criticized for being pompous and dull.

1785

Shortly after the New Year, in Milan, Mrs. Piozzi heard of Johnson's death. Her diary entry was not so emotional as Boswell's, simply, "Oh, poor Dr Johnson!!!" [78] — perhaps a true expression of her thought of him for the past three years. Her informant was Samuel Lysons,[79] a young friend whom Mrs. Piozzi had met not long before in Bath. Lysons wrote: ". . . No less than Six persons have engaged to write his life Sir J. Hawkins Dr Kippis [80] Mr Davies & Mr Boswell are of the Number. I suppose you have been or will be applied to for anecdotes of him." [81] This was true; within a short time a letter came from Hawkins' publishers requesting her anecdotes for his biography.

Mrs. Piozzi refused, but the request made her realize that the mo-

[78] *Thraliana*, II, 624.

[79] Samuel Lysons (1763–1819) had met Mrs. Thrale after she had broken off with Piozzi, and taken Queeney, Susan, and Sophy to live in Bath. He was a serious, very intelligent, and orderly young man, a year older than Queeney. He had a talent for drawing and a deep interest in literature and literary talk.

In October 1784 Lysons came to London to study law at the Inner Temple, and he continued his friendship, after Mrs. Thrale's marriage to Piozzi, by correspondence. Lysons was later to become a distinguished antiquarian and a favorite of the royal family. In 1803 he would be appointed Keeper of the Records of the Tower of London.

[80] The two perhaps unfamiliar names on the list: Dr. Andrew Kippis (1725–1795) was a nonconformist divine and biographer, who had edited *Biographia Britannica*, an undertaking once offered to Johnson (*Life*, III, 174); Thomas Davies (1712?–1785) was an actor, author and bookseller, and it was at his shop, on May 16th 1763, that Johnson and Boswell had first met. Davies semed a likely candidate, for he had known the great man well and long, and had had experience in biography, having written the *Memoirs of the Life of David Garrick*. But Davies was never given the chance to write such a book, for he died in this year.

[81] Samuel Lysons to Mrs. Piozzi, 29 December 1784. MS. Letter: Rylands Eng.MS.552. *Thraliana*, II, 624, n. 4.

Lysons, a born collector, was saving all pertinent newspaper reports. This clipping is pertinent: "There are no less than seven lives preparing in the press, for Dr. Johnson. 'He must be immortal at this rate,' exclaims a gentleman. 'No,' replies the other, 'tis rather to be feared, they will *press* him to death!' "

An octavo volume of Lysons' collection of Piozziana survives: the cuttings are pasted onto pages approximately 9½ by 5½ inches, sometimes with marginal comment. The accounts are hard to follow, except by context, for the name of the newspaper and the date are rarely given. Also, the book has no pagination. Most of the cuttings deal with events between 1784 and 1786; there is none later than 1788.

The volume belonged to Colonel F. R. Grant, later to Lieutenant Colonel Ralph H. Isham, then to Professor Chauncey B. Tinker. The last presented it to Professor James L. Clifford, and he in turn gave it to Columbia University in 1967.

The volume is hereafter referred to as Lysons' *Book of Cuttings*.

ment for her own decision could not long be delayed. What should she do with the Johnsoniana she had collected for almost twenty years? Should she make use of it herself? She and Johnson had often talked about the Lives that would one day be published: "rescue me out of all their hands My dear, & do it *yourself* said he: 'Taylor Adams & Hector will furnish you with juvenile Anecdotes, & Baretti will give you all the rest that you have not already . . .' " [82]

She realized now, to her sorrow, that she had gathered nothing from the first three, and Baretti and she had fallen out, so she could no longer approach him. She wrote to Lysons of her problems:

I wish you would get *me* all the Anecdotes you can of the *early* and *late* Parts of a Life, the *middle* of which no one knows as well as myself, nor *half* as well: Do not however proclaim either your Intentions or my own, which are scarcely settled yet; I shall tell Sr. Lucas Pepys in confidence, as I keep no Corner of my heart from *him*: & you may sh[ew] *him* my Letters at any Time if you like it.[83]

There were many difficulties about her undertaking a book. Her recent marriage made her sensitive about competition; through her marriage she had also lost most of her friends in the Johnson circle, as well as the position of respect in which she had once been generally held. She dreaded asking for help where it might be denied, and she feared the insults which publicity would bring; yet she realized that publishing a book offered the opportunity of describing Johnson in her own way and of vindicating her "Fame" (Johnson in his rough answer to her announcement of marriage had wounded her deeply by saying she had forfeited it). Doubts and problems filled her mind. She was tempted but hesitant; Piozzi encouraged her to try her talents. She wondered how comprehensive Boswell's long-contemplated book would be. She could not decide what to do.

Boswell was in a quandary himself. His *Life of Johnson*, already well known by title, was in no state of forwardness — it was simply an enormous, amorphous mass of material: entries in his Journals, almanacs, notebooks, jottings, scraps — hundreds of papers apart. Exhaustive further collection of material was necessary, sorting, organizing, outlining, to say nothing of the actual writing. He was determined to proceed deliberately with his "Magnum Opus" and not to

---

[82] *Thraliana*, II, 625–626.
[83] Mrs. Piozzi to Samuel Lysons, from Milan, 20 January 1785. MS. Letter: Hyde.

publish until he was ready. Dilly, his publisher, protested that the public's interest in Johnson, now at a high pitch, would soon wane. Boswell answered that he could offer within a short time, his Journal of a Tour to the Hebrides with Samuel Johnson; this would serve as "a good Prelude to my large Work his *Life*." [84]

In January Boswell read his manuscript Journal to a number of friends in Edinburgh with this idea in mind. They enjoyed it and agreed that the manuscript could be published with certain revision. He decided to go to London (a trip having nothing to do with his earlier determination to move there eventually); this stay was for the purpose of seeing his *Tour* through the press — of making final revision of the manuscript and correction of proof. Along with this work he planned to conduct a thorough search for essential material for the *Life*. He drew up a long list, and wrote to persons whom Mrs. Piozzi had in mind, but only in mind: he wrote to Johnson's early friends, Edmund Hector, Dr. Taylor, and Dr. Adams; he also wrote to Anna Seward, the Lichfield poetess whom he had met in 1776.[85] As has been said, Boswell could not bring himself to write to Mrs. Piozzi, but he did not show his present aversion to her by re-interpreting any passage concerning her in the *Tour*. He let her pleasant picture remain, as a description of the happier past; he deleted none of the compliments Johnson paid her, and openly acknowledged her enchantment over his hero.[86] Only once in the *Tour* did he refer to Johnson's rough treatment of her.[87]

[84] Boswell to Charles Dilly, 23 December 1784. From Boswell's Letter Register: Yale (M255). *Waingrow*, p. liv.

[85] Anna Seward (1742–1809), known as the "Swan of Lichfield," was well aware of her endowments, both physical and intellectual. She was a prolific writer, and though her verse lacked novelty and imagination, it had considerable sense and vigor. Her mother's father was the Rev. Mr. John Hunter, the headmaster of the Lichfield Grammar School and Johnson's teacher. Another connection was that Joseph Porter, a Leghorn merchant, and the younger of Johnson's step-sons, was engaged to Anna's sister, Sarah Seward, in 1764, but they had not been married when Sarah died. It was said that Joseph Porter had first paid attentions to Anna, and that he tried to renew his suit after her sister's death, but that Anna discouraged him, as she did other suitors — she had a number. All her life she lived in the family house.

Anna Seward disliked Johnson, and he reciprocated her dislike: she suffered from "affectation," something he could not abide. When he guided the Thrales around Lichfield in 1774, he would "not suffer [Mrs. Thrale] to speak to Miss Seward." *Life*, V, 429, n. 1.

[86] *Life*, V, 14.

[87] "I have seen even Mrs. Thrale stunned". *Life*, V, 288. The force of "even" is interesting, for it again shows Boswell's acknowledgment of the power Mrs. Thrale had over Johnson.

EDMOND MALONE
BY SIR JOSHUA REYNOLDS
Reproduced by permission of the
National Portrait Gallery

Camille Des Moulins. anglice
Joe Miller Orateur vif & sans Culotte

JOHN COURTENAY
A CONTEMPORARY CARICATURE OF COURTENAY
AS A FRENCH REVOLUTIONARY, BY JAMES SAYERS
Reproduced by permission of
Mr. Wilmarth S. Lewis

By the time Boswell left Scotland in March he had received good packets of Johnson letters and anecdotes from both Hector and Dr. Adams, and on his way south he stopped in Lichfield, paid court to Anna Seward, and gathered in her anecdotes as well.[88]

Upon arrival in London on the 30th of March, his serious purpose was forgotten for a month, while he gave himself over to the same low distractions he so often found it impossible to resist. But to compensate for this waste of time, he made firm, during this stay, two of the most important and influential friendships of his life — with Edmond Malone,[89] the brilliant Shakespeare critic, and John Courtenay,[90] the politician and writer, both a year younger than himself. Malone and Courtenay — particularly Malone — took a deep interest in the *Tour* and gave Boswell direction, encouragement, and assistance. Throughout June, July, and August he worked closely with Malone, most of the time at his house. Malone's assistance virtually amounted to collaboration, and Boswell showed his appreciation by dedicating the *Tour* to him.

[88] Later, Boswell was not happy about the facts delivered him by Anna Seward. He felt that they "were tinctured with a strong prejudice against Johnson." *Life*, II, 467, n. 4.

See *Life*, I, 92, n. 2, for his amusing altercation with the lady over Johnson's verse on "A Sprig of Myrtle." In his second edition Boswell says: "Mr. Hector has lately assured me that Mrs. Piozzi's account is in this instance accurate." See also note 633 below.

[89] Edmond Malone (1741–1812), the critic and editor, was born in Dublin. He was educated at a private school and later received a B.A. from Trinity College, Dublin. His first visit to England was an excursion in the summer of 1759; in 1763 he came to London as a student of the Inner Temple, and it was during this period that he met Johnson. Malone later practiced at the Irish bar, and when time permitted wrote for the newspapers. In 1776 he began an edition of Goldsmith's works, published in 1780.

In 1777 Malone settled in London as a man of letters; his main attention was given at first to Shakespeare criticism and later to an authoritative edition of his plays. Malone was a frequent visitor to Johnson's house, and he became a close friend of Sir Joshua Reynolds. In 1782 he was elected a member of The Club.

[90] John Courtenay (1741–1816), Member of Parliament and man of letters, was, like Malone, born in Ireland. A grandson of the Earl of Bute, he entered political life under the sponsorship of Viscount Townshend, and when Townshend was Lord-Lieutenant of Ireland, 1767–1772, Courtenay served as his secretary.

After coming to England to live, Courtenay became the Member of Parliament for Tamworth in 1780, and was re-elected in 1784. In Parliament he spoke frequently and with considerable style. His speeches were filled with literary allusions, irony, humor, and sometimes violence. Courtenay was well read in both classical and modern literature and often tried his own hand at short productions; he was particularly adept at essays and verse.

Mrs. Piozzi had no such good fortune; she lacked professional experience and had no skilled literary advisers to guide her. She was far from the center of action, and her travels were to continue until the spring of 1787; a very long wedding trip. She lacked material — all she had with her in Italy were the six quarto volumes of *Thraliana*, which contained only anecdotes. She felt many reservations and fears, but she had courage, and with a little provocation, she determined to publish a book on Johnson.

Boswell would have been astounded if he had known that *he* was responsible for her decision. It was a case of mistaken identity, and the offense which provoked Mrs. Piozzi was that of another, but her false assumption of Boswell's guilt dictated her course.

It happened in this way: Mrs. Piozzi was following the London magazines and papers as they came to her irregularly in Italy, and she read with pleasure the first biographical sketch of Johnson by Thomas Tyers.[91] This appeared in *The Gentleman's Magazine* for December 1784, and gave a highly complimentary account of the Thrales. But soon thereafter she was incensed by a review of the sketch in *The St. James's Chronicle* of January 8th, 1785, for this treated both the Thrales and Piozzi with rough sarcasm. She was sure it had been written with personal malice by someone who had enjoyed her hospitality at Southwark and Streatham. When the anonymous author wrote another review on January 11th, not mentioning the Thrales, but containing an enthusiastic commendation of Boswell's projected *Life of Johnson*, she suspected that the reviewer was Boswell himself. When, shortly afterward, Boswell wrote a letter to the paper inquiring the name of the reviewer, she was convinced that this was a device to puff his own book, and that Boswell himself must be the offensive *Chronicle* reviewer. In truth it was George Steevens,[92] but her unjustified assumption launched her upon a book.

With her decision to publish, Mrs. Piozzi faced many difficulties. She needed her Johnson letters and important miscellaneous papers, but these were in her London bank vault and she was fearful of giving

---

[91] Thomas Tyers (1726–1787), a graduate of Pembroke College, Oxford, and later joint manager of Vauxhall Gardens. Tyers was an amusing companion and a dilettante author of considerable capability. He had been a great favorite with Dr. Johnson, who described him as "Tom Restless" in *Idler*, No. 48.

[92] George Steevens (1736–1800) was an able and systematic editor of Shakespeare, whose achievement was impaired by his lack of taste and temper. This was a typical example of his satiric criticism.

SAMUEL LYSONS
BY SIR THOMAS LAWRENCE

DR. MICHAEL LORT
SKETCH FOR THE PORTRAIT BY JOHN DOWNMAN
Reproduced by permission of the
Fitzwilliam Museum, Cambridge

anyone the power of access; she was further hesitant about shipping this precious cargo to Italy. She lacked material for Johnson's early years, and she urged Lysons to intensify his search for juvenilia to round out her stories. She now asked two other friends in England, whom she esteemed, to help her collect material — Dr. Michael Lort [93] and Sir Lucas Pepys,[94] the physician to whom she felt very close. These men were kindly disposed but they were not eminently qualified for the task, nor were they very industrious: fully occupied with their own affairs, their somewhat perfunctory appeals were not effective.

Boswell was not only having success in gathering material; he was talking to Johnsonian authors as well — Thomas Tyers, the "first" biographer,[95] and Sir John Hawkins, the "official" biographer, now hard at work. Boswell recorded in his Journal for May 7th, that at his meeting with Hawkins "I did very well." [96] Later in May, Boswell also did well when he made an appearance at Court and George III honored him with a brief conversation on his Johnsonian labors. The King was under the impression that the forthcoming volume would be the *Life*, but when informed that it would be the *Tour*, he said, "There will be many before you."

[93] Dr. Michael Lort (1725–1790), antiquary, had been Regius Professor of Greek at Cambridge and held numerous but not lucrative preferments. He also had experience as a librarian to Dr. Mead and possibly to the Duke of Devonshire; now, in 1785, he was librarian at Lambeth Palace.

"Artless simplicity formed the basis of his character," according to John Nichols. Lort was a man of great learning, a collector of valuable books and of curious bits of information. He "loved to say little oddities" (*Life*, IV, 19). He wrote not much himself but gave "great assistance to some of the most approved writers of his time, by his communication, advice, and his correction" (Nichols' *Literary Anecdotes*, quoted in *Life*, IV, 533).

On 10 December 1782 Johnson had proposed Lort for membership in The Club; but he was blackballed on the 17th when Johnson was absent.

[94] Sir Lucas Pepys (1742–1830) has been referred to earlier as one of Thrale's doctors; in 1784 he was created a baronet. He had been educated at Eton and Christ Church, Oxford, and had studied medicine at both Edinburgh and Oxford. In the 1770's Pepys had a highly successful social practice in London (he practiced in Brighton in the summer). At the College of Physicians he held the successive posts of fellow, censor, treasurer, and president.

Since 1777 Pepys had been physician-extraordinary to King George III, whom he would later attend during his mental disorders in 1788–1789 and 1804. Sir Lucas' first wife was the Countess of Rothes, his second (1813), Deborah Askew.

[95] *Boswell Papers*, XVI, 86, 87, 103 (12 May, 14 May, 29 June 1785).

[96] *Ibid.*, 84 (7 May 1785).

Boswell: I wish first to see them all, Sir.

King: There will be many foolish lives first. Do you make the best.

Boswell: I cannot presume to say I can do that, Sir. But I shall do as well as I can.

King: I believe you knew him more intimately than any Man.

Boswell: He was very good to me, Sir. And I was very forward with him.[97]

Boswell was convinced that his natural, reasoned, unhurried, legal approach was the proper one for his great work. He continued his countless appeals for letters and information, stressing the point that no fact was too small nor too trivial to be of interest. In July he made an investigation which would have infuriated Mrs. Piozzi had she known of it. With his friend Courtenay, he went to Streatham to see Johnson's notes about books in the Thrales' library (they were not Johnson's, he found upon examination) but the incident shows that he was not suffering from timidity as Mrs. Piozzi was. And his straightforward requests were rewarding: in the same month he received good Johnson letters from Sir Joshua Reynolds and Richard Brocklesby, one of the physicians who attended Johnson in his last illness.

Mrs. Piozzi's helpers could give no such account of success. Lort sent the news that Dr. Adams had already given his material to Boswell; Lysons that Hector had done the same. William Seward, for whom she no longer had friendship because of his scorn of Piozzi, had given his information to Kippis and Hawkins. She wrote to Lysons angrily from Florence:

. . . concerning the Trick Mr Seward has serv'd me; giving the Anecdotes to others which he originally had I suppose from me, and I am sure of it indeed — Basta! as the Italians say; I have always honour'd his Virtues, respected his Abilities, and lamented his Health, too much to take amiss that futile & unkind Behaviour which he has thought proper to shew in every Transaction betwixt him & me . . .[98]

While Boswell's *Tour* was being printed, Mrs. Piozzi was struggling

[97] *Ibid.*, 91 (20 May 1785). Boswell also discussed his *Life of Johnson* with the King on 15 June 1785 (*Boswell Papers*, XVI, 99–101) and on 21 September 1785 (*Boswell Papers*, XVI, 125).

Boswell wished in the Advertisement to the second edition of the *Life* to use a version of the remark the King made at the 20 May 1785 interview: " 'There will be many lives of Dr. Johnson: do you give the best' — I flatter myself that I have obeyed my SOVEREIGN'S commands."

Malone vehemently protested against this "wild Rhodomontade." Malone to Boswell, 13 May 1793. MS. Letter: Yale (C1927). *Waingrow*, p. 530.

[98] Mrs. Piozzi to Samuel Lysons, 27 July 1785. MS. Letter: Hyde.

to bring the first kind of arrangement into her sketchy materials. Her plan was still not clear, but on June 7th she wrote to Thomas Cadell, the bookseller and publisher, offering a book, which she still hoped would be a combination of anecdotes, letters, and verses. Cadell accepted at once and, as requested, put an advertisement in the papers announcing her forthcoming book. He urged her to have Johnson's letters sent to Italy for editing; she was still opposed to doing this; there were too many risks. Finally she decided to limit her book to a collection of anecdotes alone.

By autumn, when his *Tour* was at press, Boswell added a notice at the end of the volume, assuring his readers that his second book, *The Life of Johnson*, was going forward. This large work, he announced optimistically, was "Preparing for the Press, in one Volume Quarto." He stated that "Dr. Johnson was well informed of his design," [99] an answer to the official biographer, John Hawkins. Finally, he gave details about the Johnson material he was collecting, doubtless with the hope of locating more.

On the first of October, after his return to Scotland, the *Tour to the Hebrides with Samuel Johnson* was published. A few days later, Mrs. Piozzi put the copyist's transcript of her *Anecdotes of the Late Samuel Johnson* aboard a ship at Leghorn. She had worked with extraordinary speed and under great difficulties; she hoped that her manuscript would serve its purpose. She wrote Lysons, "I wish *my* Anecdotes may be found less trivial than Boswell's." [100] She trusted that her manuscript would soon be in England. This was not to be the case; by the end of the year Cadell had not received it.

In London, Boswell's *Tour* was greeted with immediate success, requiring a second edition almost at once.[101] Comment was mixed: some critics were highly complimentary, but others were disparaging. Horace Walpole, the fastidious man of letters, called it a "most absurd enormous book . . . It is the story of a mountebank and his zany." [102] Sir Joshua read the *Tour* twice through and was lavish in its praise,

[99] See first edition of *The Journal of a Tour to the Hebrides with Samuel Johnson, LL.D.* London: Charles Dilly, 1785. Hereafter referred to as *Tour*.

[100] Mrs. Piozzi to Samuel Lysons, from Rome, 4 November 1785. MS. Letter: Hyde.

[101] "The success of our Book is very flattering indeed," Boswell wrote to Malone on 29 October 1785. At this time, since Boswell was still in Scotland, Malone was taking care of detailed corrections for the second edition. MS. Letter: Yale (L922). Not in *Waingrow*.

[102] *Clifford*, p. 259.

but he thought that Boswell was not "sufficiently warm & hearty"[103] towards Johnson. Wilkes[104] joked that Boswell had "now fired a pocket pistol at Johnson's reputation" and soon planned to "discharge a blunderbuss," while "Madam Piozzi is to stab at him with a stiletto."[105] Boswell liked that word "stiletto," and would later make use of it.[106]

The recording of actual conversation and the description of personal idiosyncracies were scandalous novelties. Many passages were disputed, and that involving Sir Alexander Macdonald, a host on the Hebridean tour, very nearly provoked a duel. Another passage launched the public quarrel between Boswell and Mrs. Piozzi. It was a comment which gave great offense to Mrs. Montagu, Queen of the Blue Stockings, a circle in which Mrs. Piozzi had recently been a star. Boswell's text recorded Johnson as saying: "Reynolds is fond of [Mrs. Montagu's *Essay on Shakespeare*],[107] and I wonder at it; for neither I, nor Beauclerk,[108] nor Mrs. Thrale, could get through it."[109]

Boswell had been undecided how to treat this passage. He had

[103] Malone to Boswell, 5 October 1785. MS. Letter: Yale (C1895). Not in *Waingrow*.

[104] John Wilkes (1727–1797). As demagogue and firebrand, and Member of Parliament for Aylesbury, Wilkes was outspoken in his attacks against Lord Bute's government. Strong action was finally taken against him, and he retreated abroad in 1763, living mainly in France, though he traveled upon occasion, and indeed in Italy in 1765 became friendly with Boswell. Wilkes returned to England in 1768, and suffered punishment for his past incendiary actions. Upon release from prison, he re-entered public life.

Wilkes was by nature a man of fashion, with fine manners and an inexhaustible supply of wit and humor. His interest in literature and art was keen and he had a lively talent of making himself agreeable, even to those who thoroughly distrusted him.

[105] Malone to Boswell, 19 October 1785. MS. Letter: Yale (C1896). Not in *Waingrow*.

[106] See below, pp. 109 and 113.

[107] Mrs. Montagu had been offended by Voltaire's contempt for Shakespeare, and her book was a refutation of his criticism. She compared Shakespeare with Greek and French dramatists, and showed how well he held his ground. London literary opinion generally held that her *Essay* was a sympathetic and sensible book, which had fulfilled its purpose.

[108] The Hon. Topham Beauclerk (1739–1780). This urbane friend of Johnson was a discerning reader, who had interest in many fields of literature, and had collected a library of thirty thousand volumes. Topham Beauclerk was a fellow student with Bennet Langton at Trinity College, Oxford, when he first met Johnson — one of "the young dogs of this age" that held such attraction. Perhaps Beauclerk came by his high spirits naturally, for he was a great-grandson of Charles II and Nell Gwynne.

[109] *Tour*, p. 299. *Hebrides*, p. 208. *Life*, V, 345.

been liberally paid for any thing he has done for Shakſpeare. If I ſhould praiſe him, I ſhould much more praiſe the nation who paid him. He has not made Shakſpeare better known. He cannot illuſtrate Shakſpeare. So I have reaſons enough againſt mentioning him, were reaſons neceſſary. There ſhould be reaſons for it."—I ſpoke of Mrs. Montague's very high praiſes of Garrick.—*Johnſon.* "It is fit ſhe ſhould ſay ſo much, and that I ſhould ſay nothing. Reynolds is fond of her book, and I wonder*ed* at it; for neither I nor Beauclerk could get through it."

Laſt night Dr. Johnſon gave us an account

BOSWELL DELETED MRS. THRALE'S
NAME IN HIS MANUSCRIPT JOURNAL
(23 SEPTEMBER 1773); RESTORED IT
IN THE PUBLISHED *TOUR*, 1785

*Both reproduced by permission
of the Yale University Library*

Thou art a Retailer of Phrases,
And dost deal in Remnants of Remnants,
Like a Maker of Pincushions.

Congreve's Way of the World, Act IV Scene 9

A SATIRIC VIEW OF BOSWELL'S PUBLICATION
OF THE *TOUR TO THE HEBRIDES*

vacillated, whether or not to include Mrs. Thrale's name. He cancelled it in the manuscript,[110] restored it in proof,[111] then took it out again. He said to Malone and Courtenay:

Why should I set two women to pull one anothers caps? Besides had Mrs. Thrale been still in the state she formerly was, I might have been less scrupulous; but now that she is under a cloud and may probably desire to have the protection of Mʳˢ Montagu should she venture to return to England, it might hurt her; and I dare say she would deny it. Upon these considerations I struck it out, and some hundreds of the first edition were actually thrown off without it. Sir Joshua Reynolds's copy has it not. Mr Courtenay however insisted that as Dʳ Johnson had done Mrs Thrale the honour to quote her as an authority on taste and to class her with himself and Beauclerk, I had no right to deprive her of such a distinction to which she had an authentick title under her own hand. I was convinced and ordered her name to be reinstated.[112]

Mrs. Piozzi had not read Boswell's *Tour* by December, but considerably before this, the distasteful passage had been brought to her attention by several correspondents who reported its mortifying effect upon Mrs. Montagu. Mrs. Piozzi desperately wanted to keep her friendship and wrote Lysons:

Mʳ Boswell did me very great Injustice in saying I could not get through Mʳˢ Montagu's Performance, for the Elegance and Erudition of which I hope I am not wholly without Taste or Cognizance; and as for Dʳ Johnson, he had to my certain Knowledge a true Respect for her Abilities, and a very great Regard & Esteem of her general Character.

It is hard upon me that I am not at home to defend myself, but Mʳ Boswell is well qualified to be witty on the *Dead* and the *Distant*.[113]

Mrs. Piozzi begged her three loyal supporters to contradict the report in whatever manner they thought most effective, and to assure the public of her high esteem for Mrs. Montagu. Unfortunately, though her indignation was sincere, her refutations, written to various people, including Mrs. Montagu herself, could not be. Her strong assurances of admiration and affection only confirmed the story.

Boswell was back in London by mid-November [114] and he continued

[110] *Hebrides*, p. 208, n. The manuscript is at Yale.

[111] The proof is at Yale.

[112] Boswell to Malone, 31 March 1786. MS. Letter: Yale (L934). This portion of the letter not quoted in *Waingrow*.

[113] Mrs. Piozzi to Samuel Lysons, from Naples, 31 December 1785. MS. Letter: Hyde.

[114] Boswell's itinerary for the last months of 1785:
  24 September, set out for Scotland (*Boswell Papers*, XVI, 126).

to forage for his great work. On the last day of his visit, he chanced
to meet Francis Barber, long Johnson's servant — now his residuary
legatee. Boswell received an unexpected windfall from Barber, for
he "promised to search for every scrap of his Master's handwriting and
give all to [him]." [115]

1786

On the 27th of January, after a brief stay in Scotland, Boswell again
headed toward London. He was putting in motion his plan of estab-
lishing residence there. He would practice at the English Bar, and
what time he had free he would devote to serious work on the *Life*.
He was now searching for a house in which his family could live, and
when this matter was settled he would send for his wife and children;
the latter, but not the former, were eager to come.

Boswell was advised upon his arrival that London, as a scene for
steady living, was a very different place from that enjoyed by a visitor,
and he soon realized the contrast between being a "settled" rather
than an "occasional" man. [116] He wrote in his Journal, "the truth is that
imaginary London, gilded with all the brilliancy of warm fancy as I
have viewed it, and London as a scene of real business, are quite different." [117]

It proved to be increasingly so. From the time he was called to the
Bar in February until November he had only one brief. His anxiety
and despondency were great; he felt ineffectual and had no comfort in
existing. His old hero, General Paoli, was stern with him: "You are
past the age of Ambition. You should determine to be happy with
your Wife and children." [118] Boswell endlessly consulted friends and
acquaintances as to the wisdom of his decision and if he should not
reverse it; the variety of the answers he received plunged him into
deeper uncertainty. One day, as he walked along the street, considering
a return to Scotland, he was so depressed that the tears ran down his
cheeks. [119]

His most successful activity was further collecting for the *Life*; he

---

12 November, set out for London (*Ibid.*, 127).

22 December, set out for Scotland (*Ibid.*, 148).

[115] *Ibid.*, 148 (22 December 1785).

[116] *Ibid.*, 283 (Boswell to Mrs. Boswell, 18 May 1786).

[117] *Ibid.*, 159 (27 January 1786).

[118] *Ibid.*, 202 (6 July 1786).

[119] *Ibid.*, 201 (4 July 1786).

received valuable material from Lucy Porter, Johnson's step-daughter; from Dr. Taylor of Ashbourne; from Thomas Warton, the historian of English poetry; W. G. Hamilton, the Parliamentarian; Thomas Percy, the Bishop of Dromore; and Bennet Langton, the close Lincolnshire friend. He was animated by such acquisitions, but as he approached the formidable labor of actual *writing*, he became paralyzed, overwhelmed by the very bulk of material he had amassed. Day after day, he sorted papers, unable to make a start. Malone counselled him on June 9th "to make a Skeleton with references to the materials, in order of time."[120] Boswell confined himself to his house[121] and day after day "sorted till stupified." On July 9th he began to write, as Malone directed, the "Narrative" in one pile beside him, and the illustrative "Papers Apart" in another. When he had brief sections in draft, he took them to Malone and Courtenay; they listened attentively, made suggestions, and drove him on.

Meanwhile, the Piozzis continued to enjoy the enchantments of Italy. Her *Anecdotes of the Late Samuel Johnson* were being put through the press, under the kind, if not masterly, supervision of her three friends.[122] Only when the copy was delivered to Cadell did Lysons have the opportunity to read the manuscript from beginning to end. He was greatly disturbed by the passage following Johnson's Latin epitaph on Thrale. It concerned the scurrilous letter about the Thrales which had been printed in *The St. James's Chronicle*; Mrs. Piozzi had intuitively identified Boswell as the author, and, outraged by his attack on Thrale, who had provided generous hospitality for years and was no longer able to defend himself, she wrote in her book:

in order to distress the unoffending Survivor, [Boswell] dares even to deride the sacred Dead . . . [he] delights in the Uneasiness that he can cause to a Family,

---

[120] *Ibid.*, 192 (9 June 1786).

[121] Boswell's London residence: On the 2nd of February Boswell started negotiation to lease Hoole's house in Great Queen Street (*Ibid.*, 160). "Entered my House," he records in his Journal the 16th of May (*Ibid.*, 188). The date chosen for his taking over, as often before, was the anniversary of a significant event in his life — twenty-three years ago on this day he had met Johnson.

Boswell did not hasten to send for his family; his lack of success at the Bar and his absorption in the *Life* made their coming at once seem unwise. In letters to his wife, he lamented the terrible distance that separated them, but he feared for her health; she was to decide when she thought it the right time to come with the family (*Ibid.*, 281–284).

[122] Samuel Lysons "made a bargain" with Cadell the bookseller, and Mrs. Piozzi "received £300, a sum unexampled in those days for so small a volume." *Hayward*, II, 305.

where Mr. Boswell never received anything but Civilities. Surely such Men make Aaron the Moor a Model for their Imitation! [123]

Lysons doubted that Boswell had written the review as well as the letter, and wisely looked into the matter. He discovered, as has been mentioned, that the offender was George Steevens, and realized that the passage must be suppressed. Lysons talked to Sir Lucas Pepys, Dr. Hinchliffe (Bishop of Peterborough), and Dr. Lort — all strongly agreed. Since there was not time to consult Mrs. Piozzi in Italy, they took authority upon themselves and cancelled sheet K, Dr. Lort contributing an innocuous translation of Johnson's epitaph on Thrale to fill the vacant space.

When Mrs. Piozzi heard the true story, she was wholeheartedly grateful. She wrote to Lysons at once from Rome (as it happened, on the day that the *Anecdotes* were published in London):

Oh! pray thank them all, and say how much I love them, and how much I feel obliged to them, and how kindly I take their interposition — till I have time to tell them so myself. Why, my shoulders would have ached for a year with the blows I should have received! And justly, there's the astonishment; for I protest to you I thought I had seen that Mr. Boswell returned thanks for the impudent letter of the 8th of January, and very angry I was naturally enough; but one gets the papers here so irregularly — and, in short, I made a gross mistake, and have been happy enough to light on true friends who were sufficiently interested in my welfare to correct me.[124]

Mrs. Piozzi's friends had saved her from the wrath of Boswell by making the deletion, but ironically they proceeded to incur it, themselves, by an addition. They decided that the publication of the book presented the perfect opportunity to make a statement of the author's appreciation of Mrs. Montagu's *Essay on Shakespeare*. They devised a Postscript using her own words in a letter to Sir Lucas which concluded with something serviceably less ambiguous than her other apologies, ". . . few things would give me more concern than to be thought incapable of tasting, or unwilling to testify my opinion of its excellence." [125]

This Postscript was an unfortunate inspiration, as her literary advisers, if they had had any imagination, should have realized; Mrs.

[123] *Clifford*, p. 262.

[124] Mrs. Piozzi to Samuel Lysons, 25 March 1786, in *Bentley's Miscellany* (London), XXVIII (1850), 443.

[125] Hester Lynch Piozzi, *Anecdotes of the Late Samuel Johnson, LL.D.* (London: 1786), [p. 307]. Hereinafter referred to as *Anecdotes*.

MRS. MONTAGU
BY SIR JOSHUA REYNOLDS

S Harding del.   *Pub.d Sept.r 1, 1794, by E & S Harding, Pall Mall.*   *R Clamp sculp.t*

SIR JOHN HAWKINS
BY JAMES ROBERTS

Montagu had been pacified by Mrs. Piozzi's letter of apology [126] and Boswell, unprovoked, was silent. The incident was nearly forgotten. But when the *Anecdotes* were published the Postscript created a stir out of all proportion.

For months, interest in Mrs. Piozzi's promised account of Johnson had run high, there was constant reference to it in the papers, and much talk and speculation. Before evening on the day of issue, March 25th (Lady Day), the first edition of a thousand copies was sold out. For the King, whose interest in Johnsonian biography has been followed, the publisher had to beg a copy from a friend — the Sovereign proceeded to stay up all night reading it. [127] Many lesser lights in society reacted with similar absorption and the complaint was soon heard that the book excluded all other topics of conversation. [128]

Mrs. Piozzi had published her book with considerable trepidation; she had no false notions of its importance. She knew that she was an inexperienced writer and that the piece was something of a Johnson potpourri, without proper form or chronology, it was disjointed and repetitive, sometimes inconsistent; it rippled on in waves. She herself called the book a "slight performance," [129] an *"ill-strung* selection," [130] "a piece of motley Mosaic," [131] "trifling memoirs," [132] and freely admitted that she had known only one side of Johnson, the family picture — and only in the middle years. But this was a long and rich period and she was able to tell the story as no one else could. Within limitations, her treatment of Johnson was excellent, lively, entertaining, and for the most part honest. She asserted that Johnson was "the

[126] Malone to Boswell, 27 March 1786: "[Mrs. Piozzi] has written a most flaming letter of panegyrick to Mᵣˢ Montague [*sic*], which Mᵣˢ M. says she considers as the greatest honour that ever was done her. So the ladies, you see, will be bien d'accord, when Mᵣˢ P. arrives . . ." MS. Letter: Yale (C1907). This portion of letter not in *Waingrow*.

[127] *Hayward*, II, 305.

[128] Hannah More, a prominent Blue Stocking, complained, as did Horace Walpole, who commented amusingly on the controversial matter of Mrs. Montagu's *Shakespeare* and concluded by saying that Mrs. Piozzi, "Boswell, and their Hero, are the joke of the public. A Dr. Wolcot, *soi-disant* Peter Pindar, has published a burlesque eclogue [*Bozzy and Piozzi*, London: G. Kearsley and W. Foster, 1786] in which Boswell and the Signora are the interlocutors, and all the absurdest passages in the works of both are ridiculed." *Hayward*, I, 286–287.

[129] *Anecdotes*, p. viii.

[130] *Ibid*., p. 300.

[131] *Ibid*., p. 240.

[132] *Ibid*., p. 249.

best and wisest man that ever came within the reach of my personal acquaintance," [133] and did much to show his admirable qualities. By showing his faults as well, she was in part following the precept which Johnson himself had set down for biography; but also in part, as Boswell and others were quick to detect, she was using his short-comings to excuse her own behavior, illustrating how great a burden and bondage it had been to endure Johnson's company for twenty years.

Boswell was out of London at the time of publication, riding the Northern Circuit, but Malone was keeping him informed,[134] and Dilly dispatched a copy of the *Anecdotes* to Lancaster. This, Boswell received on the 30th and "devoured" at once, writing to Malone next day: "She is a little artful impudent malignant Devil . . . It is *clear* that she *means* to bite me as much as she can, that she may curry favour with Mrs. Montague [*sic*]." [135]

As for his own appearance in the book — it was insignificant. Mrs. Piozzi had omitted virtually all reference to him, mentioning him only once in the text by name, when saying that Johnson "was in the Isle of Sky [*sic*] with Mr. Boswell." [136] Beyond this, there was one indi-cation of him by initial, "Mr. B—," [137] in the anecdote on the defense of Bacchus. This passage was doubly offensive, not only for the "Mr.

[133] *Ibid.*, p. 295.

[134] Malone to Boswell, 25 March 1786: "Mʳˢ Piozzi's book came out this morn-ing . . . It is very entertaining — but the stories are *strung* too thick on each other — and she does not *dramatise* sufficiently. She has got many of your unpublished stories & some of them not so well as you have them. — The last leaf of the book relates to you" (and Malone reported her Postscript defense of Mrs. Montagu's essay). MS. Letter: Yale (C1906). Not in *Waingrow*.

Again, on 27 March 1786, Malone wrote to Boswell: "I have read Mʳˢ Piozzi's book twice through . . . She does not, I think, write about Johnson *cordato animo* . . . She contradicts all the former part of her book, & wᵈ have the reader think that the eighteen years intercourse with J. was a *bondage*, which she endured *to please Mʳ Thrale*, but when he was dead it became insupportable; — & so she was forced to fly to Bath: — when in truth she was flying not *from* Dʳ J. but *to* a new husband: who does not appear upon the canvass." MS. Letter: Yale (C1907). *Waingrow*, pp. 140–141.

[135] Boswell to Malone, 31 March 1786. MS. Letter: Yale (L934). *Waingrow*, pp. 142–143. Boswell also wrote in this letter (a portion not in *Waingrow*): "It is strange that she has heard *every one* commend Mʳˢ Montagus Book, for she surely cannot reckon Dʳ Johnson *nobody* and it is very well known how *He* talked of it. . ."

[136] *Anecdotes*, p. 162.

[137] *Ibid.*, p. 261.

B—," but also because Mrs. Piozzi had had the story from him in the first place; she had persisted in telling it inaccurately and he remembered having corrected her.

He was offended by a passage, said to be a speech by Johnson, but actually a parody of one of Burke's fine speeches on American taxation. "Vile agents in the House of Parliament," he hoped was not used for the Americans there. He further resented Mrs. Thrale's saying that she had asked Johnson for particular indulgence to "write it down directly" before she forgot "the force of the expression." Direct recording was something she never practiced, she said, "nor approved of it in another." She did not name Boswell, but he recognized himself well enough.[138]

Something else he resented was her report of a discussion with Johnson on the subject of his future biographer, for Boswell's obvious candidacy was not mentioned, though hers was discussed at length.[139] Another unkind omission: Boswell's name was not included among the friends for whom she said Johnson had the strongest affection — Reynolds, Murphy, Burke. She went out of her way to ignore him and to give compliments to friends of her own, who had meant little to Johnson, such as Sir Lucas Pepys. She well knew that Johnson had been devoted to Boswell, but no uninformed reader would have realized the fact.

Mrs. Piozzi was extremely vulnerable in the way she had handled the matter of Mrs. Montagu's *Shakespeare*, and Boswell realized that

---

[138] *Ibid.*, p. 44. On this point Boswell wrote Malone, 31 March 1786: "P. 44 is *undoubtedly* levelled at me; for it *describes* what the Jade has often seen me do — but with Dr. Johnson's *approbation*; for he at all times was flattered by my preserving what fell from his mind when shaken by conversation, so there was nothing *like* treachery. I must have the patience of *Job* to bear the Book of *Esther*. But I shall trim her *recitativo* and all her *airs*." MS. Letter: Yale (L934). *Waingrow*, pp. 142–143.

The marginal annotation on this passage in *Life Limited Edition*, III, 380, was: "had he *not* used the Words, *The Lady* could never have invented them: I knew not at the Moment that Burke was meant." Boswell had said in the *Life* that if Burke had used this phrase "in an extempore effusion, I wish the lady had not committed it to writing."

[139] *Anecdotes*, pp. 31–33. Johnson agreed with Mrs. Thrale that Goldsmith could write his life the "best" but with "malice." Johnson then named the persons who knew most of the facts of his life and said: "I intend, however, to disappoint the rogues, and either make you write the life, with Taylor's intelligence; or, which is better, do it myself, after outliving you all. I am now (added he), keeping a diary, in hopes of using it for that purpose some time."

this was a good point for attack. Suddenly he remembered that he possessed strong evidence against the statement in her Postscript. He had her own letter of May 18th, 1775, thanking him for letting her read the manuscript Journal of his *Tour*. She had seen the Montagu passage at that time and had raised no objection. Excitedly, he wrote to Malone

>   Lancaster
>   3 April 1786.
>
> My Dear Sir.
>   O brave we! I am now completely armed against Signora Piozzi — She read the three volumes of my original Journal, and did not deny as to Mrs Montagu. Only think of my not recollecting this when I last wrote to you.
>   As you are upon the spot & can better judge than I can of the *effect* of her *denial* which from le bon *Dilly's* account is *strong*, you will please to decide whether the enclosed should not be immediately put into the newspapers. Consult with Courtenay. I will not send it to the venal *Chanticleer*. But I am sure the *Publick* — the *St Jamess* and probably the Morning Post will insert it liberally. I should think too the Gentlemans Magazine would
>
>   give
>
> [page 2]
>
> give it a place. I myself think it ought to appear, & that I should pay for it rather than that it should not. Its appearing speedily too I think of some consequence; otherwise it might do in my THIRD EDITION — with a Postscript concerning Signora Piozzi; I *shall* at any rate have such a Postscript. But It appears to me that an *immediate* trimming may be of service.
>   I leave it to you entirely to correct vary abridge enlarge my Reply, as you think best
>   May I not appeal to Sir Joshua who often heard our friend upon Mrs Montagu's Essay — particularly ⟨if⟩ when Shakespeare has ———— [140] for his rival & Mrs M for a Defender, he is in a pitiful state indeed. Might we not add Mr Langton & others. Pray see as to this
>   I have put the passage as
>
>   to
>
> [Page 3]
>
> the great Brewer's Wife within hooks, for consideration. It would I dare say

[140] Robert Jephson (1736–1803) the dramatist, author of *Braganza*, the *Count of Narbonne*, *Julia*, and the *Law of Lombardy*. Jephson had been a childhood friend of Malone and they remained on close terms through life. It was probably Malone who asked Boswell to suppress Jephson's name in the passage in the *Life* (II, 89) which relates the story that when *Braganza* was read to Mrs. Montagu: "she is reported to have said that she trembled for her favourite bard, lest the splendor of his dramatic works should be eclipsed by the superior blaze of Mr. Jephson's production." This statement was another example of George Steevens' satiric fun. *Life*, II, Appendix B, p. 487.

vex her; but is it not too coarse? Yet it shews *how* she might talk *differently* then from what she now does of M^rs M.

Shall the addition with xxx appear at all? and if it does would it be better to be inserted *before* my subscription?

Would it be proper to introduce into this Reply the Account of the passage being first left out &c — & the pulling of caps, and the *prophesy* that she would *deny*? ¹⁴¹ You can indent it charmingly if you think ⟨proper.⟩ fit.

I am quite ashamed, or rather am sensible I *ought* to be ashamed of giving you so much trouble. But

I

[page 4]

I am conscious I would do as much for you, if I could have an opportunity.

I long much to see Courtenay's Poem in print, & I hope it will come to me here in franks. After this you will direct to me no more at Lancaster; for we leave it, I beleive on thursday or friday. If my Cause in the House of Lords is to come on the 12, I shall proceed directly to London. If it is put off, I shall go round by Lichfield & Oxford. I have not yet written to Mr Thomas Warton, which is wrong. I may delay it now, till I have read his communications, in case I do not pay him a visit. I expect every day a letter from the Solicitor in the appeal to inform me as to the time fixed.

I long much to be with you again. Yet I am vastly well upon the Circuit. My accessions of knowledge please me much, & I value myself on my assiduity. I was counsel for a prisoner on Saturday, & cross examined boldly

Yours with great regard. J.B.

I have had a charming letter from Downpatrick. I believe I shall be quite comme il faut very soon.

[Enclosure]

Having read a Postscript (dated *Naples*) to *Signora Piozzi's* Anecdotes of Dr Johnson in which after mentioning that: it is *said* in my Tour to the Hebrides that *She could not get through Mrs Montagu's Essay on Shakespeare*", she declares /as follows/ ⟨that⟩: *On the contrary* ⟨she⟩ I have *always* commended it myself, and heard it commended by *every one* else." ———— I beg leave to observe that it would have been /⟨but⟩/ fair/er/ to have mentioned *who* said it, which was not *I* but *Dr Johnson* for whom she once professed both respect and affection /whatever/ ⟨however she may now⟩ / ⟨venture to⟩ / ⟨treat his memory⟩ she at last felt from his frowns, and however she may venture to treat his character N.L.¹⁴² (And as there seems to be an oblique *stiletto* in the paragraph, the *Signora* will pardon *me* for /now/ saying that I trust more to the accuracy of the Report in my Journal, than to her memory

at

[page 2]

at this distance of time, especially when it is a little biased.

---

¹⁴¹ See p. 101. Boswell to Malone, 31 March 1786.
¹⁴² Boswell's notation for a new paragraph.

My reasons for this confidence are /first/ that the Report so far as Dr Johnson himself is concerned is perfectly agreable to the opinion which he at all times expressed of Mrs Montagu's Essay, for which I shall appeal to Sir Joshua Reynolds; and I *wonder* that he *never* expressed it to Mrs *Thrale*. *Second* He would not have told the circumstance of Mrs Thrale's not relishing the Book had he not been *sure* of the fact and as he read over my Journal he would have corrected the passage had I mistaken him. But *Third* ⟨it must be considered that⟩ Mrs *Thrale herself* /many years ago perused/ ⟨read over⟩ my Journal in the original manuscript as far as to the Isle of Col; ⟨as far as to Dunvegan when She⟩

⟨was⟩

[page 3]

⟨was recovering from her last childbirth,⟩ as to which I *have a letter under her own hand* in very flattering terms; and /therefore/ as the passage in question ⟨occurs before Dr Johnson & I left⟩ the mainland ⟨of Scotland and therefore⟩ was /read/ ⟨perused⟩ by /her/ ⟨the *Signora*⟩, she certainly would have objected to it, had she *then* thought it erroneous. |But she was *then* the great Brewer's Wife in all the pomp of wealth.|

If *Signora Piozzi* wishes to make the experiment of returning to England, and taking a place in the *Bluestocking* Circles, it is very proper that she should pay her court to Mrs Montagu. But I do not chuse that she should do it *in this way*.

Lancaster 3 April   James Boswell.
      1786.

*** I shall by and by /soon/ have occasion to speak more fully concerning the above, and several other passages of Signora Piozzi's Book.[143]

Malone answered: "C[ourtenay] agrees with me in thinking that it will be very right to make some reply to the *Signora*, in the course of this month, and not to defer it to a note in your third edition . . . but great *address* will be necessary in constructing the answer, — which we will sit down to, when you return to town . . ."[144]

Boswell returned to London on April 10th, and he discussed Mrs. Piozzi's Postscript with Malone and Courtenay on that day and again on the 12th; on the 15th he breakfasted with them "*and we* concerted my Answer to Mrs. Piozzi."[145]

His friends felt the style of his draft was arrogant, inflated, and egotistical. They did not want him to weaken his case with the rodomontade which he was now too often employing. They were, however, as eager as he was to hit hard, perhaps even more so; and they

---

[143] MS. Letter and enclosure: Hyde.
[144] Malone to Boswell, 7 April 1786. MS. Letter: Yale (C1908). Not in *Waingrow*.
[145] *Boswell Papers*, XVI, 185 (15 April 1786).

were under no obligation for past favors — not even being acquainted
with the lady. They had egged Boswell on with his first discourtesy,
and now they helped him prepare a strong attack upon a woman whom
they considered worthless and despicable.[146]

The concerted answer began in a courteous way. It stuck to the
point at issue and hammered home arguments with unsparing, legal
precision. The personal slanders Malone and Courtenay made Boswell omit: "the oblique stiletto," the bracketed passage about "the
great Brewer's Wife in all the pomp of Wealth," the rough allusion
to Mrs. Piozzi's treachery to Johnson, also the gibe about the possibility of her awkward return to London and her desire to pay court
to Mrs. Montagu and the Blue Stocking Circle at his expense, and
they made him change her title "Signora" to "Mrs." The one point
they insisted upon was Boswell's claim "for the strictest fidelity."
"My respect for the Public," the concerted reply read, "obliges me
to take notice of an insinuation which tends to impeach it."

Copy for this judicial statement, in Courtenay's hand, survives in
the Hyde Collection, written on two sheets of unequal size, one on the
page of Mrs. Piozzi's Postscript itself. This statement, over Boswell's
signature, was printed in various newspapers, including *The St. James's
Chronicle*, *The London Chronicle*, *The Public Advertiser*, and *The
Gentleman's Magazine*. Boswell also included it in the third edition
of his *Tour*, which came out in this year.[147]

In this way the literary quarrel between Boswell and Mrs. Piozzi
began. The hostility of the two biographers was now clearly exposed
to public view, and though this created entertainment for the literary
world in general,[148] it needlessly tormented the principals. Mrs. Piozzi

[146] See *Life*, Appendix I, Vol. IV, 467–468. Beyond this, the editor of the *Life*,
L. F. Powell, has expressed this opinion in a letter, "I sometimes think that Malone
hated Mrs. Thrale or at any rate disliked her, rather more than Boswell did."

[147] *Tour*, 3rd ed. (1786), footnote on pp. 247–248.

[148] Three cuttings from Lysons' collection illustrate the point:

1. *St. James's Chronicle*, 5 April 1788, said that if Boswell and Mrs. Piozzi "intended to do Honour to the Memory of Dr. Johnson, they have certainly
failed of Success," they prove only to posterity that he was "the very Quin-
tessence of *Ill-Nature*, *Ill-Manners*, and *Pedantry*."

2. Another: "The *Caledonian Journalist*, and the *Warbler's cara sposa* have so
tried to make Dr. Johnson ridiculous, that they fully deserve the satirical
attacks of *Peter Pindar*. As Bozzy is a *good-humoured* fellow he will perhaps
join in the laugh at himself; but considering the *nature* and *connections* of
the lady, it is not to be supposed that she will be consoled before she has
had a few airs upon the occasion, both *vocal* and *instrumental*."

had been provoked by something Boswell had not done, and he, in turn, had been incensed by an action about which she knew nothing. If any communication had existed between them, the public break would not have occurred, but in their indignation and isolation, open warfare was declared.

In his official attack Boswell had the good sense to listen to Malone and Courtenay, but, characteristically, he could not let the incident rest without some independent show of spirit. He turned, as he often did, to verse, writing some *Piozzian Rhimes*,[149] in which he employed

---

3. Summing up the matter, an "Impromptu" in *The General Evening Post*, in early limerick form:

> "The Ladies all cry — Pozz up —
> The Scotsmen all cry — Bozz up —
> They do not contend
> Of the two which is best
> But cry, which is worst is a — toss up."

[149] *Piozzian Rhimes*

> Thinking, no doubt, to rival *Bozzy*,
> From Naples comes Signora *Piozzi*,
> Bringing (like former wits to *Tonson*)
> Her curious scraps of SAMUEL JOHNSON;
> Old tales and private anecdotes,
> Growling replies, uncouth *bon-mots*;
> Latin and also English verses,
> And counsel sage for babes and nurses,
> Drest with Italian *goût* so nice,
> With sugar now, and now with spice;
> And that her bantling might not fail
> To please Monboddo with a *tail*,
> Behold a postscript! — Mark the *cue*,
> To flatter Mrs. Montagu.
>   How strange seems this to me, who knew her
> The wife of honest Thrale the brewer,
> Whose kind indulgence gave her leave
> The *Literati* to receive,
> Who at his hearty plenteous table
> Might eat and drink while they were able;
> While she, elated, took great pride
> O'er feasting, genius to preside;
> But seem'd most willing to stoop low,
> On JOHNSON honours to bestow.
>   Ah, luckless JOHNSON, hadst thou thought
> Thou shouldst be thus to market brought;
> That thy lax sayings, good or bad,
> Nay, thy dire fears of going mad,
> Should all be *cask'd*, and keept [*sic*] in store,

a good number of the points which his friends had counselled him to suppress. He submitted these verses under the name of "Old Salusbury Briar" and the issue of *The London Chronicle* for April 18th–20th shows them on the same sheet, in the opposite column from his public statement on Mrs. Piozzi's Postscript. He recorded in his Journal: "My good Piozzian verses made me hasten to Malone's . . . Neither he nor Courtenay could find me out. Both liked them."[150]

Boswell wrote another Rhyme, a scurrilous piece of eight verses, supposedly composed by Mrs. Piozzi in Italy; describing her present marital bliss, her "anecdotal book" and her courting of "old Goody of a dusky hue." The manuscript, written on both sides of a small scrap of paper, survives, fortunately unpublished, for the content is obscene and indefensible.[151]

Boswell handled "old Goody" (Mrs. Montagu) in another way, as evidenced by this newspaper paragraph in *The Public Advertiser*:

Mr. Boswell's retort courteous to the *stiletto* postscript, has played the very devil in the assembly of *stockings*, whose *colour* shall be nameless . . . *Goody Galimatias*[152] herself may well say, 'I wish that designing woman had let me alone.'[153]

At the time that Boswell was sparring with his invisible opponent, she and Piozzi were on their way to Venice. It was here that she first heard, with pleasure and relief, of the success of her *Anecdotes*. Bos-

---

For *sale*, when thou should'st be no more,
Not the luxurious board of Thrale
Not oceans of his wine and ale,
Not honey'd words from coaxing tongue,
In thy dull ears for ever rung,
Would have seduc'd thee to forsake
Thy own Bolt-court and plain beef-steak.
OLD SALUSBURY BRIAR.
The London Chronicle, 18–20 April 1786, p. 373.

[150] *Boswell Papers*, XVI, 185 (20 April 1786).

[151] Yale MS. 310.

[152] "Galimatias," a word of unknown origin, meaning: confused language, meaningless talk. Addison, *Spectator*, No. 275 (1712): "The great Cavity was filled with a kind of Spongy Substance, which the French Anatomists call Galimatias and the English, Nonsense."

[153] *The Public Advertiser*, 21 April 1786. Boswell, like Lysons, was making a collection of newspaper cuttings: "Paragraphs relative to my Life of Dr. Johnson." Boswell marked with * the contributions written by himself. This has a *. Yale (P119-3). Boswell's collection hereafter referred to as *Boswell Newspaper Paragraphs*.

well's laconic Journal entry for May 4th, "Madam's letter," hints at the remote but fascinating possibility of a communication from Mrs. Piozzi, but the only suggestion that she might have been the correspondent is the editorial note in the *Boswell Papers*: "Mrs. Piozzi is probably meant." [154]

Not until July, while visiting the lakes of Northern Italy, did Mrs. Piozzi see a copy of her *Anecdotes*, and by then she was fretting about her next publication, the promised edition of Johnson's *Letters*. Cadell had already advertised that two volumes would soon be forthcoming, and he pressed her to come home and set to work. Her friend Lysons wrote, however, that both he and Dr. Lort thought her edition of *Letters* should not be published " 'till after Sir John Hawkins's Edition of Dr. Johnson's Works, unless you wish them to be serviceable to the Knight, in his compilations — By the way, no great Matters are expected from this promised piece of Biography." [155]

Mrs. Piozzi was relieved by Lysons' letter for she did not yet wish to conclude the journey. She and her husband still had plans to see the Tyrolean Alps, Vienna, Prague, and many places in Germany and Belgium. Though she did not confess it, she also had qualms about the return to England. Her supposedly staunch friend, Sir Lucas Pepys, had written recommending humility upon her reappearance in society, perhaps staying first in Bath. He further recommended that Piozzi change his name to "Salusbury." [156] These suggestions were sufficiently distasteful to break the wonderfully warm friendship she had had with Pepys; only Lort and Lysons were left as literary advisers.

Progress of the rival biographers at the end of the year was an unequal record. Mrs. Piozzi's *Anecdotes* had gone through four editions; while Boswell was still floundering with his "Narrative" and "Papers Apart," and now a third pile, "Johnsonian Additions," notes on miscellaneous scraps of paper for material to be inserted at the proper place in the final revision. [157] He worked in London until late summer, then went back to Scotland; at home, with neglected Auchinleck problems to face, there was little time to work on his book. In September [158] he finally brought his wife, five children, and housekeeper to London;

---

[154] *Boswell Papers*, XVI, 187 (4 May 1786).
[155] *Clifford*, p. 282.
[156] *Ibid.*, p. 289.
[157] These "Johnsonian Additions" are at Yale: M155, M156, M157, M158.
[158] The Boswells arrived in London 25 September 1786. *Boswell Papers*, XVII, 3.

there, if anything, his situation was more difficult. His consumptive wife had caught a cold on the journey; the children, for whom schools had to be found, were idle, restless, and unruly. They did not show the enthusiasm for London that he had expected — though indeed he felt little himself at the moment. He was apprehensive, torpid, peevish, and deeply depressed. He was beginning to be treated with ridicule, for despite all the talk about his great work, he had nothing to show. He had delayed too long, he was told; the public's curiosity about Johnson was saturated. Once impervious to such criticism, he now feared it was true.

Malone prodded him on, assuring him that delay was justified; and one day he buoyed Boswell's spirits by surprising him "with a page of [the *Life*] on two different types, that [they] might settle how it was to be printed." [159]

[159] *Ibid.*, 7 (7 November 1786).

CHAPTER IV

ENMITY

1787 through 1791

1787

On March 10th, after they had been away for two years and seven months, the Piozzis returned to London. Their welcome could in a way be described as Johnsonian: Hawkins' *Life of Johnson* was being published; the papers were reporting that Boswell was at work; and Cadell was waiting on the doorstep with an offer of £500 for the completed copy of Mrs. Piozzi's *Johnson Letters*. One newspaper noted that the arrival of "Signor Piozzi and Signora Thrale" was highly seasonable ". . . as she may survey her learned friend Dr. Johnson *laid in state* by that grave undertaker, Sir John Hawkins." [1]

Mrs. Piozzi accepted Cadell's terms and consulted with Lysons, who agreed to help her with the editing. They both felt that, with Hawkins' *Life* published, her edition of the *Letters* should come out as soon as possible. She started to work at once; Cadell wanted the manuscript before summer. This seemed hardly possible, for Mrs. Piozzi was beset by many problems — among them, finding a suitable house, as Streatham was still leased. She chose Hanover Square, in the fashionable center of things.

[1] From Lysons' *Book of Cuttings* (source unidentified).

Another paper, after recognizing Hawkins' "entré," noted that Mr. Boswell's "gleanings" and Mrs. Piozzi's "gatherings" were about to come forth. "The Doctor's bones must be acknowledged to be the bones of a giant, or there would be poor picking, after their having furnished *Caledonian Haggis*, and a dish of *Italian Macaroni*, besides slices innumerable cut off *from the body* [by] Magazine mongers, anecdote merchants and rhyme stringers."

Boswell viewed the publication of Hawkins' *Life of Johnson* with anxiety and warned the general reader in *The Public Advertiser* (9 February 1787): "The *etiquette* of *precedency* between *Hawkins* and *Boswell*, for both of whom the public has been so long waiting, is not a little curious. The truth is, that the competition between them is not who shall be *first*, but who shall be *last*; in short which shall *see the other's back*, so as to hold the lash of animadversion."

This is marked with an *, indicating Boswell's authorship. *Boswell Newspaper Paragraphs*. Yale (P119-15).

The situation with her daughters was a matter of great distress. Their reception had been courteous but frigid. Queeney, during her mother's absence, had constituted herself guardian of her sisters and placed them in school. She, herself, had a London house and had no thought of relinquishing it.[2] "[W]e never do see them here," Mrs. Piozzi lamented, "any more than when the Sea parted us — or hardly. [T]he eldest has called twice, and we have called twice on Susan & Sophy, who refused dining here at our Invitation."[3] Little Cecilia, only ten, was still legally under her mother's control, and Mrs. Piozzi was determined to bring the child home, even if it meant a quarrel with Queeney. She removed her from Mrs. Stevenson's and brought her to the Hanover Square house. Tensions with Queeney increased.

Mrs. Piozzi's reception by her old friends, with few exceptions,[4] was as hostile as that of her daughters: Burke, Reynolds, the Burneys,[5] and Sir Lucas Pepys, whose behavior was "worst of all."[6] The Blue Stocking Ladies would have nothing to do with her, and their Queen, Mrs. Montagu, though friendly on paper, carefully avoided a meeting.

Nothing daunted, Mrs. Piozzi formed a new group of friends. This was not hard; all her life she had the facility of attracting men and women, ardently enjoying them and suddenly — if she thought them false — dropping them, and quickly forming new friendships with fresh enthusiasm. Such resilience and optimism were qualities quite foreign to Boswell.

Mrs. Piozzi's new set included persons connected with music and the theatre, also a generous sprinkling of titles, both English and foreign. Mrs. Siddons, the celebrated actress, came to fill the place in the new group that Johnson had in the old: the famous intimate who could be counted upon to illuminate parties and whose distinction gave Mrs. Piozzi the confidence of reflected importance.

[2] Queeney's house was at 30 Lower Grosvenor Street. Susan, Sophy, and Cecilia were at Mrs. Stevenson's fashionable boarding school in Queen Square.

[3] *Thraliana*, II, 679 (29 April 1787).

[4] Arthur Murphy, the introducer of Johnson to the Thrales, was one of the old friends who remained loyal, and "Dr Lort," she wrote in *Thraliana* "is attentive and kind . . . & Sammy Lysons retains his officiousness & Gratitude . . . Mrs Byron [wife of the Admiral, grandmother of the poet] seems glad of my Return, but hates my Husband cordially, Perkins's respectful Behaviour surprizes & pleases me much . . ." *Ibid.*, 681.

[5] "That Family has certainly been *too* ungrateful, they were dabbling in News paper Abuse of me all the Time I was away in Italy." *Ibid.*, 686.

[6] *Ibid.*, 681.

Mrs. Piozzi had another happy ability, that of being able to work amid diversions, and thus, despite an active social life, she was able to labor effectively at her edition of Johnson's *Letters*. Lysons was a competent and industrious collaborator, aiding her in the arrangement of the letters, as well as in their choice. Some they felt were too short, others too concerned with business, or with personal details of health. Many seemed devoid of literary interest. They soon felt that they must draw upon other sources to fill the two volumes which were promised, and she considered what other letters she had: one from Johnson to her mother and over ten to Thrale. She hoped she could persuade her daughters to contribute theirs; Susan and Sophy allowed her to use the half dozen they had between them, but Queeney absolutely refused to relinquish her collection of over thirty letters.

"[P]erhaps She keeps them for some professed Enemy of mine," her mother wrote in *Thraliana*, "it would be droll enough if after refusing them to her Mother She should give them to Sir John Hawkins as a Reward for having insulted me with every unprovoked, & undeserved Abuse. Very likely."[7] Despite her failure with Queeney, she had unexpected good fortune when forty of Johnson's letters to her were found in an old trunk, and over a hundred of her letters *to* Johnson, which had escaped destruction. The latter were discovered in his house and turned over by Francis Barber. Lysons was enthusiastic about using a selection of these; Mrs. Piozzi was opposed, but he pressed her, saying that they would lend interest and contrast. They were much needed also to fill space. Both Mrs. Piozzi and Lysons feared that Volume II would be too thin. In May they decided that a search must be made for more material, and they told Cadell that publication would have to be delayed until the following year.

During the spring, the Boswells and Piozzis, all four, were in London together, but they successfully managed to avoid a meeting — a pity for posterity's sake. Mutual friends and the newspapers saw to it, though, that a steady flow of gossip went in both directions. Samuel Lysons was watching carefully and his collection[8] of Johnson-

---

[7] *Ibid.*, 680.

[8] Mrs. Piozzi knew of this collection of books, pamphlets, ballads, and newspaper clippings. She recorded in her MS. *New Common Place Book* (1809–1820), under "SAM: Lysons," 1st July 1819: "[His] Death shocks me—shocks me strangely: So active a Mind, so restless a Body,—so *full* a Head: *every* thing had a Place there. Poor Fellow! & he a Boy—a lap-ear'd Lad when I knew him first here at Bath in 1782 or then-abouts [line and a half inked out] Poor Lysons! I do not think he ever

MRS. JAMES BOSWELL
BY GEORGE WILLISON

Four Oaks Farm

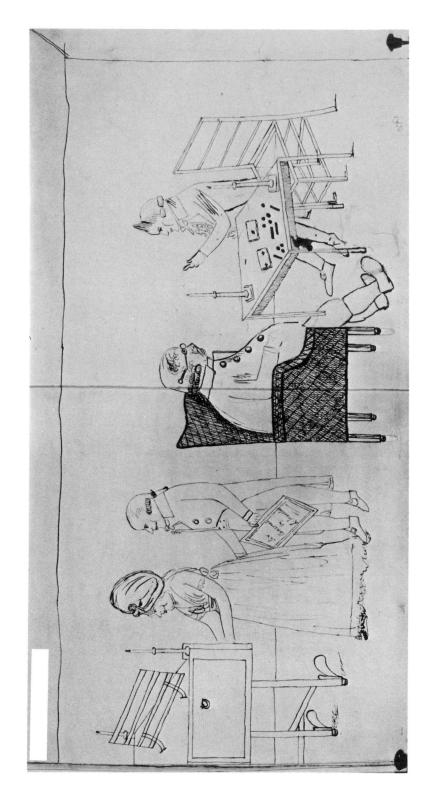

A SCENE IN THE STREATHAM PARK LIBRARY

Piozzi-Boswell was growing steadily. Mrs. Piozzi was nervous about
the stir she was causing, Boswell not a bit. He read the newspapers
with avidity and sometimes contributed paragraphs himself. He was
pleased to gather from other commentators that the Thrale wealth was
unable to sustain his rival's old prestige, and he was interested to hear
that she was planning to fill up her collection of Johnson letters with
some of her own. He let it be known that he had a very damaging communication of hers. She took fright at this — needlessly — for it was
a comparatively harmless letter, its most acid comments being upon a
gloomy party at Mrs. Montagu's, upon a "dawling" companion of her
husband's, and upon his frightening compulsion to eat.[9] The letter
was particularly damaging in Boswell's eyes, it seems, because of its
limping style.

Hawkins' "official" biography of Johnson, now published, was the
literary talk of the moment. It was felt to be a disappointing book,
ponderous and digressive. In Lysons' collection of newspaper cuttings
was one that summed up public reaction:

A gentleman, lately arrived in town, has been for several days past afflicted
with a *lethargy*, owing to the perusal of three chapters in Hawkins' *Life of
Johnson*.

Some authors put *gall* into their ink; but it is a general opinion, that the
stultified writer of the Life of *Lexiphanes* dipped his pen in opium.

Two clippings in Boswell's collection also have interest on this point:
"Sir John Hawkins — is to be *translated* into *English:* This is the work
of Johnson's black footman. The motto, '*Hic Niger*,' applying to
Hawkins himself." And another: "*Boswell's Biography* — compara-

liked me though;—& Mͬ Chappelow told me once—Years ago—that he had made
formal Proposals of Marriage to Susan Thrale, but of that I know nothing. [Neither
Susan nor Samuel ever married.] He certainly was goodnatured enough in selling my
Anecdotes of Johnson for me while I was travelling up & down Italy—When We
came home however, and were Intimate with the Greatheeds Kembles &c Sammy
Lysons invited us all to his Chambers, & gave us a Breakfast: when he shewed me a
little Collection of Books, Tracts, Pamphlets Ballads &c on a Corner of his Shelves
. . . & *Look there* said he, 'There are, I flatter myself, all the Things that ever were
written *against you* either Serious or in Ridicule—All, All; not one left out that could
be found by the most diligent Research.' Thank you was all my Reply." MS. *New
Common Place Book*: Hyde. And in a letter to Mrs. Siddons, 25 July 1819: "I
wonder if [Lysons] burned them? If he did not, I trust his brother, the clergyman
will; for he is a man with a family, and will not see any *fun* in making enemies." In
Piozziana by [the Rev. Edward Mangin] (London: Edward Moxon, 1833), p. 119.

[9] Mrs. Thrale to Johnson, 28 April 1780. MS. Letter: Hyde. *Life*, III, 421–423.

tively brightening and magnifying, from the contiguity and contrast
of trash like this, is upon the move as fast as can be, but heavy bodies
move slowly . . ." [10]

Many readers felt Hawkins' book showed a degrading picture of
Johnson, and at a meeting of the Literary Club, Malone suggested that
"a solemn Protest [be] drawn up and signed by Dr. Johnson's friends
. . . declaring that Hawkins's was a false and injurious Account. Sir
Joshua alone hesitated." Boswell resolved that the matter "should not
sleep." [11] He deeply disapproved of Hawkins' interpretation of Johnson, and though he did not say so openly, he was offended a second
time by an author's treatment; Hawkins mentioned him rarely, and
when he did, it was as a person of no significance. Boswell disliked
Hawkins' book on almost every count, but one salutary result was that
his confidence was revived; his delay now seemed justified, for his
biography would correct Hawkins' injurious picture of Johnson. He
discussed Hawkins' bias and his many inaccuracies with Malone and
Courtenay, and thereafter placed an advertisement in the papers, assuring the public that *his* Life was "in great Forwardness." He reiterated
the reason for his delay, that he had needed "to obtain much Information" from the publications of Mrs. Piozzi and Sir John Hawkins.
Now that her *Anecdotes* and his *Life* had appeared, he was forced to
admit that he was disappointed in the expectation he had had of
both. Little of "Dr. Johnson's private Life, Writings, or Conversation,
have been told with that authentick Precision which alone can render
Biography valuable." He stated that he would continue his deliberate
review of materials so that he would be able to correct these erroneous
accounts and "do Justice to the Character of his illustrious Friend."
He trusted the public would "not permit unfavourable Impressions to
be made on their Minds, whether by the light Effusions of Carelessness
and Pique, or the ponderous Labours of solemn Inaccuracy and dark
uncharitable Conjecture." [12]

Boswell was fortified when he went to a royal levee this May and
the King inquired, "When will you be done?" He answered con-
fidently, "It will be some time yet. I have a good deal to do to correct
Sir John Hawkins." [13]

[10] Neither of these newspaper clippings from Boswell's collection is marked with
*. Yale (P119–21, 22).

[11] *Boswell Papers*, XVII, 57 (27 November 1787).

[12] *St. James's Chronicle*, 12 to 15 May 1787.

[13] *Boswell Papers*, XVII, 29 (Friday, 11 May 1787).

With her publishing deadline postponed, Mrs. Piozzi was enjoying the chance to entertain for her husband. A week after Boswell's audience, the Piozzis had a very fine "Assembly" (well covered by the press). She was highly satisfied with the success of the party, "indeed in my best Days I never had finer; there were near a Hundred people in the Rooms which were besides much admired." [14] Some old friends of Streatham days had refused to come, but their absence was hardly noticed with the number of scintillating new friends present. [15] There was only one real heartache: "Miss Thrale & her Companion were asked & refused: — pass'd my Door, & looked insultingly up at the Window . . ." [16]

In June the Piozzis went to Bath, taking along their friend Count Martinengo; Cecilia they sent to Mrs. Ray's school at Streatham, so that she might enjoy the country air. Here, Queeney was quick to seize the opportunity; she took her sister away, for a trip to the Isle of Wight, she said, and later she would send her to a different school. Mrs. Piozzi wrote Queeney a firm letter, reminding her that she was legal guardian and that Cecilia belonged under her care. [17] Queeney answered with a letter so heartless that her mother thought it must have been dictated by Baretti — these letters began the estrangement which was to last for six years between Queeney and her mother.

I have got the Child home to us however, & Piozzi doats on her. — I hold her to my Heart all Day long, as Niobe did little Chloris; if they steal her away from me now, I shall lose my life: 'tis so very comfortable to have *one* at least saved out of *twelve*.

The Harrass of these Letters made me miscarry tho'; and that was a bad Thing . . . [18]

It was extremely sad, this lost chance for an heir — and she had so wanted a child by Piozzi. She was ill and anguished (Queeney had been even more cruel than she knew). Sir Lucas Pepys had to be summoned, an encounter she now dreaded; but he tended her gently and they were reconciled. "Sir Lucas Pepys & I are friends again . . . I was glad to be sick almost, that I might send for him, and make up. I

---

[14] *Thraliana*, II, 681.

[15] As a newspaper reported: "It is supposed that a vast croud [*sic*] will assemble for the occasion though but a very few *friends* of Dr. Johnson are expected." Lysons' *Book of Cuttings*.

[16] *Thraliana*, II, 681.

[17] *Ibid.*, 686.

[18] *Idem.*

love Sir Lucas Pepys," [19] she wrote in *Thraliana*, but despite the force of this statement, their relationship was never very warm again.

When Mrs. Piozzi was able to travel, a trip, a change of scene, was thought to be a proper diversion. Both she and her husband would have liked to return to the Continent. They had hoped to make frequent visits there, but Cecilia's custody posed a serious problem. If they took her with them, there would be protest; if they left her behind, Queeney would seize her again.

A summer tour to Wales, therefore, seemed advisable, with Cecilia a member of the party. It was a happy trip, at least for Mrs. Piozzi, because her husband (unlike Johnson) showed genuine enthusiasm for Wales; he said it reminded him of Lombardy. The Piozzi party stopped in Lichfield on the way to Wales, and there, in Johnson's birthplace, Mrs. Piozzi made a concentrated effort to collect more letters and anecdotes. But as she feared, Boswell had already made an effective visit while she was in Italy. [20] Several of Johnson's friends were cordial, but had nothing more to give; Anna Seward transferred her allegiance to Mrs. Piozzi, but her anecdotes she had already supplied to Boswell. She was now sorry that she had done so, and wishing to help, she was able, after considerable difficulty, to obtain the moving letters from Johnson to Miss Hill Boothby. [21] These were sent to Mrs. Piozzi in October, at the direction of Mr. Boothby, a nephew. The grudging intermediary was Johnson's old friend, Dr. Taylor, who strongly advised Mrs. Piozzi against publication. The only other letter garnered on her Lichfield visit was a copy of one to Joseph Simpson, the son of an early friend of Johnson. It was given by Simpson's cousin, Miss Adey, who said naively that she had supplied Boswell with a copy earlier, so she saw no reason why Mrs. Piozzi should not have one too.

All summer the Boswells remained in London. He was hard at work on the *Life* and thought that "January or February next at soonest

[19] *Idem.*

[20] Richard Greene, the antiquary, wrote Boswell of the party's visit to his museum: "M^r and Mrs Piozzi honour'd it lately with their presence with Miss Thrale." Richard Greene to Boswell, 9 September 1787. MS. Letter: Yale (C1398). *Waingrow*, p. 236.

[21] This pious and self-sacrificing lady is the most probable candidate of Johnson's "search," contemplated in his Journal entry for Sunday, 22 April 1753: "As I propose to try on Monday to seek a new wife, without derogation from dear Tetty's memory . . ." See *Dr. Johnson's Second Wife* by Donald and Mary Hyde. Princeton University Press: 1953.

. . . [his] volume [would] be ready for publick inspection." [22]
Toward the end of August, Boswell took his family to Scotland for a
month, and he was busy there with Auchinleck problems. Malone
wrote to him on the 14th of September reporting that he had been able
to obtain Johnson letters from Dr. Richard Farmer (Master of Em-
manuel College, Cambridge) and from William Windham (statesman
and member of the Club). Malone also told him of Mrs. Piozzi's activities in Lichfield. [23]

Boswell brought his wife and children back to London at the end of
September. Now he sat in his cluttered room, driving himself on with
the *Life*, often distracted by the sound of his wife's racking, consumptive cough. Malone advised him "to attend [Westminster Hall] laxly
this term and get on diligently with [the] *Life*." [24] Wise advice, for
no briefs were given him. Boswell recorded the days: "some *Life*," "a
little *Life*," "a great deal of *Life*." On the 24th of November when
Boswell, Malone, and Courtenay dined at Reynolds' house, Dr. Lort
was one of the guests. [25] It is disappointing that Boswell made no record
of the conversation; unfortunate too that Mrs. Piozzi was not at home
to receive a report from Dr. Lort. But early in November Mrs. Piozzi
handed Cadell the finished copy of her edition of Johnson's *Letters*; she
was now rewarding herself and her husband with a holiday in Bath.

1788

On March 8th Mrs. Piozzi's *Letters to and from the Late Samuel
Johnson* were published. In the Preface she gratefully acknowledged
her appreciation of the reception of the *Ancedotes*, which had been
welcomed "with a degree of approbation I had not dared to hope. May
these letters in some measure pay my debts of gratitude!" [26] There
had been some adverse criticism of her first book, of course, but she
noted that "the publick however has been still indulgent, though in-

[22] Boswell to the Rev. Dr. William Maxwell, 4 July 1787. MS. Letter: Yale
(L961). *Waingrow*, pp. 224–225.

[23] Malone to Boswell, 14 September 1787. MS. Letter: Yale (C1911). *Waingrow*, pp. 236–237.

[24] *Boswell Papers*, XVII, 55 (16 November 1787).

[25] *Ibid.*, 56 (24 November 1787).

[26] *Letters to and from the Late Samuel Johnson LL.D.*, Published by Hester
Lynch Piozzi (London: 1788), I, iv. This work is hereafter referred to as *Piozzi
Johnson Letters*.

dividuals have been spiteful." [27]   In the latter category Boswell was surely included.

"An Editor's duty," she stated, "is indeed that of most danger and least renown through all the ranks of literary warfare." [28] Johnson's letters, she said, were authentic, a private correspondence — and nothing more than that must be expected from them. They remained "just as he wrote them," [29] the only deletions being those "to avoid paining many individuals . . . for duty bids me defend an enemy from censure, while inclination eagerly brings forward the praises of every friend." [30]

The day before publication Dilly sent a copy of the book to Boswell,[31] who began at once and "read with assiduity till [he] had finished both Volumes." [32] Then he analyzed the book. The Table of Contents showed that Mrs. Piozzi did indeed have a great store of letters from Johnson; it had not been necessary to add many of her own — twelve in the first volume (letters I-CLXXXII) and fifteen in the second volume (letters CLXXXIII-CCCLXVII) — only twenty-seven out of three hundred and sixty-seven letters. Little supplementary material had been needed and that with which she had been "unexpectedly favoured" [33] was entirely sufficient. This included the Hill Boothby letters; a few anecdotes recently remembered; and eight Latin mottoes for the *Idler*, written on a card which she had found only "two or three weeks ago"; [34] also Johnson's gallantry (of 1755) to Miss Charlotte Cotterell, a young lady who had thought well enough of the letter to preserve it all these years, but desired that her name "remain concealed." [35] There was also Johnson's "sophistical" letter to Joseph Simpson, which it must have surprised Boswell to find in the collection; [36] and the five letters to Francesco Sastres, the

[27] *Ibid.*, II, 385–386.

[28] *Ibid.*, I, ii.

[29] *Ibid.*, I, iii.

[30] *Ibid.*, I, v.

[31] Before this (on February 8th) Boswell had seen "a sheet at the printing House . . . and observed Letter CCCXXX [Johnson to Mrs. Thrale, 24 November 1783], so that we may expect much entertainment. It is wonderful what avidity there still is for every thing relative to Johnson." Boswell to Bishop Percy, 9 February 1788. MS. Letter: New York Public Library. *Waingrow*, pp. 265–266.

[32] *Boswell Papers*, XVII, 74 (7 March 1788).

[33] *Piozzi Johnson Letters*, II, 378.

[34] *Ibid.*, 388.

[35] *Ibid.*, 385.

[36] Mrs. Piozzi was delighted to be able to publish this letter before Boswell; but

Italian translator — here because Boswell had not been home to receive them.[37] Finally came Johnson's Latin verses to his close friend, Dr. Lawrence (with translations by Mrs. Piozzi), and Johnson's translations of Boethius' *Consolatione Philosophiae*. These additions succeeded in swelling the second volume to twenty-seven pages more than the first.[38] Queeney's letters had not been needed, though one paper made the unfounded statement that her "letters from the Rambler" were "infinitely superior to those of her Mother." [39]

When Boswell had finished reading the *Letters to and from . . . Johnson,* he felt disappointed and disturbed, partly by the triviality of the correspondence — mundane subjects — and "less able and brilliant writing" [40] then he had expected. He was offended by the constant view of Johnson's devotion to Mrs. Thrale and by the almost complete absence of any glimpse of himself. He knew that Johnson had had very great affection for him and it was mortifying not to have the public see this. The only explanation he could accept for Johnson's lack of reference to him and his absorption in Mrs. Thrale was that Johnson had feigned his love for Mrs. Thrale so that he could enjoy the luxuries

---

her counsellor, Dr. Lort, was not at all enthusiastic. He thought it would be better for Johnson's reputation to consign it to the flames. *Clifford,* p. 310.

[37] Sastres wrote Boswell, c. February 1788:

"I have very often taken the liberty of calling on you with our Dear great Friend's letters to me in my pocket, but having been always so unfortunate as never to find you at home nor hearing any thing from you, I began to think that you considered them of little consequence, and was not very desirous to have them. I have been at the same time earnestly Solicitad by Mrs Piozzi to give the said letters to her, to publish them with the rest of Johnson's to herself. I have been informed, Dear Sir, that your life of Johnson is not yet ready for the press, whereas Mrs Piozzi's book will be published in a very short time; & considering within my mind that you may make the same use of the said letters from Mrs. Piozzi's publication as from the Manuscript . . . I have been induced to deliver them into her hands." MS. Letter: Yale (C2431). *Waingrow,* pp. 270–271.

[38] When the book was in proof Mrs. Piozzi and her advisers realized that their fear of a too slender Volume II had been unfounded. There was actually too much material, and sheet Ee was cancelled, omitting all of Mrs. Piozzi's own translations of Boethius, retaining only those by Johnson or those made in collaboration with her.

[39] The report went on to say: "Youth and sprightliness must have had their superior charms, even with the 'STURDY MORALIST': but MISS THRALE, with a resolution that does honour to her delicacy, however unfortunate it may be for the Publick, has declared that these *Testimonies of Confidence* shall never see the light." Lysons' *Book of Cuttings.*

Johnson's thirty-three letters to Queeney were edited by their owner, the Marquis of Lansdowne (London: Cassell, 1932). They are charming, but not comparable to her mother's collection.

[40] *Boswell Papers,* XVII, 74 (7 March 1788).

of her husband's household; but this interpretation reduced Johnson to a fawning hypocrite, and that was bitter disillusionment. He wrote in his Journal:

This publication *cooled* my warmth of enthusiasm for "my illustrious friend" a good deal. I felt myself degraded from the consequence of an ancient Baron to the state of an humble attendant on an Authour; and what vexed me, thought that my collecting so much of his conversation had made the World shun me as a dangerous companion [41]

He was disappointed that Malone [42] and Courtenay thought better of the letters than he did, "though upon looking at some of them again on saturday, they improved," [43] but not much. He was still "the *wet blanket* as Courtenay said." [44] Boswell was gratified when Langton agreed with him "that Johnson in his letters to Mrs. Thrale appeared to disadvantage, as shewing a studied shunning to speak of the friends whom he valued most, in terms such as to make her at all jealous of them. This was a stooping in the high mind of Johnson." [45] Boswell

[41] *Ibid.*, 75.

[42] Malone wrote to Boswell, 8 March 1788: "I sat up till four o'clock reading away as hard as I could, and then my candle went out and I could read no more; yet I was not able to finish the first Volume. The letters are, I think, in general very pleasing and exactly what I expected. I think you rate them too low. I would not have one of them omitted." MS. Letter: Yale (C1913). *Waingrow*, pp. 272–273. High praise from Malone, who genuinely disliked Mrs. Piozzi!

[43] *Boswell Papers*, XVII, 76 (Sunday, 9 March 1788).

[44] Boswell to Malone [8 March 1788]. MS. Letter: Yale (L936).

[45] *Boswell Papers*, XVII, 80 (15 March 1788).

Newspaper reaction was filled with both praise and blame. A friendly newspaper reported that Mrs. Piozzi's letters "mix with JOHNSON'S, and comparing as they mix, they do not suffer on a comparison.

"There is no praise beyond this, except it be for tendency. And there, what she says, is like what she does — well directed, exact, and urgent. JOHNSON'S account of her is the account of most who know her — *When we hear, we hear Wit* — *When we see, we see Virtue.*" [Johnson Letter LXVI, 17 May 1773].

Another paper wrote:

"The letters of Madame Piozzi develop her own and the character of Dr. Johnson more truly perhaps than they ever were exhibited before. We see a vain woman forcing a poor man to write fulsome letters for his daily dinner."

And one commented:

"Poor DR. JOHNSON has been served up to us in every shape — we have had him boiled to a rag, roasted, fricasseed . . .

"The letters of DR. JOHNSON, for the most part, form a salmagundi, composed of *bulls, cows, calves, cats,* and *Mr. Piozzi.*"

Still another declared:

"MRS PIOZZI, after the pleasure of publishing her own unrivalled excellence in

was annoyed with Wilkes, who took "a mischievous pleasure in point-
ing out how often Johnson had written slightingly of [him] to Mrs.
Thrale"; [46] and he was disappointed that Horace Walpole, the fastidious collector and correspondent *sans pareil*, was much pleased by the
Letters, saying they "were written in a very easy stile, and gave him a
much better opinion of Johnson, for they shewed him to have a great
deal of affection." [47] Boswell was so depressed that he lost interest in
working on the *Life*.

Suddenly, reflecting upon the wording of the Preface, Boswell
realized that the editor admitted having made deletions. He spoke with
Lysons, "and from him . . . filled up a great many of the blanks." [48]
Boswell then felt much better, for he was confident that there were
many more deletions than Lysons would admit. Mrs. Piozzi's method
was deceptive omission — he was convinced of this — it explained how
he had been made to appear insignificant. Boswell's conviction was
false, but it was strong, rekindling his spirits and sending him back to
work on the *Life* with vigor. He hoped for publication in September
or October.[49]

Actually, Mrs. Piozzi had deleted very few mentions of Boswell. As
Langton had knowingly surmised, Johnson customarily showed delicacy in not imposing one friend upon another, and he was particularly
cautious in the way he treated these two rivals. There was only one
period in the 'seventies when he felt free to pass on messages from
Mrs. Thrale. (Boswell returned compliments via Johnson.) But in
Johnson's letters to Mrs. Thrale there were no Boswell compliments
— no general appraisal of his character, no serious consideration of his
merits. He looked for evidence of the devotion he knew Johnson felt
for him; this simply was not present. For several omissions Boswell
should have been grateful. The editor left the man nameless, not even
initialled, who "goes away on thursday, very well satisfied with his
journey. Some great men have promised to obtain him a place, and

---

her letters, and enjoying the more substantial happiness of 500 £. in *hard cash*, is
determined to spread her peacock tail, and on adulation 'sup most royally.'

"At her Concerto to-night this lady expects to be installed a tenth Muse."

The four reports are from Lysons' *Book of Cuttings*.

[46] *Boswell Papers*, XVII, 84 (18 March 1788).

[47] *Ibid.*, 102 (25 April 1788).

[48] *Ibid.*, 93 (12 April 1788).

[49] Boswell to Francis Barber, 3 March 1788. *Waingrow*, p. 272. Text from Maggs
Catalogue, Spring 1922.

then a fig for my father, and his new wife." [50] In another instance, Boswell would scarcely have wanted the public to know he "paid another visit, I think, to ⟨Mrs. Rudd⟩,[51] before he went home ⟨to his own Deary⟩." [52] Such deletions were prime examples of her scrupulousness in defending "an enemy from censure."

The editor's greatest Boswellian problem concerned his claim that she had read his *Tour to the Hebrides* and not objected to the passage about Mrs. Montagu's essay. In Johnson's letters of 1775, for May 22nd and June 11th, she printed the full reference to her reading Boswell's Journal, but in that of June 19th she deliberately pasted a piece from another letter over this passage:

Do you read Boswel's Journals? He moralised, and found my faults, and laid them up to reproach me. Boswel's narrative is very natural, and therefore very entertaining, he never made any scruple of showing it to me. He is a very fine fellow . . . [53]

Mrs. Piozzi probably deleted this paragraph to spare Boswell the censure of Johnson's first remarks, but it is a pity she did not let the compliments remain, for this was exactly the kind of praise which Boswell was vainly seeking. In handling the *Tour* letters, Mrs. Piozzi followed no consistent policy. In the two letters of July 6th and 21st, 1775, after crossing out sentences showing that she had read Boswell's Journal, she then reinstated them. A curious change appeared in an earlier letter of October 23rd, 1773,[54] where she needlessly gave evidence of the fact she wished to obscure. She changed, "one of the Ladies played on her harpsichord, and I believe Boswel danced with the other" to "Boswell and Col danced a reel with the other." The details of the reel were not published in the *Tour* but were in Boswell's Journal. She could easily have erased any reference to her having read this diary, but she let all stand save one. In her treatment of this delicate subject Mrs. Piozzi seems to have been at a loss how to proceed.

[50] Boswell's father had re-married on the same day Boswell had married Margaret Montgomerie, 25 November 1769. MS. Letter: Hyde. *Piozzi Johnson Letters*, I, 324. Letter #478. *Letters*, II, 129–130.

[51] Margaret Caroline Rudd, the celebrated courtesan, who, with the two brothers Perreau, was charged with forgery.

[52] MS. Letter: Hyde. *Piozzi Johnson Letters*, I, 333. Letter #482. *Letters*, II, 133–134.

[53] MS. Letter: Johnson Birthplace, Lichfield. *Piozzi Johnson Letters*, I, 239. Letter #408. *Letters*, II, 47.

[54] Johnson to Mrs. Thrale, 23 October 1773. MS. Letter: Hyde. *Piozzi Johnson Letters*, I, 174. Letter #332. *Letters*, I, 380.

Considering the letters as a whole, she had been an honest editor according to eighteenth-century standards. She was more full and open in her presentation of Johnson's letters than Boswell was to be in the *Life*, though acknowledgedly, his use of correspondence was incidental to his narrative, reproduced simply as selective illustration. In keeping with the Johnsonian precept that "there is something noble in publishing truth, though it condemns one's self," [55] Boswell let certain strong strictures stand, but he omitted others — his deletions were extensive.

Mrs. Piozzi was certainly guilty of improving her own selected letters, the inclusion of which had been pressed by Lysons and Cadell. Boswell was quick to detect the signs of later polishing. He scorned such tampering, but her desire to appear at best advantage beside Johnson for posterity was completely understandable; and he too, in a while, would begin expanding his Journal notes and systematically improving his own utterances.

Her great sin of omission was her refusal to print the two important and angry letters at the break-up of her friendship with Johnson (his rough letter of the 2nd of July, 1784, and her bristling reply of the 4th — perhaps the finest letter she ever wrote); but though all readers would have been titillated by both, no one could reasonably have expected her to publish them. Her letter CCCLIII, announcing her imminent marriage, was immediately followed by Johnson's sad, resigned, and affectionate letter of July 8th (as letter CCCLIV), thus giving the reader the impression of a tender parting and Johnson's blessing upon her marriage. The two letters she published were captioned: "Mrs. Piozzi to Dr. Johnson" and "To Mrs. Piozzi," both incorrect, for she was still Mrs. Thrale until the 23rd of July. [56]

In her two books, quite naturally, though it was repugnant to Boswell, Mrs. Piozzi tried to show that she had not lowered herself by her second marriage, and that she continued to enjoy Johnson's respect and devotion. Her defense rested on uncertain ground, she knew, but to maintain her place in the world she felt forced to take this stand. Boswell was aware of her dilemma and was determined to have the public know as well. Her *Anecdotes* had stung him, but his indignation was mixed with amusement. With the *Letters* it was a different matter, they wounded him deeply, for they were clear proof that Johnson had loved her more than him; no reader could help but see this and Boswell

[55] *Life*, IV, 396.
[56] See discussion of these letters under July 1784, p. 89 above.

felt degraded. He no longer thought of her as a rival; he thought of her as an enemy. In time, in the *Life*, he would deal properly with Johnson's "Dearest dear Lady"; for the moment, he found relief from anger and depression — as before — in verse, an old verse, made more satiric, more coarse — to suit his mood — and for all to hear.

He "determined to publish Johnson's supposed Nuptial Ode." [57] He had it printed by Robert Faulder, back-dating the title page to 1784, when the event would have been possible. [58] The basis for the *Ode* was the "Song [on Dr. Johnson and Mrs Thrale]," which Boswell had composed in an ebullient mood immediately after Thrale's death, [59] the manuscript of which was still at hand. [60] His friend, John Wilkes, who had had "a classical and gay connection" with this first "epithalamium," may well have helped in composing the prose embellishments of the new version. The brutal prose section consisted of a "Preface by the Editor" and an "Argument." The first referred directly to the "collection of their letters, which is extant, and has been put forth in print by herself"; [61] the letter numbers used are identical with those in Mrs. Piozzi's volumes — "lett. 34," "lett. 180," "lett. 277," "lett. 303," "lett. 342" . . . Select quotations from these, exact but truncated and out of context, became ludicrous and vulgar. They show, the "Editor" says, that "the plainest familiarity" existed between Dr. Johnson, famous "for shrewd sayings and lively jokes," and this little woman "of pregnant parts." Examples: " 'I hope, in time to be like the bull.' lett. 34" and " 'On the 19th of last month I evacuated twenty pints of water.' lett. 342." [62]

The text was phrased with broad double meaning:

Signor Baretti was entertained in the house, at bed and board, to teach [the Thrale daughters] the Italian tongue; and Signor Piozzi, it is believed, was liberally rewarded for teaching them to sing, and play on the harpsichord. Mrs. Thrale had not an *ear*, as the saying is, but she had an *eye* to this her daughter's [*sic*] music-master, who, it appears, by her said publication, was permitted to *love* her. 'Piozzi, I find, is coming, and when *he* comes, and *I* come, you will have two about you that *love* you.' lett. 275. [63]

[57] *Boswell Papers*, XVII, 109 (9 May 1788).
[58] *Ode by Dr. Samuel Johnson to Mrs. Thrale upon her Supposed Approaching Nuptials.* London: 1784 [*sic*]. Hereafter referred to as *Ode*.
[59] *Boswell Papers*, XIV, 196 (12 April 1781).
[60] Yale MS. 302. See pp. 66 above and 155 below.
[61] *Ode*, p. 6.
[62] *Idem.*
[63] *Idem.*

JOHNSON'S BIOGRAPHERS, 1786

FORMERLY IN THE COLLECTION OF A. M. BROADLEY

FRONTISPIECE BY THOMAS ROWLANDSON FOR
"BOZZY AND PIOZZI" BY PETER PINDAR, 1786

This leads the "Editor" to say that the widow's final preference for Signor Piozzi over Johnson as a husband, "no doubt contributed, with other considerations, to his writing that severe answer on her informing him of her resolution, which answer she has very prudently suppressed."[64] Boswell was keenly aware of the existence of Johnson's harsh letter to Mrs. Thrale of the 2nd of July, 1784.[65]

The "Argument" of the piece was couched in highflown style, a parody of Mrs. Piozzi's grand classical allusions in her short preface to the *Anecdotes*. In the course of its brief four pages she had likened Johnson to "an oak, Trajan's column, the Nile, and Ajax Telamonius. Mrs. Piozzi herself is the archer who retires behind his comrade's shield, because fencing in the school is so different from fighting in the field."[66]

The *Ode* itself, "the sportive lay," was a parody of Johnson's verse:

[1]　If e'er my fingers touch'd the lyre,
　　　In satire fierce, in pleasure gay,
　　Shall not my THRALIA'S smiles inspire?
　　　Shall SAM refuse the sportive lay?

[2]　My dearest lady! view your slave,
　　　Behold him as your very SCRUB,
　　Eager to write as authour grave,
　　　Or govern well the brewing tub.

[3]　To rich felicity thus rais'd,
　　　My bosom glows with amorous fire;
　　Porter no longer shall be prais'd;
　　　'Tis I MYSELF am *Thrale's Entire*!

[4]　PIOZZI once alarm'd my fears
　　　Till beauteous MARY'S tragick fate
　　And RIZZIO'S tale dissolv'd in tears
　　　My mistress, ere it was too late.

[64] *Ode*, p. 7.

[65] It was quite common knowledge: a spurious version of Johnson's harsh letter of 2 July 1784 had appeared in *The Gentleman's Magazine* for December 1784 (p. 893), and Hawkins later commented on Mrs. Piozzi's deception by omission and rearrangement of letters in his *Life of Johnson* (1787), pp. 568–569. Malone in his letter to Boswell of 8 March 1788 referred to the subject: "I hope heartily *Madam* will be trimm'd well for her suppression, and evident imposition with respect to his answer to her matrimonial notification. All his documents concerning the value of truth, have been thrown away upon her . . ." MS. Letter: Yale (C1913). *Waingrow*, p. 273.

For Boswell's measured comment on her suppression of the two letters from her collection, see *Life*, IV, 339, and p. 156 below.

[66] Note by editor, George Birkbeck Hill, in *Johnsonian Miscellanies* (Oxford: Clarendon Press, 1897), I, 145, n. 3.

[5]   Indignant thought to English pride!
       That any eye should ever see
       JOHNSON one moment set aside
       For *Tweedledum* or *Tweedledee.*

[6]   Congratulating crowds shall come,
       Our new-born happiness to hail,
       Whether at ball, at rout, at drum;
          — But human spite will still prevail.

[7]   For though they come in pleading guise,
          And cry, "The wise deserve the fair!"
       They look askance with envious eyes,
          As Satan look'd at the first pair.

[8]   Ascetick now thy lover lives,
          Nor dares to touch, nor dares to kiss;
       Yet prurient fancy sometimes gives
          A prelibation of our bliss.

[9]   Convuls'd in love's tumultuous throws,
          We feel the aphrodisian spasm;
       Tir'd nature must, at last, repose,
          Then Wit and Wisdom fill the chasm.

[10]   Nor only are our limbs entwin'd,
          And lip in rapture glued to lip;
       Lock'd in embraces of the mind;
          Imagination's sweets we sip.

[11]   Five daughters by a former spouse
          Shall match with nobles of the land;
       The fruit of our more fervent vows
          A pillar of the state shall stand!

[12]   Greater than Atlas was of yore,
          A nobler charge to me is given;
       The sphere he on his shoulders bore,
          I, with my arms, encircle Heaven!

It is interesting to follow the metamorphosis of the "Song" of 1781 (eight four-line stanzas on one sheet, three on another) into this printed *Ode* of 1788 (twelve four-line stanzas). There is rearrangement, omission, addition, and revision. The fourth stanza of the "Song" becomes the first of the *Ode*, followed by "Song" stanza one ("My dearest darling," changed to "My dearest lady"). The order is this:

Ode	"Song"
stanza 1	stanza 4
stanza 2	stanza 1
stanza 3	stanza 2
stanza 4 — new	
stanza 5 — new	
stanza 6	stanza 6
stanza 7	stanza 7
stanza 8 — new	
stanza 9	stanza 10
stanza 10	stanza 11
stanza 11	stanza 3
stanza 12	stanza 8

Two stanzas were dropped from the "Song": number five, mentioning "Desmullins," "Williams," "Levet," and "Frank"; and number nine, referring to Mrs. Thrale's relieving Johnson "from lonely gloom of fretful pain," when he could be "Transported to the Blissful Bower." In the *Ode* new stanzas four and five refer to the more timely figure, Piozzi (with an allusion to Mary Queen of Scots and Rizzio from "lett. 354"), and to Piozzi's contest with Johnson for the hand of Mrs. Thrale. The *Ode*'s stanza eight predicts "bliss" but does not concede Mrs. Thrale's power for relieving Johnson's loneliness and pain.

When Boswell came to treat Mrs. Thrale's marriage to Piozzi in the manuscript of the *Life*, he chose to quote stanzas five and three, in that order: "Indignant thought to English pride!" to illustrate *"Jealousy of Piozzi"*; and "To rich felicity thus rais'd" to show *"His own Imagined success."* This page of the manuscript (981 verso) was deleted from the first edition, but in the second edition (III, 664, n. 8) Boswell gave the first three stanzas of the *Ode* (four, one, two of the "Song"). The stanza:

> To rich felicity thus rais'd,
> > My bosom glows with amorous fire;
> Porter no longer shall be prais'd;
> > 'Tis I MYSELF am *Thrale's Entire*!

seemed to Boswell the best summation of the matter, it was what he quoted, both in the manuscript and in the second edition. Boswell's editor, L. F. Powell, commented in an Appendix: "The publication of this 'poem' by Boswell cannot be defended; his indecency in introducing a specimen into the *Life* is at its grossest in the penultimate line of [this] stanza." [67]

Once the *Ode* was at press, Boswell endeavored to stir the public's curiosity. He wrote this newspaper paragraph:

Dr. Johnson's courtship of Mrs. Thrale and his rage in being rejected for Signor Piozzi, which is said now to be *promulgated* by Baretti, is one of the most extraordinary things that we have yet had concerning our great Lexicographer. Query, Did Hawkins know this? Does Boswell know it? What are we to believe? Why have we not a detail? Why not some documents? Let us have all out. [68]

Boswell also wrote "A Thralian Epigram," which appeared in *The Public Advertiser*:

> If *Hesther* had chosen to wed mighty SAM
> Who it seems, drove full at her his BATTERING RAM [69]
> A wonder indeed, then, the world would have found
> A woman who truly prefer'd SENSE to *sound*. [70]

The *Ode* was discussed in *The Monthly Review* for June, [71] but other journals took no notice of it. Boswell, now back in Scotland, [72] complained to Malone:

I see no paper but The P. A. [*Public Advertiser*] in which there has been no mention whatever of The *Ode*. Pray what became of it? Did it run at all? Or was it crushed in the bud? [73]

To this Malone replied: "The poem has gone off but badly, for want of

----

[67] *Life*, IV, 551, Appendix J.

[68] *Public Advertiser*, [12 May] 1788. Yale (P116–29*) in Boswell's Collection of "News-paper Paragraphs By myself, or relating to me. N.B. Get them all pasted." Hereafter referred to as *Boswell Newspaper Paragraphs*, cf. chap. III, note 153 above.

[69] "BATTERING RAM" referred to a phrase of Mrs. Piozzi's, with which Boswell had considerable sport. It was in the Epilogue that she had written for one of her new friends, Bertie Greatheed, for his romantic tragedy, *The Regent*, which was produced at the Theatre Royal in Drury Lane. Mrs. Siddons and her brother, John Philip Kemble, played the leading roles, and it was Mrs. Siddons who spoke the epilogue. Appealing to the audience for applause, the heroine asserted: "Our bard . . . with antiquated art/ . . . drives his battering-ram full at your heart." *The Regent* by Bertie Greatheed (London: J. Robson and W. Clarke, 1788), p. 74.

[70] *Public Advertiser*, 13 May 1788. *Boswell Newspaper Paragraphs*. Yale (P116–32*).

[71] *Monthly Review*, June 1788 (LXXVIII, 528).

[72] On 15 May 1788, Boswell left London with Mrs. Boswell, Euphemia, and Betsy. *Boswell Papers*, XVII, 110.

[73] Boswell to Malone, 2 June 1788. MS. Letter: Yale (L937).

your assistance. Finding it did not move, I made Faulder advertise it a second time." [74]

No stir was created, and Boswell wrote again to Malone in mid-July:

I am somewhat alarmed that the *Ode* though so truly good has not moved. It is I fear a slight symptom of a cooling as to Johnson. I have inquired for it at several shops here, in vain though most of the new publications are to be had. I have not seen a word about it except in the Monthly Review which allows it to be *witty*, but thinks the story improbable. Pray be so good as to inquire for me how many are sold. When I return to town, I will shew you how I shall *puff* the embers into a flame. So let Faulder carefully preserve them. 'Look to't I'll do't.' [75]

Malone answered Boswell flatly, "The poem, I fear, has done nothing." [76] It was felt that newspaper friends of Mrs. Piozzi had suppressed its mention, but Malone was not interested in the *Ode*. His concern was the important matter of the *Life*. Perhaps Boswell's agitation over the small piece covered the fact that he had done little on the great. Malone said in this August letter that if Boswell returned to London without "*The Life* complete, expect no mercy." [77] Abjectly, Boswell confessed that all summer he had "done nothing to Dʳ Johnson's Life — Literally nothing — not a single line" of the first draft he had hoped to finish. "It will require an exercise both of your philosophy and indulgent friendship to make allowance for me." [78] Boswell added, "I even think of *resolving* not to taste wine till it be done; and *that* I think will make me work hard indeed." To this suggestion Courtenay replied, "Do not think of quitting the Joys of wine — as you threaten in yʳ last; if you do — Your life of Johnstone [*sic*] will resemble — Sir J. Hawkins." [79] In the same letter Courtenay gave what encouragement he could about the poem, reporting that Jephson, [80] the dramatist, while visiting Malone, had read it and "is much pleased — with your Connubial *Ode*" to the Signora. Boswell was still hoping to "make the Ode fly." [81]

[74] Malone to Boswell, 17 June 1788. MS. Letter: Yale (C1914).

[75] Boswell to Malone, 12 July 1788. MS. Letter: first part Hyde; second part Yale (L938).

[76] Malone to Boswell, 12 August 1788. MS. Letter: Yale (C1915).

[77] *Idem.*

[78] Boswell to Malone, 18 September 1788. MS. Letter: Yale (L939).

[79] Courtenay to Boswell, 29 September 1788. MS. Letter: Yale (C838).

[80] See Chap. III, note 140 above.

[81] Boswell to Malone, 18 September 1788. MS. Letter: Yale (L939).

It remained, however, decidedly earthbound. It is curious that it did not have something of a sale, and one wonders if, at some later date, Faulder did not return folded, unstitched sheets to Boswell, for a number of these were found at Auchinleck after his death. One of the few copies which has an eighteenth-century provenance belonged to Samuel Lysons, and in it is the interesting inscription, "Written by Jas. Boswell, Esq., as he assured me." But even advertisement to the rival camp did not help; none of Mrs. Piozzi's friends even appear to have enlightened her upon the subject of this publication.

Her mind at the time was filled with a publishing project of her own. She was enjoying her role as an author and wished to bring out another book. She thought the public might be entertained by a volume on the Piozzi travels, drawn from *Thraliana* and her special travel diaries. She worked on this project all summer, and in the autumn painstakingly wrote out a fair copy for the printer. Her husband, mystified that she could be so long absorbed with "a stack of foolish papers," remarked pleasantly, "never had Man so diligent a Wife." [82] On the 10th of November, she was able to report in *Thraliana*, "I *have* finished my Book" [83] and four days later she offered it to Cadell for first refusal, the price asked: "500 guineas and twelve copies to give away." [84] He accepted with alacrity.

Things were moving in slow and painful contrast for Boswell. His summer had been spent on estate responsibilities, duties to Lord Lonsdale, his capricious patron,[85] and trying cases on the Northern Circuit. In July he wrote to Malone from York. He was anxious about his wife, and said: ". . . I suffer frequently from anxious apprehensions, which make me shrink. I sometimes upbraid myself for leaving her; but tenderness should yield to the active engagements of ambitious enterprise." [86]

[82] *Clifford*, p. 341.

[83] *Thraliana*, II, 720.

[84] Mrs. Piozzi to Thomas Cadell, 14 November 1788. *Hayward*, I, 322.

[85] Boswell in his *Letter to the People of Scotland*, 1785, had made overtures to the Earl of Lonsdale with the hope that this powerful figure might become his patron and advance his career. Lord Lonsdale did become his patron, but it was a connection Boswell soon wished he might sever. Lonsdale was boorish, brutal, and rapacious. He furthered Boswell's career little; he was jealous of any interest but his own. When full realization came to him of Boswell's devotion to his family and his dedication to the writing of the *Life of Johnson*, Lonsdale began a persecution that was relentless. *Boswell Papers*, XVIII, xiii–xv.

[86] Boswell to Malone, from York, 12 July 1788. MS. Letter: Hyde.

Soon, Boswell faced the decision, whether or not to return to London, to get on with the *Life*. It was clear that Mrs. Boswell was not well enough to accompany him. He anguished. After many misgivings he left his wife at Auchinleck, and by early November was back in London; he brought Sandie, Jamie, and Veronica with him.

Once in the city, he worked feverishly on the *Life* to make up for the wasted summer, and by the 17th of November he was able to report to Malone: "I am now half done with 1783, so that there remains no more but a year and a half of the first draught to do." [87] In the same letter he added an encouraging bit of information. He had met Mrs. Piozzi's publisher, Cadell, "in the street the other day, [and he] raised my hopes by saying he was convinced mine would be the only Life that would be prefixed to Johnson's Works." [88]

On December 5th Jamie Boswell sent a report to his mother in Scotland, reassuring but inaccurate: "papa is continuing to write his life of the great Dr. Johnson [corrected from 'Jonstone'] [89] and hopes to have it done by Christmas." [90]

1789

The rapidity with which Mrs. Piozzi was able to turn out her personal and entertaining volumes, and the money she received so easily for them, vexed and depressed Boswell. Now, her third book was at press, while his *Life of Johnson* was not even completed in rough draft. Only the Introduction and Dedication were composed. He wrote to his friend, Temple, on the 10th of January that he planned: "Whenever I have completed the rough draught, by which I mean the Work without nice correction, Malone and I are to prepare one half perfectly, and then it goes to press, where I hope to have it early in february so as to be out by the end of May." [91] At the end of January he wrote to

[87] Boswell to Malone, 17 November 1788. MS. Letter: Yale (L940). *Waingrow*, p. 281.

[88] This hope was not realized. Three years later, on 8 March 1791, he was to write Malone in Ireland: "Have I told you that Murphy has written *An Essay on the Life and Writings of Dr. Johnson* to be prefixed to the new edition of his Works? He wrote it in a month, and has received £200 for it." MS. Letter: Hyde. *Waingrow*, p. 392.

[89] "Papa," a week before he met Johnson in 1763, had also given a Scottish spelling of the name, "Johnston," in his Journal. *Boswell, the Earlier Years*, p. 119.

[90] *Boswell Papers*, XVII, 135 (5 December 1788).

[91] Boswell to Temple, 10 January 1789. MS. Letter: Pierpont Morgan Library, New York City. *Waingrow*, p. 285.

his wife: "O, if this Book of mine were done! Job says, 'O, that mine ennemy *had written* a Book!' I shall rejoice when I can speak in the *past* tense. I *do* hope to be at *Finis* in ten days." [92]

He was revising steadily with Malone, and Johnsonian materials were still coming to him; William Seward was being "very obliging" in helping him.[93] Boswell plodded on, his concentration often broken by frightening apprehensions about his wife. Her condition had become critical, and at the beginning of April he received such an alarming report that he left for Auchinleck, taking Veronica with him.[94] He found his wife worse than he had expected, and their physician, Dr. Campbell, gave no hope for recovery. Boswell tried to "soothe and console," but characteristically, finding her suffering hard to endure, he drank to excess and went frequently from home. On the night of the 16th of May, returning from a friend's house, after dining (and drinking too much), he fell from his horse and hurt his shoulder badly. The next day he received a summons from the Earl of Lonsdale to come to Lowther and accompany him to London on business.[95] Boswell was ill himself and felt great apprehension for his wife, but she "generously pressed me to be resolute. Alas! the event proved fatal. I never saw her again alive." [96]

"I shall never forget her saying, 'Good Journey!' " he wrote in his Journal.[97] He shed tears as he rode away. Boswell was in London a week, subordinating all other duties to futile attendance upon Lord

---

[92] *Boswell Papers*, XVII, 143 (28 January 1789).

[93] *Ibid.*, 142.

[94] Veronica had been attending Mrs. Stevenson's, "the great boarding school" in Queen Square — Malone teased Boswell about his fondness for grand sounds: "What has the great boarding school in Queen's Square to do with the matter? Any other place where good English manners c^d be obtained, w^d do just as well." Malone to Boswell, 12 August 1788. MS. Letter: Yale (C1915). Susan and Sophy Thrale were also still at Mrs. Stevenson's; Susan two years older than Veronica, Sophy a little less than a year — one wonders how the three got on.

Jamie was a day scholar in the Academy at Soho, and Sandie was tutoring under one of the Soho masters in preparation for Eton. The two youngest children, Euphemia and Betsy, had stayed at Auchinleck with their mother. *Boswell Papers*, XVII, 111.

[95] Boswell was asked to "appear as Recorder of Carlisle, in an Action brought against that ancient Corporation in the Court of King's Bench." Boswell's *Book of Company*, entry for Tuesday, 18 May 1789. MS: Hyde. Hereafter referred to as Boswell's *Book of Company*.

[96] *Idem.*

[97] *Boswell Papers*, XVII, 112. In entry for 19 May 1789.

Lonsdale — the case had not even come up when he received such desperate news that on the 4th of June he and his two sons, Sandie and Jamie, set out posthaste for Scotland. They arrived in Auchinleck "in Sixty four hours and a quarter" [98] and were met at the door by Euphemia, who in a burst of tears, said that her mother was dead.[99] Boswell knew the magnitude of his loss. He was overcome with remorse that he had left Scotland when she was dying. He was sunk in grief. He was also badgered by domestic problems at Auchinleck, and the difficulty of making plans for the children — all these trials he now had to face alone. The summer offered little comfort and no opportunity to work on his book.

In contrast, Mrs. Piozzi's summer was extremely happy. Her *Observations and Reflections Made in the Course of a Journey through France, Italy, and Germany* (two volumes, of about 400 pages each) appeared in June,[100] and in that month she and Piozzi, with Cecilia, started for Scotland. As before, Piozzi would rather have gone to Italy, and she would have too, but fear that Cecilia might be taken from her custody if they undertook such a journey made them plan a tour to the Hebrides instead. Those who watched her progress may well have thought that she was following in Johnson's and Boswell's footsteps, and that her next book might be a feminine version of their journey.

But Mrs. Piozzi made it clear to her friends that Johnson, not Boswell, was her inspiration and guide. She wrote to Mrs. Byron,[101] about Johnson's *Journey*, " 'Tis one of his first Rate Performances — I look it over now every day with double Delight," and then with sudden and uncalled-for asperity, "Oh how the Scotch do detest him!" [102] The Piozzis' Tour to the Hebrides never took place; bad weather and her ill health prevented it; the party advanced no farther than the Lowlands (at one point they were not far from Auchinleck).

It was in Edinburgh on July 7th that she heard the good news from Lysons and Lort of the success of her *Observations and Reflections*. Despite considerable criticism that her writing was too colloquial ("to read twenty pages and hear Mrs Piozzi talk for twenty minutes is the

---

[98] Boswell's *Book of Company*. Entry for Sunday, 7 June 1789.

[99] Margaret Montgomerie Boswell died on Thursday the 4th of June at three in the morning. (Boswell to Lord Lonsdale, 8 June 1789. *Boswell Papers*, XVII, 160.)

[100] *Clifford*, p. 343.

[101] See note 4 above.

[102] Mrs. Piozzi to Mrs. Byron, 11 July 1789. MS. Letter: Rylands Eng. MS. 546/19. *Clifford*, p. 349.

same thing," said her friend, Leonard Chappelow) [103] and despite its inconsequential subject matter and superficial treatment, the book of travels was generally well received. *The Morning Post*, as usual, condemned her, but *The World* and other papers were full of praise. The book was widely read and enjoyed. Her "Fame" increased.

By the end of August the Piozzis made their way to Wales, where they visited Mrs. Piozzi's friends and relations in the Vale of Clwyd, and took care of her Welsh business problems. She claimed to "know no more of Business" than little Cecilia,[104] but fortunately her musical husband, though untrained to administrative tasks, became exceedingly proficient in handling her financial affairs. From Wales, the Piozzis journeyed to Bath, and there had an enjoyable stay, surrounded and admired by many members of their new circle. Not until December 23rd did they return to Hanover Square, and there the pleasures of the London season lay ahead.

Boswell's life offered a bleak contrast. He had campaigned unsuccessfully in Ayrshire, and later had been obliged to go on the Northern Circuit, where he had been insulted by Lord Lonsdale and his men. On October 1st he made his sad departure from Auchinleck, returning to London with all of his children except Euphemia, whom he left in a boarding school in Edinburgh.

In his rented house in Queen Anne Street,[105] he worked along on the *Life* without heart, often idle, often in low company, often intoxicated, and always depressed. "Many a time have I thought of giving it up,"

[103] The Rev. Leonard Chappelow was a former librarian of Trinity College, Cambridge, a classical scholar, naturalist, and would-be poet. He met the Piozzis in April 1786, when their coach broke down in the Apennines. He and his fellow-traveler effected their rescue.

[104] Mrs. Piozzi to Mrs. Byron, 19 September 1789. MS. Letter: Rylands Eng. MS. 546/24. *Clifford*, p. 350.

[105] Number 38 Queen Anne Street West, Cavendish Square. A year before, when his wife was still alive, Boswell had written to her in Scotland (28 November 1788, *Boswell Papers*, XVII, 131): "I am quite sorry to leave our Queen Street House [the Hoole house where she been with the children], and as yet have found none that I could possess with any satisfaction. However, one *must* be got."

For a while he found nothing and considered selling his furniture and going into chambers, but his wife had advised him to continue his search. He settled upon 38 Queen Anne Street West. This location had the great advantage of being near Malone.

Now, in December 1789, Boswell "retook my house for another half year. I thought this might do well to keep near Malone." *Boswell Papers*, XVIII, 10 (12 December 1789).

he wrote Temple.[106]   He had a constant, sinking sense of failure: he used the word often in his Journal. This sense of failure and his lack of any other opportunities were the negative forces which drove him on. His hopes of attaining consequence and wealth were gone; there was only one way left for him to achieve his ambition of "Fame" — the "*Life of Dr. Johnson*, the most important, perhaps *now* the only, concern of any consequence that I ever shall have in this world! "[107] He worked on, saw Malone, revised with Malone, revised and revised.

1790

Determinedly, on the 1st of January, Boswell delivered the copy for his Introduction to Henry Baldwin, the printer, "that I might say my Book was *at* if not *in* the press on Newyear's day. The honest, friendly Printer was a little gruff about my mode of carrying on the Work, but I made allowance for him."[108] Though the book was *at* press, Boswell and Malone had not yet gone over the second half of the manuscript, and they were making constant changes. They revised almost daily, Boswell composed, and copy was sent, when it could be, to press. :

On the 11th of January, after a computation, it was determined that there would be some 416,000 words in the book, and Baldwin felt there would have to be two volumes.[109] This was bad news, as it meant added expense, but Malone had a scheme to over-run the type and keep 1000 copies in readiness for sale, whenever the quarto edition would be exhausted; Boswell was pleased by this.

Progress on the *Life* was being followed in the newspapers, *The Morning Post* reporting that Boswell had been assailed "by much importunity, to expunge" all that might be unfavorable to Mrs. Piozzi.[110] The same paper noted on February 22nd that Mrs. Piozzi was thought to look with terror upon the approaching biography, but *The Morning Post* assured its readers that Boswell was "honest and benevolent" and was "pursuing an Eagle," not plucking "a feather from a *tom tit*."[111]

[106] Boswell to Temple, 28–30 November 1789. MS. Letter: Pierpont Morgan Library. *Waingrow*, p. 291.

[107] *Boswell Papers*, XVIII, 286 (30 June 1790).

[108] *Ibid*., 14 (1 January 1790).

[109] Boswell suggested printing the *Life* in folio rather than the two quarto volumes. Malone said that he "might as well throw it into the Thames," for no one would read a folio. *Ibid*., 20 (13 January 1790).

[110] *Morning Post*, "1790." (No *) *Boswell Newspaper Paragraphs*. Yale (P100–4).

[111] *Morning Post*, 22 February 1790. (No *) Yale (P100–5). On 21 September

Boswell, the widower, was managing his existence in London more satisfactorily than might have been predicted. Grief for his wife was still painful, and he found the supervision of his children irksome and worrying, but his friends were kind and sympathetic. Malone and Courtenay gave him companionship and kept him hard at work, and popular Sir Joshua, "in the constant enjoyment of his art and the best Society," [112] always welcomed his company.

On the 3rd of February Boswell dined at the Turk's Head with Reynolds, Holman the actor, and others; [113] and as upon an earlier occasion under Sir Joshua's aegis, Boswell's fancy soared, not verse this time, but a drama; Mrs. Piozzi had tried her hand with an Epilogue,[114] he would attempt a five-act tragedy, to be called *Favras*.[115] The title character, the Marquis de Favras, was a gallant aristocrat, much in the news at the moment (and the night before Boswell had been "Very warm ag[ains]t [the] french Revolutionists").[116] The Marquis de Favras had tried to effect the flight of King Louis XVI and his family in October 1789, but failing, had been arrested and charged with "plotting a counter revolution." He was at the moment imprisoned, about to be executed. Boswell thought his friend, John Kemble (star of *The Regent*) would fill the tragic role perfectly, and wrote on the scrap of paper: "They say a Playwright I am a Play Taylor I shall fit on the part on my freind Jack by & by. I shall lace it or embroider it for him." [117] He continued with a mock letter to Mrs. Piozzi: [118]

Mr Boswell's comps to M^{rs} P and requests she may let him have a battering ram as a prologue to introduce his Play to the hearts of the Ladies

---

1790, *The Diary* was to report: "Mr. BOSWELL has erased from his intended biography of JOHNSON whatever was calculated to wound the feelings of Mrs PIOZZI." *Boswell Newspaper Paragraphs*. (No *) Yale (101–2).

[112] Boswell to Malone, 12 July 1788. See note 75 above.

[113] *Boswell Papers*, XVIII, 27 (3 February 1790).

[114] Epilogue written for Bertie Greatheed's *The Regent*; see note 69 above.

[115] "[While] the Press pursues its slow, but steady motion, with his Biography of JOHNSON, it seems the 'Tory Soul' of BOSWELL is employed upon a Tragedy, of which the subject is . . . deeply interesting. It is the Death of FAVRAS, one of the ultimi *Romanorum*, the faithful and heroic Martyr for the Monarchy of France," *The World*, 13 March 1790. See Lucyle Werkmeister, "Jemmie Boswell and the London Daily Press, 1785–1795," *Bulletin of the New York Public Library*, LXVII (1963), 96.

[116] *Boswell Papers*, XVIII, 26 (2 February 1790).

[117] *Favras*. MS. notes. Yale (M84.2).

[118] *Favras*. MS. notes. Yale (M855).

He also composed her reply:

Mʳˢ P's comps to Mʳ B She would gladly enable him to please the Ladies but has at present no battering ram to spare

Boswell was in high spirits — he would dedicate his play to the Empress of Russia! A great deal of merriment was had by all. "A great deal of noise," Boswell recorded in his Journal, "Heated myself somewhat." [119]

Drama and the "battering-ram," in its full erotic connotation, were much in mind, and within a few days Boswell let his fancy play with something else, a supposed entertainment given by Mrs. Piozzi upon the occasion, as he imagined it, of her revisiting the Thrale Brewhouse with her new husband. Boswell, as an artist, disliked wasting good material: dramatic situations, telling words and phrases. If these were suppressed in a serious piece, through his own good judgment or by the persuasion of others, they often reappeared in a satiric *jeu d'esprit*. This imaginary account of the Brewhouse Entertainment is a collection of things saved, among which are bits salvaged from Mrs. Piozzi's supposed verses from Italy.[120] The *Ode* is recalled, and *Favras* is not forgotten. John Kemble, the chosen hero of this play, was to be called on again.

Boswell reported the forthcoming event in the friendly *Morning Post*: [121] the Brewhouse Entertainment, he promised:

is to be truly a *Mischianza*,[122] a medley of tragedy, comedy, music, oratory; in short, of everything . . .

A grand procession is to take place, in which Mr. JOHN KEMBLE is to walk in the character of *Hamlet*, holding two miniature pictures, and repeating the well-known comparative passage, —
  'This WAS your husband,' &c.

And Signor SASTRES, the Italian master (to whom Dr. JOHNSON left 5 £.) is to exhibit himself in the fantastical dress of *Il Mercurio Italico*, for which Sir JOHN GALLINI [123] has obligingly lent him his best pair of wings.

  By way of *ground*-work there is to be a solemn dirge:
  "Down among the dead men let him lie."

[119] *Boswell Papers*, XVIII, 27 (3 February 1790).

[120] Yale MS. 310. See p. 113 above.

[121] *Morning Post*, [c. 22 February or 3 March]. *Boswell Newspaper Paragraphs*. Yale (P117-3*).

[122] Italian for "a jumble."

[123] Sir John Gallini (Giovanni Andrea, 1728–1805), dancing master, ballet dancer, and manager of the London Opera House. In the capacity of dancing master, he had met the third Earl of Abingdon's eldest daughter, won her heart, and married her.

After which, all on a sudden, a brisk *fugue* is to be played, and
    "Viva, viva la Padrona,"
To be sung by a troop of jolly *brewers*, carefully instructed by Signor SASTRES . . .

BARETTI's ghost next rises, and frowns upon the Signora; she, however, not abashed, vaults upon a *black ram*, reciting —
    "And for my Crinkum Crankum," [124] &c.
Parson ESTE [125] has, in the politest manner, engaged to present the *black ram*.

The principal air is to be —
    "By the hollow *cask* we are told
    How nobly *Thrale's entire* has sold";
accompanied by a band of *barrel*-organs: after which will be sung the good old glee,
    "He that has the best wife
    She's the plague of his life," &c
with the chorus of—
    "And ten times a day hoop her *barrel*"
The butchers of the Borough have orders to attend with their marrow-bones and cleavers.

But what has excited the most eager impatience in the ladies of Southwark is, a report that the Signora is to give after dinner, an *improvisation*, founded on the much famed line in her Prologue to the tragedy of *The Regent*,
    "And drives his *battering ram* FULL at your heart."

Boswell's flow of spirits continued during the spring; and he puffed his embryonic *Favras* in *The Public Advertiser*, "Boswell's tragedy against the Revolution in France." (His hero had been executed in Paris on February 19th.) "[W]ild-verse" it would be, "And Boswell's boisterous verse make[s] Frenchmen quake." [126]

During April and May a good deal of work was accomplished, but in June the situation changed abruptly. Boswell, though he protested, was obliged to go again to Carlisle for Lord Lonsdale. During Boswell's absence from London, Malone superintended the *Life of John-*

---

[124] "Crinkum crankum." A word that applies playfully to anything full of twists and turns. "Old Rime" in *Blount Law Dictionary*, 1670: "Here I am . . . Like a Whore as I am. And for my *Crincum Crancum* Have lost my *Binkum Bankum*."

[125] Charles Este was editor of *The World*. He was a member of the group in which Mrs. Piozzi moved, and his paper defended her in her social and literary quarrels.

[126] *Public Advertiser*, 24 March 1790. *Boswell Newspaper Paragraphs*. (Boswell *) Yale (P117-7). "Boswell having boasted that the couplet at the end of his fourth Act, which finishes with 'GOD save the King!' would undoubtedly secure *that* Act, his friend Courtenay pleasantly observed, 'I would have you end every Act with it.'"

son at press, but Malone was planning a trip to Ireland soon, and as the days passed, Boswell's impatience and melancholy increased, for the hours were being wasted in Carlisle "which you could now have given me for revising my M.S. and . . . perhaps you may be gone before I get back to town." [127] In the end, the treatment of Lord Lonsdale and his men was so humiliating that Boswell gave in his resignation of the Recordership, and returned to London. Luckily, Malone was still on hand when Boswell resumed his labors in mid-July. By then 300 pages of the book had been printed, but more than 350 pages of the manuscript had not as yet been gone over by Malone.

They now worked together under pressure, a desperate pressure for Boswell because of the imminence of Malone's departure. Boswell faced another anxiety as well. The past September the property of Knockroon, which about two hundred years before had belonged to the estate of Auchinleck, had come up for sale. Boswell could not bear to see "a piece of — as it were the flesh and blood of the family, in the hands of a stranger." [128] With the added expenses of the second volume of the *Life*, he had no right to consider its purchase. But he did; he contracted to pay £2500 for Knockroon: £1500 he was able to "borrow upon itself by a mortgage" [129] but as for the remaining £1000 needed, he had no idea how it might be raised. The offer for his manuscript of the *Life*, which he had written Bennet Langton about in April,[130] was tempting; George Robinson, the bookseller and publisher, had offered that amount to buy the copyright of his *Life of Johnson*.[131]

If he could only realize money from his own publication! By October, 56 pages of Volume II were in print,[132] but by mid-November Malone had gone to Ireland and progress was difficult. By early December, however, Boswell was able to write that 216 pages [133] were printed, and by the middle of the month, 256 pages.[134] Boswell was

---

[127]Boswell to Malone, 30 June 1790. MS. Letter: Yale (L942). *Boswell Papers*, XVIII, 284–287.

[128] Boswell to Malone, 29 January 1791. MS. Letter: Hyde.

[129]*Boswell Papers*, XVIII, 287–288, n. 1 (September 1790).

[130]Boswell to Bennet Langton, 9 April 1790. "Only think of what an offer I have for it — *A Cool thousand*. But I am advised to retain the property myself." MS. Letter: British Museum. *Waingrow*, p. 313.

[131]Boswell to Sir William Forbes, 2 July 1790. MS. Letter: Somervell Papers. A précis in *Waingrow*, p. 329.

[132]Boswell to his son, Sandie, 5 October 1790. MS. Letter: Hyde. *Boswell Papers*, XVIII, 289.

[133]Boswell to Malone, 4 December 1790. MS. Letter: Hyde. *Waingrow*, p. 353.

[134]Boswell to Malone, 16 December 1790. MS. Letter: Hyde. *Waingrow*, p. 353.

querying his adviser on many points, and Malone gave return advice and such cautions as to "take care of colloquialisms & vulgarisms of all sorts. Condense as much as possible, always preserving perspicuity & do not imagine the *only* defect of stile, is repetition of words." [135] Beyond the problems of the book, Malone was genuinely concerned about Boswell's state of health and mind; he seemed to be in a very low state. Malone asked if his depression might not be owing to "almost uniform intemperance in wine?" It was "surely *unwise* to indulge in such excesses *habitually*, and . . . the sure consequence of wild and intemperate riot for one half the year, must be the lowest depression during the other." [136]

Courtenay, who the last autumn had urged him not to give up the "Joys of wine," now took his "word and honour that till the first of [March 1791, his] allowance of wine per diem should not exceed four good glasses at dinner, and a pint after it — and this [pledge Boswell had] kept." [137] Despite resolution and industry, however, it was certain that there would be no publication of the *Life* in 1790.

During this year Mrs. Piozzi did not torment Boswell with any literary production; her vitality was absorbed in activity of a different nature — the re-establishment of her household at Streatham. The house had been leased to various tenants since 1782 and was much run down. Now, she spent over two thousand pounds on renovation and decorating. She filled the rooms with treasures acquired on the Continent, and under Piozzi's guidance, she transformed the Johnsonian house into an Italian villa. To celebrate the sixth anniversary of her marriage to Piozzi, she gave a lavish party — seventy friends for a seated dinner, thirty-six of them at "an immensely long Table in the Library."

The Plate so fine too, the China so showy, all so magnificent, and at the Time of Dinner Horns Clarinets &c wch afterwards performed upon the Water in our new Boat that makes such a beautiful, such an elegant Figure.

Never was a pleasanter Day seen, nor Weather half as favourable: the Setting Sun, & the full moon rising, were wonderfully happy Additions; and at Night

---

[135] Malone to Boswell, 23 December 1790. MS. Letter: Yale (C1921). *Waingrow*, p. 375.

[136] "Your account of yourself for sometime past is very deplorable." Malone to Boswell, 5 March 1791. MS. Letter: Yale (C1925). Portion quoted in text not in *Waingrow*.

[137] Boswell to Malone, 4 December 1790. MS. Letter: Hyde. Portion quoted not in *Waingrow*.

the Trees & Front of the House were illuminated with Colour'd Lamps, that called forth our Neighbours from all the adjacent Villages to admire & enjoy such Diversion. Many Friends swear that not less than a Thousand Men Women & Children might have been counted in the House & Grounds . . .[138]

Such was the welcome given the new Master of Streatham Park!

1791

In January Boswell moved from Queen Anne Street West to Great Portland Street.[139] He labored on with the *Life* "sluggishly and comfortlessly." Malone's continued absence in Ireland was a heavy loss and whenever he passed by his door, he "cast many a longing look." [140] "Your absence is a woeful want in all respects," he wrote, and "You will I dare say perceive a difference in the part [of the *Life*] which is revised only by myself . . ." [141] On the 10th of February Boswell reported that 488 pages of the second volume were in print and only 80 pages of copy remained, "besides the Death, as to which I shall be concise though solemn — Also many letters. Pray how shall I wind up. Shall I give the Character in my *Tour*, somewhat enlarged?" [142]

In the same letter he asked Malone what he had determined should be done about the Robinson offer. Malone was to decide. Boswell would follow his advice, though he was "very, very unwilling" to part with the copyright, and certainly would not if he could find "credit for £1000 for three or four years." Courtenay favored the sale of copyright,[143] and when Boswell talked to Dilly, this friendly publisher also pressed him to accept the £1000 from Robinson; but Boswell, characteristically loyal, could not bear to disassociate himself from Dilly "with whom [his] name had been so long connected." [144]

On Shrove Tuesday (March 8th) Boswell was able to write Malone that money matters were not so sad as before, in fact they had improved very much. Dilly and Baldwin each promised a £200 advance credit on

---

[138] *Thraliana*, II, 775 (28 July 1790).

[139] He moved 19 January 1791. Ill and depressed, he recorded in his Journal (21 February 1791; *Boswell Papers*, XVIII, 108), "I abhorred my new house, from my having been dismal ever since I came into it." Despite his dislike of the Great Portland Street house, Boswell was to live there until he died (19 May 1795).

[140] Boswell to Malone, 29 January 1791. MS. Letter: Hyde. *Waingrow*, p. 383.

[141] Boswell to Malone, 18 January 1791. MS. Letter: Hyde. *Waingrow*, p. 380.

[142] Boswell to Malone, 10 February 1791. MS. Letter: Hyde. *Waingrow*, p. 384.

[143] Boswell to Malone, 12 March 1791. MS. Letter: Hyde. *Waingrow*, p. 392.

[144] *Boswell Papers*, XVIII, 107 (20 February 1791).

the *Life* and he had been able to secure £600 credit on his rents in Scotland, "thus I shall get the £1000 [for Knockroon] paid in May." Boswell was "quite resolved now to keep the property of [his] *Magnum Opus*," and he flattered himself that he should not repent it. "I hope[d] to have published today," he wrote, but instead he looked at the printed pages before him, "560 pages of Vol. 2 & I fear I shall have 20 more." [145]

On the 14th of March he wrote his son, Sandie, at Eton: "I am now *writing* the *last sheet* of my Book . . . I mean to publish on the 15 of next month." [146] But this was not to be. On the 6th of April he was "correcting the last sheet" [147] and hoped for publication on the 25th of the month — but this was not to be either — the middle of May was now predicted. This postponement permitted Boswell to select a day of good omen, and he chose what was probably the most appropriate date of all the year — May 16th.

On the twenty-eighth anniversary of Boswell's meeting with Johnson, his Magnum Opus appeared — *The Life of Samuel Johnson, LL.D. . . .* by James Boswell, Esq. printed by Henry Baldwin for Charles Dilly.[148] This was the finished creation: the "constant plan" which, during Johnson's lifetime, had been a pleasure and diversion but which after Johnson's death had become a monstrous thing, obsessive and destructive, demanding the sacrifice of family happiness, career, and self-respect. Now finally — after Johnson had been gone for more than six years, and as many biographies had already appeared — the terrible labor was ended. Boswell had produced his Magnum Opus, activity for him was over; it was now up to the public to give judgment.

[145] Boswell to Malone, 8 March 1791. MS. Letter: Hyde. *Waingrow*, p. 392. March 8th was the publication date hoped for the past December; but when the time came Boswell was still composing. Volume II was swelling to almost 600 pages, and he feared it would look awkward beside Volume I (516 pages).

[146] Boswell to his son, Sandie, 14 March 1791. MS. Letter: Arthur A. Houghton, Jr. *Waingrow*, p. lxxiv.

[147] Boswell to Temple, 6 April 1791. MS. Letter: Pierpont Morgan Library. *Waingrow*, p. lxxv.

[148] The edition (referred to hereafter as *Life First Edition*) was 1,750 copies, two large quarto volumes, issued in blue-gray boards; 516 pages in Vol. I; 586 pages in Vol. II (the last page incorrectly numbered "588"). Thomas Tomlins, a corrector at Baldwin's press, had ingeniously suggested "thickening" Vol. I by *prefixing* the Index. (*Waingrow*, p. 382, n. 4). Boswell had also effected some cutting, so that the two volumes looked much the same size in the end.

The book was an immediate sensation. Despite the stiff price of two guineas, eight hundred sets were sold in the first week or so.[149] And, since we have been following the King's reaction: he was highly enthusiastic. At a levee he spoke about the *Life* with Burke, who said "it was the Most entertaining Book he had ever read."[150] "My *Magnum Opus* sells wonderfully," Boswell reported to Temple in August: "1200 are now gone and we hope the whole 1700 [*sic*, for 1750] may be gone before Christmas."[151]

Boswell, however, did not feel the exhilaration one would have expected at the end of his long travail, crowned with success. He felt too exhausted from the effort itself, and the leisure which now came gave him time to consider the career which he had abandoned in order to complete the undertaking. Though he had long tried, Boswell had not been able to "convince himself that the *Life of Johnson* was a sufficient reason for his existence."[152] He considered himself a failure; and the book was a symbol of defeat.

He did feel satisfaction, though, in having achieved the purpose to which he had dedicated himself. He had written the biography according to the theory he and Johnson shared. He had presented his subject faithfully, showing virtues, but not ignoring faults, showing talents and achievements, the strong qualities that made the man remarkable and revered, but not omitting the weaknesses which made him human. He had considered the whole judiciously and given what he believed was the right interpretation, well proportioned.

During the course of the narrative, Boswell had found opportunities to correct what he believed was Mrs. Piozzi's false and deprecating interpretation of Johnson. A serious charge was that in discussing his morbid melancholy she had followed Hawkins' dark hint of insanity; in this Boswell was unfair, for she had suppressed evidence she had on the subject.[153] He also dealt harshly with her account of the origin of

[149] Frederick A. Pottle, *The Literary Career of James Boswell, Esq.* (Oxford: Clarendon Press, 1929), p. 167.

[150] Boswell asked Burke if he would take the trouble to write him a statement of this interview for his "Archives at Auchinleck." Boswell to Burke, 16 July 1791. MS. Letter: Yale (L335). *Waingrow*, p. 426.

[151] Boswell to Temple, 22 August 1791. MS. Letter: Pierpont Morgan Library. *Waingrow*, pp. lxxv–lxxvi.

[152] Frederick A. Pottle, comment in *Boswell Papers*, XVIII, xix.

[153] *Anecdotes*, pp. 77, 127. Sir John Hawkins, *The Life of Samuel Johnson, LL.D.* (London, 1787), pp. 287–288. *Life*, I, 66. In *Life Limited Edition* Mrs. Piozzi made no comment on this passage.

Johnson's religious belief, composing a lengthy footnote on her "strange fantastical account" (*Anecdotes*, p. 17). In the first proof of this passage, Malone's hand, as well as Boswell's, is visible in the corrections.[154]

Under the year 1763 (the event actually took place the year before)[155] Boswell told the authentic story of Dr. Johnson's rescuing Oliver Goldsmith from his landlady's arrest for failure to pay rent. Both Mrs. Piozzi and Sir John Hawkins, he claimed, "have strangely mis-stated the history of Goldsmith's situation and Johnson's friendly interference."[156] In the first proof was the direction, "Note Paper marked P,"[157] and the resulting footnote appeared in the revised proof: "It may not be improper to annex here Mrs. Piozzi's account of this transaction, in her own words, as a specimen of the extreme inaccuracy with which all her anecdotes of Dr. Johnson are related, or rather discoloured and distorted."[158] Mrs. Piozzi's version of the Goldsmith story followed.

At the point in 1767 when Boswell wrote that he had "received no letter from Johnson this year; nor have I discovered any of the correspondence he had, except the two letters to Mr. Drummond," the Edinburgh bookseller, he gave this footnote:

It is proper here to mention, that when I speak of his correspondence, I consider it independent of the voluminous collection of letters which, in the course of many years, he wrote to Mrs. Thrale, which forms a separate part of his works; and as a proof of the high estimation set on any thing which came from his pen, was sold by that lady for the sum of five hundred pounds.[159]

Boswell's feelings on the subject of Mrs. Piozzi's edition of Johnson's Letters were very strong, and the mere mention of her publication was apt to provoke some version of this statement.

---

[154] *Life First Proof* (Hyde), I, 29–30. *Life*, I, 68–69. In *Life Limited Edition*, I, 33–34, Mrs. Piozzi's note is: "he told me this *himself*; I did not dream it, & could not have invented it, or heard it from others. I will *Swear* he told me as I told the Public . . ."

[155] *Life*, I, 416, n. 2.

[156] *Life*, I, 415: referring to *Anecdotes*, p. 119, and *Hawkins*, pp. 420–421.

[157] *Life First Proof* (Hyde), I, 224.

[158] *Life Revised Proof* (Hyde), I, 225, n. 9. *Life*, I, 416, n. 2.

[159] *Life Revised Proof* (Hyde), I, 296, n. 7. *Life*, II, 43, n. 1. In Mrs. Piozzi's edition of *Johnson's Letters*, the year 1767 is represented by one letter to Mrs. Salusbury, "Mother to the Editor," and two to herself. The Chapman edition of *Johnson's Letters* gives fifteen for the year 1767, and at least one more is now known.

No detail of inaccuracy was too trivial to escape criticism, including Mrs. Piozzi's inability to read Johnson's handwriting. In one of his letters to her, Mrs. Knowles, the Quaker, was mentioned. In Boswell's hand in the revised proof is the note:

Dr. Johnson describing her needlework in one of his letters to Mrs. Thrale Vol. I, p. 326 uses the learned word *sutile*; which Mrs. Thrale [deletion] has mistaken, and made the phrase injurious by printing '*futile* pictures' [160]

Mrs. Piozzi had already been much twitted about the word "futile" in her edition of the *Letters*. Her advisor, Dr. Lort, always interested in little things, was even asked to give a close examination of the original letter to determine a wager. And in more recent times added pleasure has been had at her expense; the editors of *The Oxford English Dictionary* give Johnson's sentence as an illustration for "sutile" (made or done by stitching or sewing). An examination of the original letter reveals a clear, long, characteristic Johnson "s"; a dash through it has been added, but the manufactured "f" could not have fooled Dr. Lort any more than it would fool a twentieth-century scholar.[161]

Boswell drew attention to the fact that Mrs. Piozzi tampered with and improved her own letters. He exhibited an unimproved specimen (the letter which caused her fright in 1787), remarking that it would probably amuse his readers "more than those well-written but studied epistles which she has inserted in her collection, because it exhibits the easy vivacity of their literary intercourse." [162] In the revised proof Boswell gave the marginal direction, "Pray compare Mrs Thrale's letter very carefully." The answer was returned, "We have no Copy to compare it by," to which he replied, "I have now compared it & have made it exact — *wench* not *girl* and an addition before the * * * *" The addition was that Thrale "has got a dawling companion to ride with him now." The * * * * perhaps stimulated the imagination, but in actuality the phrase suppressed was merely, "Captain Cotton who married Miss Aston." [163]

On the subject of Mrs. Piozzi's deletions of Boswell's name from her

---

[160] *Life Revised Proof* (Hyde), II, 223. In the margin is Boswell's direction to the printer: "If the *note* can be printed without deranging the presswork, well — If not leave it out." It was fitted in, *Life First Edition*, II, 223. *Life*, III, 284, n. 4.

[161] Johnson to Mrs. Thrale, 16 May 1776. MS. Letter: Hyde. Letter #479. *Letters*, II, 131.

[162] *Life Revised Proof* (Hyde), II, 313–314. *Life*, III, 421. See page 119 above.

[163] MS. Letter: Hyde. Letter #662a. *Letters*, II, 349.

edition of Johnson's *Letters* there was little reference; perhaps by this time he had become convinced that her cuts had not been so extensive as he had once supposed. There was a restrained footnote comment, though, after quoting from Johnson's letter to Mrs. Thrale, of the 21st of June 1780 ("I have had with me a brother of Boswell's, a Spanish merchant"): "Mrs. Piozzi has omitted the name, she best knows why." [164] His treatment of the bitter grievance of omission in a low key is a clear example of improvement caused by the passage of time and calmer judgment.

It was now his turn to exert the power of omission, and he did so in his treatment of Mrs. Thrale as an important character in the narrative. Her influence over Johnson for almost twenty years could not be ignored, but Boswell showed it in what he claimed was proper proportion to the influence of others. He minimized her importance, omitting numerous mentions from his Journals. Sometimes he revised to give a less flattering picture, and sometimes he developed a compliment into a criticism. [165] He took special pains to separate Mrs. Thrale from her husband, whenever possible placing her in opposition to Thrale, contrasting his strengths and virtues with her weaknesses and faults. He avoided giving opinions of his own; others spoke for him, often Johnson himself:

Johnson had a very sincere esteem for Mr. Thrale, as a man of excellent principles, a good scholar, well skilled in trade, of a sound understanding, and of manners such as presented the character of a plain independent English 'Squire. As this family will frequently be mentioned in the course of the following pages, and as a false notion has prevailed that Mr. Thrale was inferiour, and in some degree insignificant, compared with Mrs. Thrale, it may be proper

---

[164] *Life Revised Proof* (Hyde), II, 321, n. 7 (Piozzi *Letters*, II, 163). MS. Letter: Yale. Letter #684. Letters, II, 376. *Life*, III, 434.

[165] Examples:

Omission. (For September 1769. Papers Apart, 349. Yale.) Johnson delivered Boswell a card in the "fair handwriting" of Mrs. Thrale. Boswell preserved the card as his "first ticket to a great deal of most agreable [*sic*] society." The text of the letter followed. Omitted in *Life*, II, 77.

Presenting a less complimentary picture. (18 April 1778. Journal. J. 55 Yale.) After Johnson told Boswell that Mrs. Thrale had sneered at his invitation for the Boswells to stay at his house.

Boswell: "She is a good woman." Omitted in *Life*, III, 316.

Bland note developed into strong criticism. (30 March 1778. Journal. J.55 Yale.) "Fine Mrs. Thrale." In *Life*, III, 226, Mrs. Thrale told Boswell's story of an old man as an "old *woman*," and Boswell, in Johnson's presence, criticized her for inaccuracy.

to give a true state of the case from the authority of Johnson himself, in his own words.

"I know no man, (said he,) who is more master of his wife and family than Thrale. If he but holds up a finger, he is obeyed. It is a great mistake to suppose that she is above him in literary attainments. She is more flippant; but he has ten times her learning: he is a regular scholar; but her learning is that of a school-boy in one of the lower forms." [166]

In the paragraph, Boswell continued by describing Thrale as "tall, well proportioned, and stately. As for *Madam*, or *my Mistress*, by which epithets Johnson used to mention Mrs. Thrale, she was short, plump, and brisk." [167]

Boswell went on to say that Thrale:

understood and valued Johnson, without remission, from their first acquaintance to the day of his death. Mrs. Thrale was enchanted with Johnson's conversation for its own sake, and had also a very allowable vanity in appearing to be honoured with the attention of so celebrated a man.

Nothing could be more fortunate for Johnson than this connection. He had at Mr. Thrale's all the comforts and even luxuries of life; his melancholy was diverted, and his irregular habits lessened by association with an agreeable and well-ordered family. He was treated with the utmost respect, and even affection. The vivacity of Mrs. Thrale's literary talk roused him to cheerfulness and exertion, even when they were alone. But this was not often the case . . . [168]

This picture of Mrs. Thrale was at the beginning of Johnson's friendship, and though Mrs. Thrale was said to be a superficial scholar and not alluring in appearance, she was still made out to be vivacious, attentive and affectionate toward the new and celebrated member of the family. And the setting of the Thrale household was shown to provide all the dreams Johnson could have of family happiness. As the years passed, many instances were given of Mrs. Thrale's flightiness, flippancy, and above all her inattention to truth — but hers was not a dark portrait.

It was in the year 1784 that the characterization became harsh: Mrs. Thrale, the widow, foolish in her behavior and indifferent to Johnson. In the manuscript of the *Life* Boswell wrote that on the 16th of May

[166] *Life*, I, 494. In her annotations Mrs. Piozzi made no defense of herself. Her only significant remark on this passage for our purpose was on "English 'Squire": "no no; Mr. Thrale's manners presented the Character of a Gay Man of the *Town*: like Millamant in Congreve's Comedy, he abhorred the Country & Every thing in it." *Life Limited Edition*, I, 352.

[167] *Idem.*

[168] *Life*, I, 495–496.

1784 he found Johnson alone and listened to him talk with much concern about Mrs. Thrale. This deleted passage follows:

I could not imagine what disturbed him, for I had heard nothing to her disadvantage. He said: "Sir she has done every thing wrong since Thrale's bridle was off her neck. You must know there was an Italian Singer" — Here Dᴿ Douglas now Bishop of Carlisle was announced, and Johnson was interrupted in explaining himself to me upon a subject / an affair [written above] / which has since made much noise, but which being then totally unsuspected by me, I never afterwards asked him about it, which if I had done, I have no doubt that by my peculiar ease in questioning him I should have heard what would have been well worth being recorded.[169]

In the printed text Boswell revised this to:

On Sunday, May 16, I found him alone; he talked of Mrs. Thrale with much concern, saying, "Sir, she has done every thing wrong, since Thrale's bridle was off her neck"; and was proceeding to mention some circumstances which have since been the subject of publick discussion, when he was interrupted by the arrival of Dr. Douglas, now Bishop of Carlisle.[170]

The most difficult point in his treatment of Mrs. Thrale concerned the events two months later, in July 1784 — her final desertion of Johnson and her marriage to Piozzi. Boswell was apprehensive about this section and when, on the 22nd of February (1791), Courtenay came to Great Portland Street to have "hodgepodge," Boswell was wise enough to consult with him. Courtenay was his mainstay now, since Malone was still in Ireland. It was "about ten" when Courtenay arrived, having been kept late at the House of Commons; Boswell's other guests had gone, but Courtenay was offered his promised "hodgepodge and a bit of roast beef," and then, despite the advanced hour, the two set to work. As Boswell recorded in his Journal, Courtenay "obligingly assisted me in *lightening* my animadversions on Mrs. Piozzi in my *Life of Johnson* — for my own credit. His manly mind conveyed to me some sympathetick force." [171] This expresses well the power that Courtenay, as well as Malone, had over Boswell, the ability

[169] *Life* MS. (Yale), l. 929.
[170] *Life Revised Proof* (Hyde), II, 492. *Life*, IV, 277. This paragraph prompted no marginal reaction from Mrs. Piozzi in *Life Limited Edition*, III, 349.
[171] *Boswell Papers*, XVIII, 109. I am indebted to Professor Frederick A. Pottle for his kindness in letting me see his detailed notes on the "Animadversions."
This subject has been given thorough treatment in an article, "Boswell at Work: the 'Animadversions' on Mrs. Piozzi," by Irma S. Lustig, in *The Modern Language Review*, LXVII:1 (1972), 11–30.

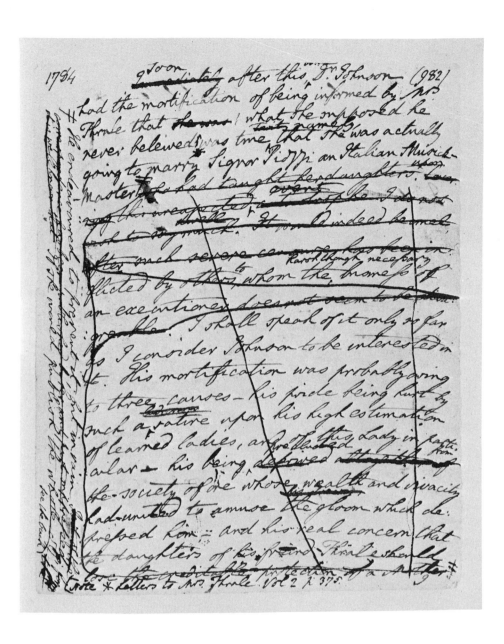

ON MRS. THRALE'S MARRIAGE TO GABRIEL PIOZZI
A PASSAGE FROM THE MANUSCRIPT OF THE
LIFE OF JOHNSON

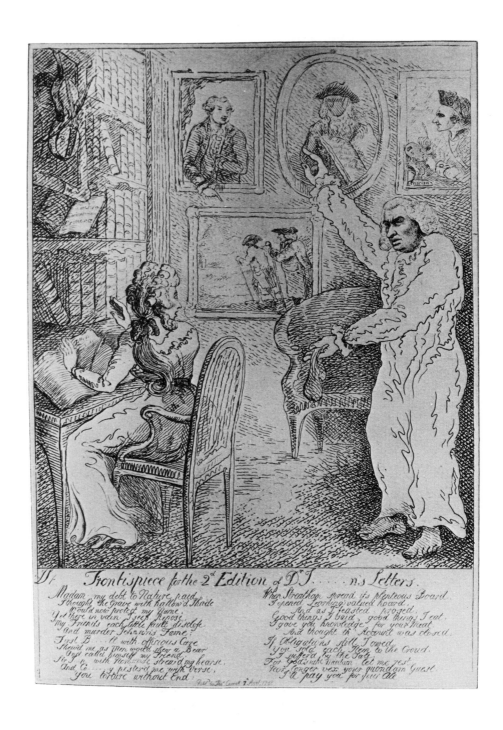

A SATIRIC SUGGESTION FOR A FRONTISPIECE TO
MRS. PIOZZI'S SECOND EDITION OF
JOHNSON'S LETTERS, 1788

to strengthen his own good judgment. The tone of his manuscript Boswell believed was right (it was not so vitriolic as one might imagine). Notwithstanding, in this final discussion of Mrs. Thrale, there were remarks of personal spleen and bits of satire which he knew should probably be deleted.

What Mrs. Thrale had done in 1784 was now past history, and for almost seven years London society had inflicted heavy censure upon her. He did not wish to give much space to her story or attach undue importance to her. He did not want to demean his book. He was interested in the "catastrophe" only so far as it concerned Johnson. Thus, with Courtenay's assistance, five sheets of his manuscript were compressed into four paragraphs. The points which Boswell wished to make about Mrs. Thrale's behavior he stated forcefully and, stripped of personal malice, the points became even stronger.

He simply let stand the statement that soon after his departure for Scotland in 1784 "Dr. Johnson had the mortification of being informed by Mrs. Thrale, that 'what she supposed he never believed,' was true, namely, that she was actually going to marry Signor Piozzi, an Italian musick-master. He endeavoured to prevent it; but in vain." [172]

He deleted the three causes of Johnson's mortification: "his pride being hurt by such a ⟨ludicrous⟩ satire upon his high estimation of learned ladies, and of this Lady in particular"; his being deprived of her lively society and the comforts of her home; and his "real concern" for "the daughters of his freind Thrale"; [173] and a fourth possible cause of mortification became a footnote, "that Johnson himself ⟨was a suitor / lover / of the Lady⟩ wished to espouse the rich widow. This I believe to be totally without any serious foundation, though I have seen him pleased to be rallied upon it." [174] As said before, these statements were followed in the manuscript by two stanzas from the *Ode*, selected "as a specimen," [175] the fifth illustrating "Jealousy of Piozzi," and the third "His own Imagined success." Boswell, doubtless with Courtenay's persuasion, cancelled the two stanzas, but information about the *Ode* was not deleted entirely. The passage was revised and transferred to p.562 of the proof, where parodies of Johnson's style were discussed.

[172] The longer passage, with deletions: *Life* MS. (Yale), l. 982. *Life Revised Proof* (Hyde), II, 528. *Life*, IV, 339.
[173] *Life* MS. (Yale), l. 982.
[174] *Ibid.*, l. 981 verso.
[175] See p. 133 above.

As an example, the first verse of an imagined Ode by Johnson on Mrs. Thrale was given — not Boswell's — but his footnote read:

Johnson's wishing to unite himself with this rich widow was much talked of, but I believe without foundation.[176] The report, however, gave occasion for a poem, not without characteristical merit, entitled, 'Ode to Mrs. Thrale, by Samuel Johnson, LL.D. on their supposed approaching Nuptials:' printed for Mr. Faulder, in Bond-street.

Boswell did not claim authorship, nor did he do so when he reprinted the footnote in the second edition. Here, however, he took the occasion to "quote as a specimen, the first three stanzas." [177]

To return to the manuscript narrative: Boswell deleted the page describing Mrs. Thrale's omissions from her published *Letters* of Johnson's "strong and earnest" attempt to avert "a very fatal measure"; and Mrs. Thrale's "high and violent" answer.[178] He revised to the single, strong general statement: "If she would publish the whole of the correspondence that passed between Dr. Johnson and her on the subject, we should have a full view of his real sentiments." [179] "As it is," he concluded, "our judgment must be biassed" by Johnson's letter to Sir John Hawkins:

Poor Thrale! I thought that either her virtue or her vice would have restrained her from such a marriage. She is now become a subject for her enemies to exult over, and for her friends, if she has any left, to forget, or pity.[180]

Boswell deleted the manuscript passage in which he had said that Mrs. Thrale "assiduously courted" Johnson, and with him "in her possession" her vanity was amply repaid by being courted "by numbers of eminent persons," turning "a Wolf dog into a lap dog." [181]

[176] *Life Revised Proof* (Hyde), II, 562, n. 6. *Life*, IV, 387. Mrs. Piozzi's marginal comment: "I believe so too!" in *Life Limited Edition*, III, 438.

[177] *Life*, Second Edition, III, 664.

[178] *Life* MS. (Yale), l. 983.

[179] Quoted from *Life Revised Proof* (Hyde), II, 528. Cf. *Life* MS. (Yale), l. 982 verso; *Life*, IV, 339.

[180] *Life* MS. (Yale), l. 982 verso. *Life Revised Proof* (Hyde), II, 528. *Life*, IV, 339. The letter was Johnson to Hawkins [July 1784]. Letter #978. *Letters*, III, 183. Hawkins published the quoted excerpt and no more of the letter in his *Life of Johnson*, p. 570.

The location of this letter has never been traced. R. W. Chapman, editor of Johnson's *Letters*, commented: "I do not remember that J elsewhere ever writes 'Thrale' in a letter. But the lack of ceremony is not necessarily contemptuous; 'Williams,' 'Burney,' &c, are quite common in his letters and diaries."

[181] *Life* MS. (Yale), l. 985.

He deleted his charge of the "pecuniary advantage which she has made of Johnson having received for her Collection of Letters alone five hundred guineas." [182] This he had already mentioned in the text which had been printed (*Life Revised Proof*, I, 296, n. 7). And apt though the lines were on the subject of "full compensation" and being "quit," he had the good sense to delete Prior's "Epigram." [183] Boswell also omitted his observation that this lady had claimed to have shown extraordinary kindness to Johnson "without which he would scarce have lived and kept his faculties entire; a cruel inuendo!" [184]

Boswell simply stated that Johnson was indebted to Henry Thrale for the enjoyment and benefit found in the family's house and he quoted Mrs. Thrale herself to prove the point: her own words from an *Anecdote*, that Johnson's presence was a "yoke" her husband put upon her and "contentedly bore his share for sixteen or seventeen years," but after his death she was unable to support the burden by herself. [185] Boswell concluded with one sentence, the only expression of his own opinion: "Alas [alas *deleted*]! how different is this from the declarations which I have heard this Lady [*originally* her] make in his lifetime without a single murmur against any of his peculiarities or against any one circumstance which attended their intimacy [*originally* or any one circumstance in / of their intimacy] . . ." [186]

It was doubtless very late by the time these revisions were settled, too late to give the same attention to leaves 986–999 of the manuscript. Boswell's handwriting, on the verso of 996, testifies to his exhaustion. This second section dealt mainly with the correction of Mrs. Piozzi's anecdotes, which gave a false impression of Johnson's character, and there are comparatively few deletions in the manuscript. The first edition text, however, has many changes and so, presumably, Boswell made further corrections and deletions in the first proof. The revise is very lightly marked. [187]

Mrs. Thrale's inaccuracy was what Boswell wanted to stress, but he deleted Johnson's remark that, "if she could but make a story better in the telling, she did not care what she *added* to it, a practice which he

---

[182] *Idem.*

[183] *Ibid.*, l. 986.

[184] *Ibid.*, l. 985 verso.

[185] *Anecdotes*, p. 293.

[186] *Life* MS. (Yale), l. 983 verso. *Life Revised Proof* (Hyde), II, 529. *Life*, IV, 340.

[187] *Life Revised Proof* (Hyde), II, 529–534.

thought very blameable." [188] He also omitted the fact that Malone had made a collection of her inaccuracies. [189] He simply referred to an eminent critic's opinion that the "severe things" which Mrs. Piozzi reported Johnson to have said were given undue emphasis. In twenty years doubtless severe things were said, but to have so many in two hours' reading was a distortion.

He defended Johnson from the charge of rudeness by examples of her inaccuracy. He gave her anecdote of Johnson telling a celebrated lady not to "choak" him with flattery, followed by the genuine, much kinder account. [190] As another instance, he gave Mrs. Piozzi's anecdote (told her, she had said, by her husband) of a gentleman who dined at a nobleman's house; in defending King William's character, the gentleman contradicted Johnson and received a stern rebuke from him. Boswell said that he had the true story from one present, Sir Joshua Reynolds (whose name he omitted in the *Life*). The dinner was not at a nobleman's, but at the house of Mr. Fitzmaurice (his name also omitted). Mr. Thrale was not present, and Dr. Johnson had said nothing to the gentleman. [191]

Boswell then took up Mrs. Piozzi's disapproval of instant recording, a criticism he had taken personally. [192] He said that her commonplace book [*Thraliana*] of which she "boasts" would have been less full of error if she had recorded directly. [193] This he let stand as well as most of the passage. The major deletion was an example of her writing down from Johnson's own lips an Epigram he made on a temple to the winds "at *Lord* Ansons (meaning Mr. Anson's in Staffordshire)" and Boswell quoted the lines. Later, he struck out the whole reference, probably because it was not precisely on the point; for here she was recording on the instant and was still inaccurate. [194]

Boswell took up the charge that Johnson was not a generous friend,

[188] *Life* MS. (Yale), l. 987.

[189] *Idem*, and l. 988.

[190] *Ibid.*, ll. 988–989. *Anecdotes*, p. 183. *Life Revised Proof* (Hyde), II, 529. *Life*, IV, 341.

[191] *Anecdotes*, p. 202. *Life* MS. (Yale), ll. 989–990. *Life Revised Proof* (Hyde), II, 530. *Life*, IV, 342–343.

[192] *Anecdotes*, p. 44. See p. 308 above for Boswell's letter of 31 March 1786 to Malone on this subject.

[193] *Life* MS. (Yale), ll. 990–991.

[194] *Ibid.*, l. 991.

citing her statement that Johnson was: "Admirable at giving counsel; no man saw his way so clearly; but he *would not stir a finger* for the assistance of those to whom he was willing enough to give advice." [195] He left in the manuscript, but cut in the first proof, Malone's observations that Mrs. Piozzi painted two pictures of Johnson: when he was " 'Guide Philosopher and Freind,' " she extolled him; but when he was "the indignant upbraider of Signora Piozzi" she belittled the great man in every way. [196]

In the published text Boswell answered her charge of uncharitableness by giving a quotation from the *Anecdotes* in which she contradicted herself upon the subject. [197] He then said he was "certain that a *more active freind* has rarely been found in any age," [198] and he cited prominent men still alive who could attest to this fact. He followed this with instances of Johnson's kindness to the Thrale family: campaign advertisements for Thrale, epitaphs for him and for Mrs. Salusbury, playful verses and letters to the Thrale daughters, but this Boswell deleted: "and above all can she forget his taking the trouble through such a series of years to honour her with so many letters . . ." [199] and he again suppressed the statement that she had sold Johnson's letters for five hundred guineas. [200] He also struck out: "It is not easy to suppress the indignation that I feel upon this subject; but [*originally* to refrain from warmth and strong expressions of disapprobation when such things are; but] I *will* refrain both from delicacy to one / her [*of deleted*] with whom I once lived in the cordiality of the Johnsonian School [*alternatively* delicacy to a lady], and for my own decorum [*alternatively* for the decorum of my own Work]." [201]

In the revised proof, the Cholmondeley anecdote followed, though manuscript directions to the printer give it a different placement. [202] This anecdote Mrs. Piozzi used to illustrate Johnson's rudeness, his continuing to fix his eyes on a book and not to acknowledge a friend. [203]

[195] *Life Revised Proof* (Hyde), II, 531. *Life*, IV, 343–344. *Anecdotes*, p. 193.
[196] *Life* MS. (Yale), l. 992.
[197] *Anecdotes*, p. 193.
[198] *Life* MS. (Yale), l. 993.
[199] *Idem.*
[200] *Ibid.*, l. 994.
[201] *Idem.*
[202] *Ibid.*, l. 995 verso.
[203] *Anecdotes*, pp. 258–259. *Life Revised Proof* (Hyde), II, 532. *Life*, IV, 345.

Boswell asserted that, if Mrs. Piozzi found it "an absolute necessity" to mention the story, she should have stated the circumstances which softened it: that Johnson had apologized to Cholmondeley and that in Johnson's letter of 25 October 1777, he had told her that he was "utterly unconscious" of the story, but if true, he was "very sorry, and very much ashamed."

Mrs. Piozzi's charge of Johnson's "musing" and of his conversation being "fatiguing," [204] Boswell answered, as he had done before, with her own contradiction.[205] In the manuscript (but deleted in the revised proof) Boswell wrote that he could "scarcely beleive" that she could have found such a fault when he had "so often beheld" her listening "with rapture," she who had said to him, "Many people admire and reverence Mr. Johnson; but you and I *love* him." [206] The sentence which followed was deleted in the manuscript: "I have never seen her since she chose to retire, 'where she knew Mr. Johnson would not follow her' [*Anecdotes*, p. 292] never since she became the wife of Signor Piozzi, and therefore though I read the words which I have quoted, my imagination revolts at their being hers." [207] Boswell deleted before the revised proof: "Her *double picture* occurs here again . . ." and further on, also deleted: "she can without remorse give a hideous caricature of *Him* to whom she was under the greatest obligations . . ." [208] In the revised proof he let the charge of fatigue be answered by her own quotation: "like the Sage in 'Rasselas,' he spoke, and attention watched his lips; he reasoned, and conviction closed his periods." And Boswell added himself that Johnson's conversation, indeed, was so far from ever fatiguing his friends, that they regretted when it was interrupted or ceased, and could exclaim in Milton's language, "With thee conversing, I forget all time." [209]

In the manuscript paragraph which followed he let stand (but deleted before the revised proof) the charge of Mrs. Piozzi's "carelessness and inaccuracy in general, and after a certain event the prejudice ⟨& spleen⟩ . . ." [210] Also left in the manuscript, but struck out before the

[204] *Anecdotes*, p. 23.
[205] *Ibid.*, p. 302. *Life Revised Proof* (Hyde), II, 532.
[206] *Life* MS. (Yale), l. 994.
[207] *Ibid.*, l. 995.
[208] *Idem.*
[209] *Idem. Life Revised Proof* (Hyde), II, 532. *Life*, IV, 346.
[210] *Life* MS. (Yale), l. 995.

revised proof, was his comment on the story of Johnson's berating a totally unfortunate woman because she claimed to be happy.[211] Pure cant! Boswell wished to show Johnson's intolerance of "affectation," but he was wise to delete this example, for Johnson's rebuke was likely to horrify a reader, as it had horrified Mrs. Thrale.[212]

Boswell considered another story to illustrate Johnson's intolerance of "affectation" and to clear him from the charge of "heartlessness." In the manuscript he gave the version in "Johnson's own words to me." [213] When on the trip to France, Thrale had jumped out of his carriage, fearing an overturn — his wife had "screamed out in an agony of fright." Johnson saw that Thrale was safe, and "*she* saw he was safe," but she continued to scream. Johnson "kept his eyes close fixed on a Book . . . not to be duped by her tricks." Not only was Boswell unable to give an *Anecdote* reference, but the story was also a double-edged sword, again more likely to make the reader think Johnson "unfeeling" than Mrs. Thrale "affected." Boswell deleted the passage from the manuscript.

As a better example of Mrs. Thrale's "affectation," Boswell let stand the manuscript refutation of her anecdote about the larks, and Johnson's "Prithee, my dear . . . have done with canting . . ." [214] and later, his angry rebuke. Boswell endeavored to tell the story with authenticity, letting the circumstances appear fairly, as related by a gentleman who was present. One day as Mrs. Thrale was dining on larks, she abruptly exclaimed, "O dear Mʳ Johnson do you know what has happened . . . our poor [cousin in the American war has had his head] taken off by a cannon ball." Johnson, shocked at the fact and her "unfeeling" manner of telling it, said, "Madam it would give *you* very little concern if all ⟨those⟩ your relations were spitted like those larks, and drest for Presto's supper." [215] (Presto was the Thrales' dog that lay under the table.) There were added details from the gentleman who was present (Baretti): the fact that she had no friendship for Thrale's first cousin, and that when she spoke, she "was got to the seventh or eighth" [216] lark;

[211] *Anecdotes*, pp. 284–285. *Life* MS. (Yale), l. 996.

[212] *Anecdotes*, p. 284.

[213] *Life* MS. (Yale), ll. 998–999.

[214] *Anecdotes*, p. 63.

[215] *Life* MS. (Yale), l. 996 verso. *Life Revised Proof* (Hyde), II, 533. Here, the phrase is "O, my dear Mr. Johnson . . ."

[216] *Life* MS. (Yale), l. 997. Boswell had written to Malone, 31 March 1786, di-

these, Boswell omitted, but the rest of the story he let stand, made more ludicrous by a footnote giving a pigeon anecdote, contributed by Wilkes.[217]

However "smart and entertaining" Mrs. Thrale's *Anecdotes* were, Boswell said, they should not be held as evidence against Johnson, for in every example of "harshness" and "severity," though there might be "*some* foundation," her manner of narration made the story "very unlike the real fact." In his summing up, he wrote in the manuscript that he was "sorry to have been obliged to expose Mrs. Thrale's foibles so much,"[218] but reworded this to "animadvert on the inaccuracies" — a much better phrase. He changed "Mrs. Thrale" to "Mrs. Piozzi" and cut the word "extraordinary" in describing Johnson's "intimacy with her"; and he wisely deleted the final direction to the printer, "Take in Piozzian Rhimes."[219] Rather than this comic finale, the revised proof and printed text gave this dignified dismissal of the lady from his book:

It is with concern that I find myself obliged to animadvert on the inaccuracies of Mrs. Piozzi's *Anecdotes*, and perhaps I may be thought to have dwelt too long upon her little collection. But as from Johnson's long residence under Mr. Thrale's roof, and his intimacy with her, the account which she has given of him may have made an unfavourable and unjust impression, my duty, as a faithful biographer, has obliged me reluctantly to perform this unpleasing task.[220]

As soon as Boswell's *Life* was off the press, Mrs. Piozzi was reading it at Streatham:

I have been now laughing & crying by turns for two Days over Boswell's Book: That poor Man should have a *Bon Bouillon* and be put to Bed, — he is quite light-headed. yet Madmen, Drunkards, & Fools tell Truth they say: — and if Johnson was to me the back Friend he has represented — let it cure me of ever making *Friendship* more with any human Being — let it cure me![221]

She anticipated Macaulay in her description of Boswell, but unlike him saw no quality of greatness in the book. His writing ability she rated

---

rectly after reading the *Anecdotes*: "The story of spitting her relations is I suppose exaggerated [*sic*]; or she must have provoked him confoundedly by *affectation* of grief." MS. Letter: Yale (L934). *Waingrow*, p. 143.

[217] *Life Revised Proof* (Hyde), II, 537. Boswell has written in the margin: "Sheet yyy is with M! Wilkes to look at a note."

[218] *Life Revised Proof* (Hyde), II, 533. *Life* MS. (Yale), l. 999.

[219] *Idem.*

[220] *Life Revised Proof* (Hyde), II, 533–534. *Life*, IV, 347.

[221] *Thraliana*, II, 809–811.

JAMES BOSWELL
BY SIR JOSHUA REYNOLDS

*Reproduced by permission of
the National Portrait Gallery*

MRS. PIOZZI
BY JOHN JACKSON

Four Oaks Farm

very low.[222] Certain scenes, however, had powerful emotional impact:

The Death of my Son so suddenly — so horribly produced before my Eyes, now suffering from the Tears then shed — so shockingly brought forward in Boswell's two Guinea Book, made me very ill this Week, very ill indeed; it would make the *modern* Friends all buy the Work I fancy, did they but know how sick the *ancient* Friends, had it in their Power to make me: but I had more Wit than tell any of 'em.[223]

She worried about the reaction of her haughty daughters: "I wonder whether those Girls read Boswell's Book? & whether they enjoy the Insults offered to their Mother — perhaps they have forgotten who, what, or where She is though . . ."[224]

In contrast to Boswell's purposeful absorption with Mrs. Piozzi's two Johnson books, resulting in his public charge of their inaccuracy, her absorption in the *Life* was purely personal; she made no public statement in rebuttal. But, unlike Boswell, who dismissed her books from his mind when he had finished the *Life*, she continued to be drawn to this book, reading and re-reading it over the years. She annotated two copies, a fifth edition (1807) and an eighth edition (1816).[225] She made hundreds of marginal notes, not emotional responses like those recorded in *Thraliana*, which were immediate and private. Now, she wrote with an audience in mind; time had passed and memory took the place of involvement. Some of her answers to Boswell's strictures were still bitter, but in the main her comments show that she was entertained; she made queries and indulged in reminiscence. Without admitting it, she was giving proof of the enduring power of Boswell's book. He had been right when he wrote his friend, George Dempster, on the eve of publication, ". . . I really think it will be the most entertaining Collection that has appeared in this age."[226]

She annotated the fifth edition in 1808, at Brynbella, the house she and Piozzi had built in Wales, in the Vale of Clwyd. Piozzi was by

[222] In discussing the argument between Boswell and Anna Seward over Johnson's "Sprig of Myrtle," she claimed that "his Opponent out-writes him — Miss Seward has ten times his Powers." *Thraliana*, II, 878.

[223] *Ibid.*, 811.

[224] *Idem.*

[225] Fifth edition (1807): Hyde. Eighth edition (1816): Harvard. Mrs. Piozzi annotated a number of books for her own amusement and that of others.

[226] Boswell to Dempster, 30 April 1791. MS. Letter: Yale (L423). *Waingrow*, p. lxxv.

then an invalid, wracked by violent attacks of gout. Such an occupation was a diversion from the sick room.[227] The eighth edition, if annotated in 1816, was done seven years after Piozzi's death — and twenty-one years after Boswell's death — virtually all the old friends were gone. In 1814 she had given Brynbella to her adopted heir, Piozzi's nephew, John Salusbury Piozzi Salusbury [228] and his young bride; Mrs. Piozzi, now an old lady of seventy-five, was living in Bath.[229] She made her last visit to Brynbella in 1818, when she spent the summer with the Salusburys; perhaps she presented the book then, in the hope that her spirited marginalia would make her remembered by descendants with pride and pleasure.

All that is known with certainty is that both her annotated copies of the *Life* were at Brynbella when John Salusbury ordered her library to be sold in 1823, the year after her death. A surviving marked copy of the sale catalogue gives Lot 643 as the fifth edition and lot 644 as the eighth. No price is recorded for the fifth edition (perhaps it was withdrawn or perhaps the two were sold together). After the eighth edition is the price £4/17/6.[230]

In both editions Mrs. Piozzi was eloquently silent concerning crucial passages: her reading of Boswell's *Tour*, young Harry's death, her neglect and abandonment of Johnson, her marriage to Piozzi, even on the death of Johnson — no comment. She made no answer to Boswell's judgment of her as a person; she put up no defense on large issues. She concerned herself with small matters. Ladies are often accused of this waste of energy, but in her case there were important reasons for silence: these were painful passages, and they included Boswell's personal attack. She had no desire to open up old wounds, nor to expose the hurt for others to see.

It was a different matter when it came to Boswell's attack upon her publications. She did not accept this criticism silently. She was indig-

[227] "Alas! Alas! & now Johnson & Boswell & Blair & Robertson & Garrick & Reynolds — & almost *all* the People named in [this book] add to the dead cold List — Alas Alas! cries the Survivor in 1808." *Life Limited Edition*, II, 105.

[228] Sir Lucas Pepys's advice, given in 1786, to take the Salusbury name, had not gone entirely unheeded. See p. 114 above.

[229] In 1816, since her daughters would not help with the burden of upkeep, Mrs. Piozzi was forced to sell the contents of Streatham (they brought £3921 7s.); she then leased the place unfurnished. Having "shaken off this load of splendid misery," she took a house for herself in Bath, 8 Gay Street, near the Crescent.

[230] *Catalogue of the Library . . . of Mrs. Hester Lynch Piozzi* (Chester: 1823), p. 33. Marked copy: Hyde.

nant and articulate. She countered with charges of *his* inaccuracy, concealment, bad taste, poor style — and such details as grammatical error. In his special section of criticism on the *Anecdotes*,[231] she defended herself when she could, and when she could not, she added side information. In the story of excessive flattery given Johnson by a celebrated lady, she identified her as the Blue Stocking writer, "Hannah More."[232] Concerning the anecdote of the gentleman defending King William's character and being rebuked by Johnson, she defended her phrase "nobleman's house" by saying the dinner was at Thomas Fitzmaurice's, the son of Lord Shelburne, so he was "noble enough — on *one* Side at least." And she stated positively that her husband had been one of the company.[233] As for the Cholmondeley story, she noted, "look at a Letter of his own Saying what you tell me of Cholmondeley *shocks me.*"[234] Since Boswell himself quoted from Johnson's letter a few lines further on in the text, Mrs. Piozzi's annotation would appear to have been instant, before she had finished reading the paragraph.

Against her anecdote about Johnson's heartlessness, the cousin's death, and the larks, she wrote: "Boswell appealing to Baretti for a Testimony of the *Truth* is comical enough,"[235] and concerning the larks: "Mrs. Thrale never *saw* a Supper in those Days, never eat a Lark for Supper in England; & dar'd as well have swallow'd the Lark *alive* as have said O my dear Johnson! She never address'd him with any such familiarity."[236]

As for Boswell's remarks on her edition of Johnson's *Letters*, his footnote that she valued his correspondence so greatly that she sold it for five hundred pounds provoked an agonized "how spiteful!"[237]

She held no animosity, however, against Boswell for the *Ode* on her approaching nuptials with Johnson. When she came to this passage, she asked, "Whose silly Fun was this? Soame Jenyns's?"[238] In the

---

[231] At Boswell's first mention of her *Anecdotes* (and Johnson's verses, dictated to his mother when he was three, after he had trod on a duckling and killed it): ". . . I do protest he told them to me himself as I printed them; & I believe he made them." *Life Limited Edition*, I, 12.

[232] *Ibid.*, III, 397.

[233] *Ibid.*, 397–398.

[234] *Ibid.*, 400.

[235] *Ibid.*, 401.

[236] *Idem.*

[237] *Ibid.*, I, 388.

[238] *Ibid.*, III, 438. Soame Jenyns (1704–1787), miscellaneous writer. As Malone said, he "looked at everything with a view to pleasantry alone." *Life*, III, 289, n. 1.

margin beside Boswell's three stanzas (also anonymous), she again asked, "whose Fun was this?" and commented "It is better than the other." [239] What, in the days of passion, would have roused her to justified anger, now, as an old lady, caused only a pleasant flutter of remembered excitement. As for authorship, it seems she was no more aware of Boswell's hand at the time she made this note, than she had been in 1781 and in 1788.

She had no defense for Boswell's charge that she had tampered with her own letters. Her marginal comment at this point was indignation that her own letter had been purloined by Johnson's servant, Francis Barber, and bribed away from him by Boswell "for half a Crown to have a little Teizing in his Power." But, she commented, though he "*Then* made a Bustle & a Rout as if he had got a great Prize; It is a complete Nothing." [240]

On the suppression of Boswell's name in a Johnson letter, she misunderstood Boswell's footnote and thought his brother was meant. Her comment was, "I never heard his Name." [241]

In response to Boswell's criticism that she could not correctly read Johnson's handwriting, that the word is "sutile" not "futile," she generalized in the eighth edition: "It was no Mistake . . . as *Pictures* they are futile . . . The Moth, the Sunshine every thing may destroy the beautiful Work — Alas!" In the fifth edition, she had been more specific: "on the Contrary it is a plain f . . ." but she showed Boswell's attack was warranted by concluding in confusion, ". . . Mr. Lysons said it should be *sutile* — I car'd not which it was; I knew he

---

Boswell allowed that "Jenyns was possessed of lively talents . . . and could very happily play with a light subject, either in prose or verse; but when he speculated on that most difficult and excruciating question, the Origin of Evil [in *A Free Inquiry into the Nature and Origin of Evil*], he . . . was exposed by Johnson, both with acute argument and brilliant wit." *Life*, I, 315. Shortly after Johnson's death, Jenyns had the bad taste to print an "Epitaph" in which the lines occur:

> "[Johnson's] actions, sayings, mirth, and melancholy,
> *Boswell* and *Thrale*, retailers of his wit,
> Will tell you how he wrote, and talk'd, and cough'd, and spit."
> — *The Gentleman's Magazine*, LVI:1 (1786), 428.

[239] *Life Limited Edition*, III, 439.
[240] *Ibid.*, 108. See pp. 119 and 151 above.
[241] *Life Limited Edition*, III, 117. Johnson to Mrs. Thrale, 21 June 1780. MS. Letter: Yale. *Piozzi Johnson Letters*, II, 163. Letter #684. *Letters*, II, 376. *Life*, III, 434, n. 1. See also page 152 above.

wrote futile. Against Mrs. Knowles I could have no malice, I knew her not." [242]

Her defense against Boswell's reiterated charges of carelessness and inaccuracy was not strong. In many instances she made no comment; frequently she gave recognition and half-confession by an underscoring or a marginal line. On one occasion she was provoked to an example of feminine logic that would have delighted him. Against Boswell's accusation that she had repeated a story of his about an old man in a stagecoach, changing his gender, she remarked spiritedly, "Mrs. Thrale knew there was no such Thing as an old Man: when a Man gets Superannuated they call him an old Woman." [243] She answered Boswell's charge that the Thrales kept Johnson under restraint by exclaiming, "What Restraint can he mean? Johnson kept every body else under Restraint." [244] And Boswell's comment, immediately following this, that Johnson was required to talk for the entertainment of the Thrales' company, made her say: "I do not believe it ever was suggested."

The most surprising marginalia were sudden thrusts of asperity against Johnson, which gave unexpected support to Boswell's charge of harsh treatment. Opposite Boswell's statement, "A dog will take a small bit of meat as readily as a large, when both are before him," she wrote, "Which Johnson would never have done." [245] In the margin, against Johnson's letter to Boswell about his journey with the Thrales in 1774, "Wales, so far as I have yet seen of it, is a very beautiful and rich country, all enclosed, and planted," she protested, "yet to please Mr. Thrale he feign'd Abhorrence of it." [246] Against Boswell's apology for having kept Johnson up too late and his replying: " 'No, Sir, . . . I don't care though I sit all night with you.' This was an animated speech from a man in his sixty-ninth year," Mrs. Piozzi commented "not from Johnson, who delighted to sit up all Night, & lie a Bed all Day." [247] To Boswell's remark that Johnson had told him he was to be Taylor's heir, she added: "His fondness for Reynolds too . . . Ay & for Thrale; had a Small dash of Interest to keep it warm." [248] In

[242] *Life Limited Edition*, III, 1.
[243] *Ibid.*, II, 441.
[244] *Ibid.*, II, 264.
[245] *Ibid.*, I, 423.
[246] *Ibid.*, II, 108.
[247] *Ibid.*, II, 423.
[248] *Ibid.*, II, 405.

answer to Boswell's "Mrs. Thrale knew Johnson's character so super-ficially, as to represent him as unwilling to do small acts of benevo-lence; and mentions, in particular, that he would hardly take the trouble to write a letter in favour of his friends," she stressed the identity of the person involved, the painter, Lowe: "Yes — to get the Man a Dinner: he was a very poor Man. [Johnson] would not have written Letters for Barry & Benjamin West." [249] On the editorial note [by Kearney]: "It seems to me, that there are many pathetick passages in Johnson's works, both prose and verse," Mrs. Piozzi expressed herself with violence: "Where? The End of his Preface to the Dictionary certainly does call a Reader to lament with & for the Author — but it was mere Autobiographical Pathos: Johnson neither felt nor Could excite Concern for others — unless they wanted a Dinner: he laughed at distresses of *Sentiment*." [250]

Mrs. Piozzi, in marginal comments, gave her frank opinion of Bos-well. She had at one time thought him comical and good natured, but she never liked him. Johnson's message in a letter to Boswell, "You continue to stand very high in the favour of Mrs. Thrale," she answered, as has already been noted, with "Poor Mrs. Thrale was forced to say so in order to keep well with Johnson." [251] To another letter message, "Mrs. Thrale loves you," she protested, "not I, I never lov'd him." [252] She matched Boswell's charge that Johnson's attraction to the Thrales was based upon material comforts, by saying that Boswell was at-tracted to Johnson only because of his celebrity. He wanted his letters "chiefly for the Pleasure of shewing them." [253] If Johnson had been in distress, ". . . Bozzy would not have cared a Pin for him." [254] Against Johnson's statement that a journal of one's own life gave later satisfac-tion, she wrote, "Would it? a Journal of a Life like Boswell's?" [255] As for his setting down facts at the moment they were observed, she com-mented sarcastically, "how clever all this is!!" [256] Repeatedly, she noted that Boswell's dominant characteristic was curiosity and, on this sub-

[249] *Ibid.*, III, 283. James Barry and Benjamin West were two of the most popular painters of the day.
[250] *Ibid.*, III, 160.
[251] *Ibid.*, II, 48.
[252] *Ibid.*, I, 465. See HLP list of "Profess'd Enemies," Small 1820 Almanack. Rylands Eng. Ms. 616.
[253] *Ibid.*, II, 105.
[254] *Ibid.*, III, 303.
[255] *Ibid.*, I, 307.
[256] *Ibid.*, III, 120.

ject, she made the mordant generality that "Curiosity carried Boswell further than it ever carried any Mortal breathing." [257]

A true friendship between Boswell and Mrs. Thrale was never possible. She was not the kind of woman he liked, nor was he the kind of man she liked, although both were very partial to the opposite sex. Mrs. Thrale responded to conventional gallantry in polite society; she enjoyed the stimulation of men's minds. Boswell was invigorated by a contrasting assortment of persons and places, high company and low company. He found no stimulation in women's minds. He thought of all females as "potential mistresses or potential wives" and "though he was attracted to every variety of greatness in men, no matter how unconventional, [he] actually disliked superior intelligence in women." [258] Mrs. Thrale was a Blue Stocking, and he felt ill at ease and intimidated by any display of superior feminine intelligence. He wanted complaisance, not competition.

Mrs. Thrale did not want competition either: she enjoyed, as much as he did, being the center of attention. Informed, witty, entertaining, they both wanted to shine — both were independent and proud. Praise from her close friends kept Mrs. Thrale irrepressibly youthful (a quality very annoying to her daughters). The same praise gave Boswell confidence and self respect. Despite their differences in temperament — she, practical and optimistic; he, impractical and hypochondriac — both shared a zest for life and both depended upon a band of supporting admirers to buoy their spirits.[259] Both needed an idol for inspiration. Johnson perfectly fitted this role — hero, mentor, father, friend. And since he was over thirty years their senior, he was not in the least competitive; he no longer felt the jealousy he once had for Garrick and Goldsmith, in the early days of bitter struggle. Johnson's place in the world was well established now. His young friends amused and comforted his old age, and he gratefully gave his devotion and totally unselfish help for any project either one of them envisioned or undertook.

It was Johnson's "Fame" which first attracted the Thrales, as well as

[257] *Ibid.*, II, 260.
[258] *Boswell Earlier Years, Pottle,* p. 144.
[259] As Boswell's wife said (she had a remarkable ability for appraisal), his "spirits [were] like brandy set on fire. If not constantly stirred the flame will go out." Boswell to Malone, 3 October 1785. MS. Letter: Yale (L923).

Boswell, but genuine affection soon became the dominant
for him by them all. Once established in the Thrales' house
son was able to bring the three together and make things run
very well. This happy state of affairs would have continued
nitely if Thrale had lived, still content in "the Johnsonian."
Boswell found Mrs. Thrale agreeable and, like many men,
himself by thinking he was a delightful guest. He believed that
Thrale appreciated him as a person and admired his literary pow
she did not. Mrs. Thrale was gracious and supported the patt
hospitality — she giving, he receiving. For years she patiently
dured his company, but she always knew his opinion of her and
opinion of her literary ability. Just as Boswell valued Thrale like
"*useful dish or vase of fine metal,*"[260] she felt that he valued her for
her Johnsonian treasure. By her own testimony, she never liked Boswell, but he was too insensitive to realize the fact.

If Mrs. Thrale had not become Mrs. Piozzi, Boswell would undoubtedly have continued his courting of her Johnsoniana (like his
"courting" of Anna Seward's anecdotes). I think it would have been
a futile pursuit, but Boswell surely did not think so. He would have
gone on trying, doggedly. Her marriage to Piozzi, however, changed
everything. Boswell's repugnance for her behavior made it impossible
for him ever again to communicate with her upon any subject.

If only there had been some kind of correspondence between them,
even desultory, the mistakes and misunderstandings, the comedy of
errors, which precipitated their public quarrel, would have been avoided, their personal feelings would have been spared, and much needless
pain and offense not given. But, as it was, both refused to seek the
truth directly and, even when enlightened by friends, they refused to
make a single conciliatory move. Their conflict was an extraordinary
one, occurring after all personal connection had ceased. Apart, filled
with suspicion, they became increasingly defensive, each supported by
cohorts egging them on. Soon, they were central figures in a paper war,
with the general public enjoying each new battle.

Mrs. Piozzi's desire for a little "Fame," and her self-defense were
understandable, if not commendable. Boswell, in his indignation over
her interpretation of Johnson in her two books and his insistence that he
must defend him from her aspersions, was praiseworthy, but this was

[260] *Boswell Papers,* X, 158 (28 March 1775). See page 28 above.

not a complete statement of his purpose. He had been piqued by her indifference to his importance in the *Anecdotes*, and deeply hurt by the *Letters*, for they showed that Johnson had greater affection for Mrs. Thrale than for himself; more humiliating than that, they showed that Johnson and Mrs. Thrale had often joked about him.

While she had enjoyed carefree years of protection and happiness, prosperity, and applause, he had endured years of loneliness and melancholy. He had struggled through family tragedy, financial pressure, and professional failure. Her trifling volumes had succeeded, while he had little to show for his years of labor. His case, in the end, was even stronger than hers for self-preservation; on his merits as an author, he finally entrusted his last hope, his long-held ambition for enduring "Fame."

With the publication of *The Life of Johnson*, Boswell ceased his attack — their conflict was over and posterity would be the final judge. Mrs. Piozzi's publications have merit. She was able to picture the intimate, family side of Johnson, of which Boswell had far less knowledge than she. At the time, her books were extremely popular but, even then, they were acknowledged to be slight accomplishments; and as the years have passed, her little "Fame" has diminished. On the other hand, Boswell's performance was massive and has become classic. He was able to establish his interpretation of Johnson, enlarge his own stature, and reduce his rival to insignificance.

In this impossible friendship, which turned into enmity, the victory goes to Boswell, but the sympathy goes to Mrs. Thrale.

APPENDIX

I. Boswell's "Epithal[amium]
on D[r] J. & M[rs] T."
Yale Ms. 302

[Sheet 1. Boswell's writing is on both sides of a sheet (with seal), addressed to "S[r] Joshua Reynolds"]

My [*originally* Now] dearest darling view your Slave
Behold him as your very Scrub
Ready [*originally* Whether] to write as Author grave
Or govern well the brewing tub

While to [*alternatively* To rich] felicity thus raisd
My bosom glows with amorous fire
Porter no longer shall be prais'd
Tis I myself am Thrale's entire

Five daughters by your former spouse
Shall match the [*alternatively* with] nobles of the land
The fruit of our more fervent vows
A pillar of the State shall stand

If e'er my fingers touch'd the lyre
In satire fierce or pleasure gay
Shall not my Thralia's smiles [*originally* Thralia now] inspire
Shall Sam refuse the sportive lay.

Desmullins now may go her ways
And poor blind Williams sing alone
Levet exhaust his lungs in praise
And Frank his Master's fortune own

Congratulating crowds shall come
Our new born happiness to hail
Whether at ball at rout at [*alternatively* or] drum
Yet human spite we must [*alternatively* envy will still] berail

For though they come in pleasing guise
And cry the Brave [*alternatively* wise] deserve the fair
They look askance [*originally* view us still] with envious eyes
As the fiend hated [*alternatively* looked at] the first pair

Greater than Atlas was of yore
A higher power [*originally* bliss] to me is given
[He bore *deleted*] The earth he on his shoulders bore
I with my arms encircle heaven

[Sheet 2. Boswell has written on one side of a quarto sheet, docketed
　　　　　on verso: ". . . Epithal on Dᴿ J. & Mʳˢ T. . . . . . .
　　　　　1781."]

From thee my Mistress I obtain
A manumission from the power [*originally* woe]
Of lonely gloom [*originally* gloomy solitude], of fretful pain
Transported to the [*originally* I migrate to a/ At once
　　　　　　　I reach the] Blissful Bower

No more [*deleted, the beginning of a new stanza*]

Charming Cognation! With delight
In the keen aphrodisian spasm
Shall we reciprocate all [*alternatively* each] night
While wit & learning leave no chasm.

Nor only are [*originally* shall] our limbs entwind
And lip in rapture glew'd to lip
Lock'd in embraces of the Mind
Fancy's [*alternatively* Imaginations] enchanting sweets we sip

II. Chronological List of the Correspondence between
Boswell and the Thrales
Present location given when known

1769

Boswell to Mrs. Thrale, 5 September 1769.   [Hyde]
A card from the Thrales inviting Boswell to Streatham,
   30 September 1769 (See *Life*, II, 77).
     (a) MS. card.   [Hyde]
     (b) text of card,
       quoted in Materials for the *Life* (Papers Apart 349).   [Yale]

1773

Boswell to Henry Thrale.
   According to Boswell's Letter Register, sent 19 March 1773.   [Not known]
Boswell to Henry Thrale, 29 July 1773.   [Rylands]
Henry Thrale to Boswell, August 1773.
   "A few lines," enclosing a letter to Johnson.
   Referred to in Boswell's letter to Henry Thrale of
     22 November 1773.   [Not known]
Boswell to Henry Thrale, 22 November 1773.   [Hyde]

1774

Boswell to Henry Thrale, 13 May 1774.   [Harvard]

1775

Henry Thrale to Boswell, 1 April 1775.
   A card asking Boswell to dine (See *Boswell Papers*, X, 170).   [Not known]
Mrs. Thrale to Boswell, 18 May 1775.   [Yale]
Boswell to Henry Thrale.
   According to Boswell's Letter Register, sent 30 September
    1775.   [Not known]
Boswell to Henry Thrale.
   According to Boswell's Letter Register, sent 18 December
    1775.   [Not known]

1776

Boswell to Mrs. Thrale, 29 March 1776.
     (a) draft on the pages of an almanac.   [Hyde]
     (b) the letter.   [Hyde]
Mrs. Thrale to Boswell, 20 June 1776.   [Yale]
Henry Thrale to Boswell, 25 July 1776.   [Yale]

Boswell to Mrs. Thrale, 30 August 1776.
   (a) the letter.   [National Library of Scotland]
   (b) copy of the letter, in hand of Boswell's clerk,
      John Lawrie.   [Yale]

1777

Mrs. Thrale to Boswell, 15 August 1777.   [Hyde]

1778

Boswell to Mrs. Thrale.
  According to Boswell's Letter Register, sent 18 April 1778. [Not known]
Mrs. Thrale to Boswell.
  According to Boswell's Letter Register, received 21 April
  1778.   [Not known]

1779

Boswell to Henry Thrale.
  According to Boswell's Letter Register, sent 22 January 1779
  (See *Life*, III, 372).   [Not known]

1781

Henry Thrale to Boswell, (in Johnson's hand), Wednesday [21 March 1781.]
  Boswell "found a card of invitation to dine at Mr. Thrale's." The Thrales were
  now in Grosvenor Square. (*Boswell Papers*, XIV, 171).   [Hyde]
Boswell to Mrs. Thrale, 26 April 1781.
   (a) the letter.   [Rylands]
   (b) copy in Boswell's hand.   [Yale]

1782

Boswell to Mrs. Thrale, 19 March 1782.
  (a) draft. According to Letter Register, letter sent 18 March
    (18 changed to 19 in draft).   [Hyde]
  (b) the letter.   [Sold in 2–4 June 1908 Sotheby Sale, Lot 768]
Mrs. Thrale to Boswell, 13 May 1782.   [Hyde]
Boswell to Mrs. Thrale, 25 May 1782.
  (a) the letter.   [Hyde]
  (b) copy of the letter in hand of Boswell's clerk, John Lawrie. [Hyde]
Mrs. Thrale to Boswell, 3 June 1782.   [Hyde]
Mrs. Thrale to Boswell, 4 July 1782.   [Hyde]
Boswell to Mrs. Thrale, 9 July 1782.
  (a) the letter.   [Belonged to W. K. Bixby]
  (b) copy of the letter in hand of Boswell's clerk, John Lawrie. [Hyde]
Boswell to Mrs. Thrale, 20 December 1782.
  (a) the letter.   [Hyde]
  (b) copy in hand of Boswell.   [Hyde]

INDEX

Account of Corsica, An, by James Boswell, 11

Adam, R. B., xii

Adams, Dr. William, 1706–1789, Master of Pembroke College, Oxford: visited by S.J. and J.B. (1776), 34; visited by S.J. and J.B. (1784), 88; to provide Mrs. Thrale with anecdotes of S.J.. 93; asked for material by J.B., 94

Addison, Joseph, 1672–1719, essayist and critic: S.J.'s advice concerning, 7

Adey, Mary, 1742–1830: S.J. letter given Mrs. Piozzi by, 122

Agnew, Geoffrey, xvi

Anecdotes of the Late Samuel Johnson, by Hester Lynch Piozzi: rivalry with J.B. shown in, xiii; ms. sent to Cadell, 99; in press, 103; publication of, 104; success of, 105; J.B.'s reaction to, 106–108, 171; J.B.'s note in reply to, 108–112; seen by Mrs. Piozzi, 114; attacked in *Life,* 159–162

Anson, George: Mr. not Lord, 158

Argyll Street, Mrs. Thrale's house in, 77, 80

Ashbourne, Derbyshire: S.J. and J.B. visit Taylor at (1776), 35, 36; meeting of S.J. and J.B. at (1777), 45–47; S.J. to (1779), 54; (1784), 90n

Aston, Elizabeth, 1708–1785, of Stowe Hill, 45, 90n

Auchinleck, Ayrshire: described by J.B., 3; meeting of S.J. and J.B.'s father at, 23; S.J. invited to (1783), 84, 87; J.B. to (1787), 123; Mrs. Boswell too ill to leave (1788), 137, dies at, 139; the Piozzis near, 139; J.B.'s departure from (1789), 140

Auchinleck, Alexander Boswell, Lord, 1707–1782, Scottish judge and J.B.'s father: on J.B.'s career, 1, 3–4; illness of, 10; meeting with S.J., 23; death of, 76

Austin, Gabriel, xvi

Balderston, Katharine C., xiv

Baldwin, Henry, ca. 1734–1813, London printer: printer of *Life of S.J.,* 141, 147, 148

Barber, Francis, 1745?–1801, S.J.'s Negro servant: account of, 9–10n; learning Latin, 11; at Bolt Court, 47, 48n; Boswell requests him to save Johnsonian mss., 52, 53; S.J.'s sole nurse, 83, 85; asked by J.B. for bulletins, 86; S.J. writings promised by, 102; Mrs. Thrale's letters returned by, 118

Barclay, David, 1728–1809, banker: sale of brewery to, 71

Barclay, Robert, ca. 1740–1828, nephew of David, 71

Baretti, Guiseppe, 1719–1789, critic and miscellaneous writer: at the Thrales' in Southwark, 27; to Bath, 37; Reynolds' portrait of, 59n; included in Italian trip, 60–61; dinner guest, 64; to provide Johnsonian anecdotes, 93; possible author of letter to Mrs. Piozzi, 121; mentioned in "Nuptial Ode," 130; in Brewhouse Entertainment, 144; quoted by J.B., 161, 165

Barry, James, 1742–1806, painter, 168

Bate, W. Jackson, xvi

Bath, Somersetshire: Mrs. Thrale and Queeney to (1776), 37; Thrales and S.J. to, 39; Thrales in (1780), 57; riots in, 58; Mrs. Thrale and daughters to (1783), 79; Mrs. Thrale awaiting Piozzi at (1784), 89; Piozzis to (1787), 121, (1789) 140; Mrs. Piozzi buys 8 Gay Street in, 164

Bathurst, Richard, Colonel, d. ca. 1755, father of Dr. Richard Bathurst. and West Indian planter, 9n

Bathurst, Dr. Richard, d. 1762, physician, 9n

Beattie, William, xvi

Beauclerk, the Hon. Topham, 1739–1780, friend of S.J.: quoted in *Tour,* 100

Beaverbrook Art Gallery, Fredericton, N.B., xvi

Beinecke Library, xv

Bevan, Sylvanus, 71

Birmingham, S.J. and J.B. to (1776), 35

Blackshiels, Midlothian: S.J.'s departure from, 24

Boethius: S.J.'s translation of, 7, 125

Bolt Court: S.J. moved to, 34; inmates of, 48n; J.B. to, 61, 62, 80; S.J. writes Mrs. Thrale from, 77

Bond, William H., xvi

Book of Company, by James Boswell, xiv, 76

Boothby, Miss Hill, 1708–1756, friend of S.J.: S.J.'s letters to, 122, 124

Boscawen, Hon. Edward, 1711–1761, Admiral, 40

Boscawen, Capt., son of Admiral Boscawen: introduced to J.B., 40; entertained in Edinburgh, 41–42